The Acoustic Guitar
BIBLE

Published by **SMT**®
an imprint of Bobcat Books Limited
14-15 Berners Street, London W1T 3LJ, UK.

Exclusive Distributors:
Music Sales Limited
Distribution Centre, Newmarket Road,
Bury St Edmunds, Suffolk IP33 3YB, UK.
Music Sales Corporation
257 Park Avenue South, New York, NY10010, USA.
Music Sales Pty Limited
20 Resolution Drive, Caringbah, NSW 2229, Australia.

Order No. SMT1408R
ISBN 978-1-84492-063-1
© Copyright Eric Roche, 2004
published under exclusive licence by SMT, an imprint and registered trade mark of
Bobcat Books Limited, part of The Music Sales Group.

Cover image courtesy of Photosearch.
Music engraving: Cambridge Notation/Alan Heal.

Printed in the EU.

A catalogue record for this book is available from the British Library.

www.musicsales.com

The Acoustic Guitar
BIBLE

Eric Roche

ACKNOWLEDGEMENTS

First of all, a huge 'thank you' to Candy and Stefan for putting up without me while I spent most of the recent months in the basement office; the sound of typing and tuning told them that I was probably still alive down there. Thanks to my first guitar teacher Benny O' Carroll for lighting a flame in me, to Ed Speight for adding fuel to the fire and to Thomas Leeb for that spark.

Thanks also to Iain McGregor, Albert DePetrillo, Dicken Goodwin, Alan Heal and Chris Bradford at SMT. To Chris Francis at Cambridge Notation for his patience. To Phil Brooks and Martin Kennedy at ACM for their support. To Keith Dudley for input and support. To Nick Benjamin for his great guitar building. To George Lowden and the folks at Avalon for all those lovely guitars. To Peter Sprot for the pep talk. To Phil Hilborne and David Mead at *Guitar Techniques* magazine. To Tony Gravel at Tascam, Alison Hildyard at Big I Am Promotions and James Taylor at P3 music. To Adam Pain for his help with the audio and Tudor Morgan-Owen for the photography. To Martin Taylor and Tommy Emmanuel for inspiration and encouragement. To all of the great people and musicians who have helped me along the way – thank you.

CONTENTS

ABOUT THE AUTHOR

Eric Roche is an internationally respected guitarist, performer, teacher and columnist. He is Head of Guitar at the UK Academy of Contemporary Music and a regular columnist for *Guitar Techniques* and *Guitarist* magazines. He has performed and given guitar masterclasses all over the world.

Eric has performed with many of the world's other leading fingerstyle guitarists, including concerts with Martin Taylor, Tommy Emmanuel, Doyle Dykes, Jacques Stotzem and many others. He presents regular residential guitar workshops and is member of the board of trustees of the Bath International Guitar Festival.

Eric has recorded a number of solo guitar albums, including *The Perc-U-Lator* (1999), *Spin* (2001) and *With These Hands* (2004). He plays guitars by Nick Benjamin, Lowden and Avalon, and he also endorses Fishman, D'Addario and AER products.

You can find out more about Eric Roche and his music, concerts, albums and workshops at www.ericroche.com

FOREWORD

To the reader,

The guitar is both a demanding and humbling instrument. One day you pick it up and say, 'I'm going to master this thing,' and the next day you pick it up and feel like a fool. The only way to truly get anywhere with it is to be totally dedicated to it. I hope that the information and knowledge in this book opens doors for you to become a better musician and express yourself on this box made of wood and wire. I thank Eric for his dedication to the guitar and have enjoyed watching his commitment, love and passion for playing. I wish him all the very best in the future and for those who have bought this book. I hope you enjoy the adventure that playing music on such a beautiful instrument will bring you!

Yours fretfully,
Tommy Emmanuel, cgp.

INTRODUCTION

I have been a student of the guitar for most of my life. It has brought me pleasure and frustration in almost equal measure, but I am so in love with the guitar and what it allows me to be that I can easily forgive it. For the things I have seen and felt, for the people I have met and the places I have been, for the music I have been able to make, I am truly thankful.

So many guitarists speak of falling into a rut on their guitar journeys, of being unable to improve or move on. Sometimes many months and years can pass when it seems that there is no progress, and then suddenly you find yourself on the next level. It's like the children's song about the bear climbing over the mountain. What do you think he saw?

The guitar is not logical; unlike the linear logic of the piano, its tuning and design all conspire against symmetry and regularity. The strings are different gauges and the frets get smaller and smaller. Scale patterns change shape all over the fingerboard. Lulling us into a false sense of linearity, notes appear and disappear. We even use different tunings. And as for trying to tune it...!

Yet, underneath all that, there is a sort of guitar logic. The guitar is the music world's paintbrush. No instrument can compete with its tone colours and sounds. The guitar – particularly the acoustic guitar – is very responsive to our expression. We hold and cradle the instrument to play it.

It takes two hands to make a single note. The acoustic guitar has the dynamics of an orchestra. But how do you discover all these qualities?

You *practise*. You practise to refine your technique. In the words of Tommy Emmanuel, 'Technique lets you fly your kite.' Find a good teacher. I was blessed to have a great teacher for many, many years. In this day and age it is more and more difficult to find that powerful kind of relationship, so I am grateful for that.

Of course, guitarists today have other advantages. There are countless teaching videos, books, guitar magazines, schools and courses. The standards of guitar playing and instruction continue to improve. We just keep getting better and better at our game. Look to the great masters of the instrument, both present and past. Be inspired by their music and lives. Take their legacies and carry them forward.

Don't be distracted by the progress of others around you. Focus on what you're doing right now. There is no deadline. Take things one day, one song, one note at a time.

In all my guitar-playing years I have seen enough ruts, mountains and plateaus to fill a book. So that's what I've done. In my life I can pinpoint particular concerts, albums, musicians, songs, music lessons, moments of fear and joy when the impasse was broken and I found myself moving forward again. Be present and alert, because you never know when the inspiration will touch you!

Eric Roche
Suffolk, England
Summer 2004

HOW TO USE THIS BOOK

When I set out to write *The Acoustic Guitar Bible*, I wanted the book to be a reference book for acoustic guitarists, and so there are numerous exercises and technical studies in the book. There are also chapters on music theory, altered tunings, accessories, harmonics and arranging. The accompanying CD will give you an audio reference for all of the exercises and pieces in the book. I've also included thoughts on amplification, performance and recording. There is an outline of the acoustic guitar's history and even a section about nail care!

In summary, *The Acoustic Guitar Bible* can be dipped into at any point and used as for reference and, hopefully, a source of inspiration for you on your guitar journey. Let me know your thoughts about the book by email at author@ericroche.com.

Enjoy!

A Note About The Audio Examples

The accompanying discs feature 158 audio examples of the material covered in the book. CD 1 has 78 tracks that relate to chapters 1–3, while CD 2 has 82 tracks covering the material in chapters 4–10. The vast majority of the tracks were recorded in my studio using a Tascam 2488 hard disc recorder. I used my Nick Benjamin OM custom steel string for all these tracks. The guitar was recorded direct to disc via a Fishman Rare Earth Blend pick up system - featuring separate microphone and magnetic signals. I mixed these tracks on the Tascam with minimal EQ and processing.

A small number of the recordings were previously recorded by Phil Hilborne for *Guitar Techniques* magazine and thanks to him for the permission to reuse them. These are tracks 19 and 31 on CD 1 and tracks 80 and 81 on CD 2. "Eight Years" originally appeared on my second album *Spin* while tracks 45, and 77–79 originally appeared on my debut album *The Perc U Lator*. These album tracks were all performed on my 1991 Lowden O10 via a Fishman Rare Earth Blend pickup system. Track 19 on CD 1 and track 80 on CD 2 were recorded on my Ramirez nylon-string guitar.

All the audio tracks for *The Acoustic Guitar Bible* were mastered by Adam Pain at ACM. I am very grateful to all these individuals and manufacturers for their assistance in making this recording.

1 IN THE BEGINNING...

There Was Only Acoustic Guitar – And It Was Good

'For a musician, music is the best way to unite with God.' – Inayat Khan

The guitar family is so wide and varied that it is sometimes hard to recognise its members as being relatives at all. From the modern 7-string electric guitars to traditional 6-string flamenco guitars, from 12-string guitars to vintage arch-tops, the term 'guitar' means different things to different people. Each of these distinct instruments has a history, culture, terminology and repertoire that sets it apart from others.

Guitarists generally tend to put any guitar-like instrument into one of two broad categories: acoustic and electric. But, even then, certain instruments straddle the border. All guitars are acoustic in a sense. Strings tightened across the instrument cause it to resonate. While solid-body guitars need electric amplification to make their relatively low resonance audible, semi-solid and acoustic guitars rely on their bodies to amplify these vibrations and project them away from the instrument.

All these relations in our 'guitar family' are the result of hundreds, even thousands of years of evolution, cross-breeding and natural selection. Example 1.1 shows the main stages in the evolution of the guitar:

2500 BC
The Lyre and the Kithura (Greece). The first "Chordophones" – instruments working on a "vibrating" string principle are created.

2000 BC
The Nefer (Egypt). The earliest recorded existence of string instruments with a "neck and body" construction.

400 BC - 400 AD
The Cithara and Fidicula (Rome). The Romans, as they spread across Europe bring their own "Chordophones" with them.

700 AD
The Oud and Quitara. The invasion of Spain by the Moors, brings these middle eastern instruments further west.

1500 AD
The Guitarra and Vihuela (Spain/Europe). The emergence of the modern "guitar". These instruments are much smaller than the modern guitar but have the familiar "waist" curved "bouts". They have five "courses" (strings in pairs). The Guitarra tends to be smaller than the Vihuela. Gradually the top pair of strings is replaced by a single string. The tuning tends to be AA dd gg bb e'.

Late 18th – mid 19th Century
Late 18th – mid 19th Century The six course guitar emerges in Spain and France and, by 1800 the 5-course guitar has disappeared. By 1850 the double string courses have been replaced by single strings. Modern bracing patterns develop. Staufer (Germany) develops the modern fingerboard design of extending the fingerboard over the body as far as the soundhole. In America, CF Martin develops the x bracing system.

Early 20th Century
The modern steel string guitar emerges with the development of steel strings. Guitars and their bracings become bigger and stronger. The Dreadnought guitar is developed by the Martin guitar company and the popularity of Flat Top acoustic guitars increases. Companies such as Gibson and Washburn turn their attention to the flat top acoustic market. The Blues and Country music and, later, the Folk revival of the 1960's cement the worldwide appeal of the instrument.

Example 1.1: The evolution of the acoustic guitar

In this book we are zooming in on one particular branch of this wide and varied species – the acoustic steel-string guitar. We will meet some of the close relations later on in the book, but for now we'll take just a moment to make ourselves thoroughly acquainted with one particular member!

Construction

By way of introduction, let's look at a detailed diagram of the modern acoustic steel-string guitar, as shown in Example 1.2. In this diagram you can see the many different parts of the instrument. The *neck* supports the fingerboard and

its *frets*. Many centuries ago the guitar had movable frets made of gut string which was tied around the neck at set intervals. These days the frets are fixed at scientifically derived points on the neck. Guitar necks are of widely varying lengths, and each *luthier* (guitar maker) and guitar company will have a neck length that suits its design.

The *strings* cross the neck and operate on a particular section – from the *nut* at the top of the neck to the *bridge* on the guitar soundboard. The 12th fret marks the halfway point of the string length and is known as the *scale length*. From this fret the luthier calculates the positions of the remaining frets.

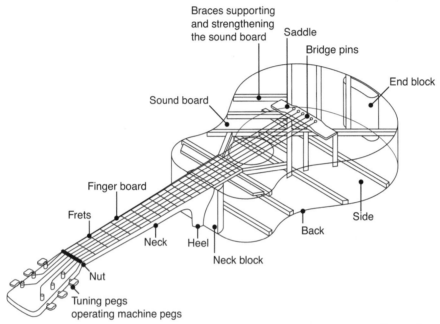

Example 1.2: The acoustic guitar

The acoustic guitar behaves in a highly complex way. The soundboard is the real sound generator of the guitar. When a note or a chord is sounded, the strings vibrate and cause

the soundboard (also known as the *top*) to vibrate in sympathy. The string vibrations work on many different planes at once:

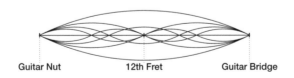

Example 1.3: A vibrating string showing the fundamental and the first three overtones

The vibrations of a tightened string have been documented in great detail by mathematicians, physicists and acoustic engineers. The key discovery has been that a single, struck string produces not only one note but, in theory, an infinite series of notes. In practice, the number of notes is limited, but still quite large. The 'fundamental' note produces the series of 'overtones' in diminishing percentages of volume. Example 1.4a shows the first few steps in the 'overtone series' produced from an open low E string. This series of intervals occurs with all vibrating strings. Example 1.4b shows where these overtones can be found on any open string. The first overtone (harmonic) can be played at the 12th fret. Lightly, but without pushing, touch the string directly over the 12th fret. Pluck the string with the right hand and you should produce a harmonic. (This technique is explained in greater detail later in the book.) The subsequent overtones can be found at the 7th fret, the 5th fret and at the locations marked in Example 1.4b. With practice and careful listening you can hear these various overtones.

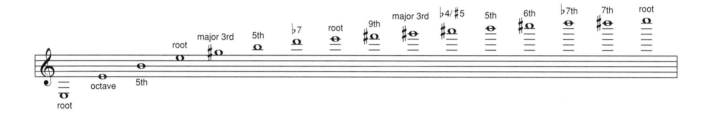

Example 1.4a: The overtone series based on an E fundamental

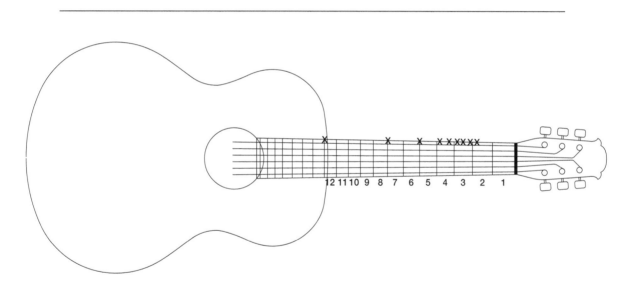

Example 1.4b: Overtones as found on an open string

Many factors affect the quality and quantity of these overtones. The relative mix of the fundamental note and its overtones affect the tone of the sound produced. Here is a short list of some of them:

- String length;
- String gauge;
- Condition and age of the string;
- String material;
- Type and quality of wood in the soundboard;

- Size and shape of the guitar soundboard;
- System of braces beneath the guitar soundboard;
- Depth and volume of the soundbox;
- Type of wood in the back and sides of the guitar;
- Point on the string where the string is plucked;
- Intensity of attack when the string is plucked;
- Type, density and shape of the material used to pluck the string (eg fingernail, thumbnail, flesh, plectrum and fingerpick).

The list can go on to include which finger is used to fret a note, the type of wood used in the guitar neck, the shape of the bridge and saddle system, the height of the frets, the height of the strings above the fretboard (the action), the shape, quality and design of the nut. All of these factors are effective even before we amplify the instrument, at which point many more factors affect the tone of each string.

The overtones correspond with the natural harmonics on an open string. There is a detailed description of these and the various techniques associated with harmonics in a later chapter.

The Soundboard

This string motion is also reflected in the movement of the soundboard. The soundboard is the prime source of the guitar's amplification. It has to be flexible enough to react efficiently to the vibration of the strings, while being strong enough to withstand the pull and pressure of 80kg of string tension.

The guitar soundboard vibrates in different ways at various points on its surface. To control this movement, guitar makers over the centuries have devised various 'bracing' systems. A simple ladder-bracing system was popular among ancient luthiers but has been virtually abandoned in favour of more complex systems. One of the most copied is the X-bracing system, designed by CF Martin in the 19th century for the Martin Guitar Company. Variations have included the double X-bracing system, the A-bracing system etc. One particularly innovative bracing system is that devised by Australian luthier Greg Smallman, who designed a complex lattice system of bracing for his nylon-string guitars. Example 1.5 shows a few examples of these styles:

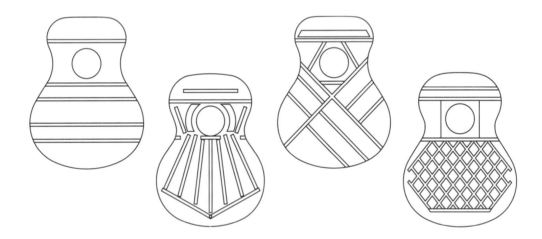

Example 1.5: Four guitar bracing systems.
From left: ladder-, fan-, X-brace and Smallman lattice

The choice of material for the soundboard is also critical in creating the 'voice' of a guitar. Over the years, luthiers have settled on spruce, cedar and redwood as being the most efficient in transforming the energy of vibrating strings into vibrating air around the soundboard. These woods have a high stiffness-to-weight ratio that makes them particularly suitable for soundboard construction. Mahogany and koa have also been found to be suitable.

Key Developments And Innovations In Acoustic Steel-String Design

The instrument that most people now refer to as an 'acoustic guitar' has been around for only the past 150 years or so. It is constantly undergoing design changes and developments by luthiers. Recent scientific explorations of the physics of guitar production and sound have led contemporary luthiers to develop many new construction techniques and designs.

Here are some of the key developments in the construction of the instrument:

- **Early 19th Century** – Development of 'single course' (ie single gut strings) and wound bass strings.

- **Mid-Late 19th Century** – Development of fan-bracing, which was a radical development of the more traditional and less effective ladder-bracing. Martin Guitar Company develops the X-bracing system.

- **Turn Of The 20th Century** – Continued development of

the steel string and the Martin Guitar Company's X-bracing system. Guitars are now competing with much louder instruments and luthiers start to develop larger and stronger instruments that can withstand the increased tension of heavier strings.

- **1930s** – Development of the Dreadnought guitar by Martin Guitar Company and the adjustable truss rod (neck-strengthening system) by Gibson.

Over the past 20 years, the traditional dovetail joint that connects the neck to the body of the guitar has been replaced widely in favour of bolt-on neck joints.

The Future Of Acoustic Guitar Construction And Design

Most guitar builders will tell you that the future of acoustic-guitar design is already here, with the replacement of traditional building materials. The timbers that have been used for centuries are in short supply, and to meet market demands guitar companies are turning to synthetic materials such as carbon fibre and fibreglass. Presuming that the acoustic guitar remains even remotely fashionable, builders this century will most certainly have to use these synthetic substitutes if they are to produce affordable yet efficient instruments.

Intonation

The ability of an instrument to play in tune in all positions on the fretboard and in all keys is the aim of all respectable guitar makers. However, due to the complexity of relationships between notes and their overtones, instrument builders face a number of difficulties. Without getting too deeply into the mathematics of intonation, let's take a simple example. The note C appears in many different keys. However in each of these keys the role of that C note is different. The C in the key of C major should have a slightly different pitch (that is, frequency) than the C that appears as, let's say, the third note in the key of A♭ major. This is because in one key it is the *tonic*, and in the other it is the *major third*.

Now, violinists and vocalists are free to express these slight variations of pitch, as their instruments are not restricted by a fixed tuning system or frets. Guitarists, on the other hand, generally have to play these notes as the same frequency.

Have you ever played a chord or sequence of notes low down on the neck and then found that playing the same sequence in a different key much further up the neck sounded out of tune? If the keys are not closely related (for example the key of C and the key of A♭) there can be a noticeable discrepancy in the intonation. Even with the most

well-maintained instrument and strings, there will always be this slight discrepancy. Over the centuries, instruments have been built that are fixed in pitch (take the overbearing accordion, for example) and don't allow for these differences. In the 18th century it was the intonation of the keyboard that caused the most arguments. In fact, at that time certain keys were unplayable. The keyboard is set with a fixed series of pitches that have to accommodate every key equally. However, to overcome the slight differences explained above (discovered by Pythagoras many thousands of years earlier and called 'Pythagoras's comma'!) each key had to be compromised slightly to average out these differences. After many years of experiments and suggestions a system was finally agreed upon, grudgingly, and the modern system of intonation was put in place.

With its varying string gauges (used for different ranges of pitch), the guitar has some additional problems. Builders have experimented with movable bridge pieces (almost standard now on all electric guitars), split bridge systems (like that designed by George Lowden), the 'zero' fret system (involving a fret placed just after the nut) employed by certain builders and 'kinked' frets. Guitar virtuoso John McLaughlin has experimented with interchangeable fretboards in his concerts to help him achieve the most accurate intonation for each piece of music!

While this is obviously impractical for the large majority of guitarists, it should help you to appreciate the importance of playing in tune. From my concert-going experience two players stand out as having remarkable intonation – the German fingerstyle guitarist Peter Finger and England's Martin Simpson. These two players are constantly aware of the pitch of every note they are playing, whether it is in a melody or in a chord.

Although the frets are fixed, the guitarist has control over the fine tuning of notes by bending notes slightly sharp with the fretting hand, or bending notes slightly flat by pushing the guitar neck gently forward. These techniques will help you to improve your intonation.

Concert Pitch

It wasn't until the 1980s that there was finally international agreement on the standard for concert pitch. Concert pitch is now globally recognised as A = 440Hz. This A note, which can be played at the 5th fret on the high E string, is the same A note used by all musicians and instrument makers everywhere as a common reference point. Before this, the A note had drifted over the past 300 years from as low as 419Hz to as high as 483Hz. Even today many musicians experiment with concert pitch; the Australian guitarist Tommy Emmanuel tunes his guitar to A = 444Hz, while jazz-guitar legend Martin Taylor prefers to tune his guitar to A

= 442Hz. Both players feel that this slight shift in pitch enhances the clarity and tone of the instrument.

Tuning The Guitar

A later chapter discusses the origins of 'standard tuning' and the enormous variety of 'alternate tunings'. In this section let's discuss the various ways of tuning the guitar accurately in standard tuning. For clarity in the rest of the book, the open strings of a standard tuned guitar are named more accurately, using Helmholtz notation, as...

E A d g b e'

from low to high. In other words the low E string (the 6th string) is named with a capital E while the top E string (the 1st) is known as e'. The E note that appears on the 2nd fret of the 4th string (the d string) is named e. The E note that appears on high e' string at the 12th fret would be e". In practice there are four E notes on the guitar fingerboard E, e, e' and e". When discussing lower notes we add apostrophes to the capital letters so that, for example, the low e string on a bass guitar would be known as E'. Going down another octave on a piano would bring us to E" and so on.

Electronic Tuners

While they are extremely useful, portable, inexpensive and accurate, there is a price to be paid for taking this route. In my experience, guitarists who tune with electronic tuners, particularly in their formative years, bypass a whole learning curve of pitch differentiation and development of a critical ear. By learning to tune with their 'eyes', these players often end up with no appreciation for the subtle variations in pitch required for accurate intonation. (These tuners do have their place though, in studios where tuning to concert pitch is necessary, and perhaps in noisy performance environments.)

If you're going to invest in an electronic tuner, I recommend the type with a needle marking the pitch and one that also can be calibrated. The tuner can then be calibrated for different tuning standards, such as a' = 441Hz or a' = 444Hz. Often these tuners will allow you to plug in either via a guitar cable or via a small built-in microphone. Ideally you would use an electronic tuner in conjunction with your ears. You can set up a correctly tuned reference pitch (eg the open high e' string) and tune the rest of the strings from this one note.

Tuning From A Pre-tuned Reference Point

This could be from a piano (or electronic keyboard), which can generally be taken to be in concert pitch (A = 440Hz); a tuning fork; or the recording of a work which is known to be in concert pitch.

With experience and practice you can train yourself to recognise when a note is in concert pitch or not. Like any of the human senses, there will be days when your ear is more accurate than others. Be gentle with yourself and allow yourself to extend your skills gradually over months and years rather than hours and days.

Once you have successfully determined this note (it could in theory be any note but I suggest that you work from an open string to begin with, preferably any E or A note) then find this note in other positions on the guitar fingerboard and do a 'like for like' comparison.

The Fifth-Fret Method

This method is well documented in many guitar books and by numerous guitar teachers worldwide. In quick summary, the method is as follows:

Tune the open high e' string to a concert e', either from memory or a trusted reference point, then compare the pitch of this string with the note at the 5th fret of the b (2nd) string. These two notes should be identical. If they're not, tune the b string until its pitch at the 5th fret matches that of the open e' string. At this point the two strings are in tune and you can proceed to the g (third) string. Because

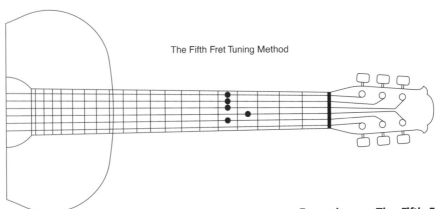

The Fifth Fret Tuning Method

Example 1.5: The Fifth-Fret tuning method

of the pattern of intervals in the standard tuning of guitars, you should now compare the open b string with the note on the 4th fret of the g string. Again, tune the g string until the pitch at its 4th fret is identical to the pitch of the open b string. The method continues at the 5th fret, comparing the notes of previously tuned open strings with the note on the 5th fret of the adjacent string.

Inconsistencies Of The Fifth-Fret Method

While this method is good for ballpark tuning, it is not particularly accurate. It all comes back to intonation and a slight blip in the mathematics of pitch and the cycle of fifths (see below for a detailed explanation).

With the fifth-fret method, the strings are tuned at one particular point on the string. As explained above in the section 'Intonation', you will find that being in tune at the 5th fret won't necessarily mean that the instrument is in tune at the 10th or other frets.

Equally, tuning the six open strings with an electronic tuner or any other means will not necessarily mean that the guitar is in tune all over the fingerboard. A more accurate tuning can be achieved as follows.

Tuning With Harmonics
The Accurate Method

There are many methods of tuning with harmonics. Unfortunately, many of them produce poor results. As mentioned above, the world of tuning and intonation is not as simple as it might seem. (For example, a C note in the key of C is not the same as the C note that belongs to the key of Bb., or G or Ab.) Here's the science bit – now pay attention!

Example 1.6 shows the 12 steps of the chromatic scale (a 12-step scale made up of semitone steps) arranged in a cycle. Each clockwise step on the cycle is an interval of a perfect fifth. Each semitone (equivalent to a movement of one fret on the guitar) can be subdivided into 100 equal divisions called *cents*, so an octave (12 semitones) is 1,200 cents. If you start at C (at the 12 o'clock point) and tune the G perfectly to the C (an interval of a perfect fifth), then continue by tuning the D a perfect fifth above the G and so on clockwise around the cycle, you will eventually arrive back at C. However, if you have tuned correctly at each stage you will find that the C at the end of the process is 24 cents sharper than the C you started with! This is the 'comma' in Pythagoras's comma mentioned above. Its originator conveniently ignored it, acknowledging that one day it would rear its ugly, out-of-tune head! It took a couple of thousand years, but eventually, in the 18th century, things came to a raging boil as musicians and composers argued about the most effective way to accommodate all the keys on all instruments but in particular on the keyboard. People retreated in various opposing camps as numerous tuning 'temperaments' were devised. Eventually 'equal temperament' (the division of the octave into 12 equal steps of 100 cents each originally conceived by Marin Mersenne in 1636) came to be regarded as the best solution, although even to this day musicians will adhere to other methods.

But back to our 24 cents' worth of difference on the cycle of fifths. The 24 cents represent almost a quarter of a semitone – quite noticeable when those two C notes are played together. By tuning each of the fifths a little flat by two cents (almost imperceptible), the 'error' can be

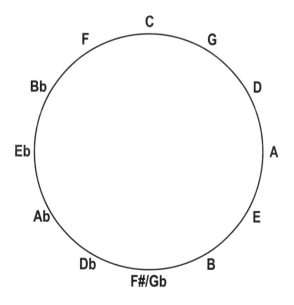

Example 1.6: The Cycle of Fifths

corrected. Of course, it isn't an error at all. The 'perfect fifth' is a naturally occurring interval (see Example 1.4a). We have had to devise man-made intervals to allow our ears to deal with nature's wonderful variety! By tuning each fifth a couple of cents flat, the cumulative effect over a whole octave is to counterbalance the 24 cents in difference.

The octaves and unison intervals remain pure while all the other intervals are slightly out of tune. Of course, these differences are very small and make themselves known only in large position shifts on the guitar fingerboard or in unusual key changes (say, the key of A major to the key of C minor, which share only one note, D). For the most accurate tuning you should restrict yourself to only unison or octave intervals. In addition, you should aim to make these intervals at a wide variety of points over the first 12 frets. The following method will prove to be very accurate.

The Failsafe Tuning Method

Tune the e' string (the open 1st string) as the reference point. Play the 12th-fret harmonic on the b string and compare it to the fretted note at the 7th fret on the high e' string. Tune the second string to the first. Next, play the 12th-fret harmonic on the g string and compare it to the fretted note at the 3rd fret on the high e' string. Remember that you are tuning the third string by comparing its pitch with the first string. Now play the 12th-fret harmonic on the d string and compare it to the fretted note at the 3rd fret on the b string. Play the 12th-fret harmonic on the A string and compare that note to the fretted note at the 2nd fret on the g string. Finally, play the 12th-fret harmonic on the low E string and compare it to the fretted note at the 2nd fret on the d string. Example 1.7 summarises these steps:

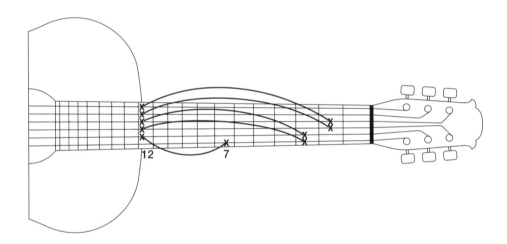

Example 1.7: The failsafe method of tuning with harmonics

Even after tuning with this method you will need to fine-tune all the strings again as the act of tuning each string changes the tension of the other strings ever so slightly. With practice you will find that you can tune with this method quite quickly. Once you feel you are in tune, try the following chords. Their voicings are designed to highlight any tuning gremlins! These voicings contain many of the four perfect intervals (unison, fourth, fifth and octave), intervals that are very 'vocal' when out of tune! Other intervals, such as seconds, thirds and sixths, are a little more flexible and our ears will more easily forgive these intervals when they are slightly sharp or flat. The 'tuning by harmonics' method helps to average out the inconsistencies of pitch caused by varying string gauges and tension as well as the mathematical differences discussed above in 'Intonation'.

The chords in Ex. 1.8 are sensitive to inaccurate tuning:

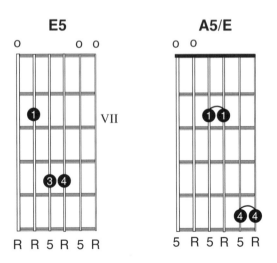

Example 1.8: Two chords sensitive to inaccurate tuning

Practice Makes Perfect

First, let's look at some hand science! This section will introduce some exercises to get our left and right hands warmed up (left-handed readers should make the obvious edits, while ambidextrous readers...you're just being greedy!).

Let's start with a description of how the human hand functions. There are about 60 muscles in the arm and hand. In Example 1.9 you will see that the thumb and four fingers are controlled by muscles in the arm, primarily the forearm. These muscles are attached via ligaments to tendons. The tendons are enclosed in a sheath and lubricated with *synovial fluid*. The tendons encased in these sheaths pass through the carpal tunnel in the wrist – a complex series of bones forming a flexible structure that allows the wrist to move in many directions. Having passed through the carpal tunnel, these tendons are attached to the bones in the fingers via ligaments. Hold your hand and wrist out parallel to the floor and move your fingers quickly in a 'typing action'. You should see the tendon flexing on the back of your hand and over the first knuckles.

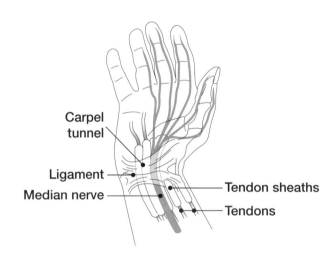

Example 1.9: The structure of the human hand

The common problems that can occur in the hands of guitarists are tendonitis and carpal-tunnel syndrome. These are examples of the common 'overuse' injuries – also known as RSI (Repetitive Strain Injury) – that can affect guitarists. How do they occur? They can happen quite suddenly, due to a trauma to the system, or by over-use of a particular muscle, bone or tendon, or gradually, through poor practice methods.

Too Much Of A Good Thing
Tendonitis

Tendonitis in guitarists is rarely manifested as damage to the tendon itself, but more commonly as damage to the muscle attached to the tendon. When the muscle, bone or tendon is stressed beyond its physical limit, an over-use injury occurs. This injury is caused by numerous microscopic tears that cause a little bleeding and swelling in that region.

Tendonitis can be acute or chronic. Acute tendonitis happens when a guitarist learns a new chord, stretch or phrase and practises it repetitively for many hours with little or no break for relaxation. The injury will often take a few hours' or a night's sleep before it is noticed as a dull, painful stiffness of the hand or arm. Chronic tendonitis takes a bit longer to manifest itself and is often the result of poor technique and/or posture which is used over many weeks and months. When this type of tendonitis is inflicted on the system, it can seem quite mild at first but will become more severe as the weeks and months pass.

Treatment Of Tendonitis

Tendonitis is often treatable with a period of rest. Cooling the inflammation with packs of ice will often help to alleviate the pain also. More extreme cases can be treated with medication and should be administered with the advice of a qualified physician.

Carpal Tunnel Syndrome

CTS (Carpal Tunnel Syndrome) is a very specific injury to the median nerve that runs from the arm in through the wrist and into the hand. The nerve goes to the thumb, forefinger, middle finger and ring finger along the palm side of the hand but not to the little finger. It passes through a small tunnel in the complex wrist bone system and the carpal ligament called the *carpal tunnel*. Any swelling of the carpal ligament can cause pressure on the nerve and result in varying degrees of discomfort and restriction of movement.

The symptoms of CTS can be more dramatic than those of tendonitis. It usually begins with a 'pins and needles' tingling in the hand affecting all the fingers, bar the little one. It also creates sharp pains in the hand and sends pain shooting up the arm. Over-bending of the wrist can inflame the carpal ligament and lead to CTS. Guitarists who arch their wrists over the neck or overbend their right wrist in the classical approach can be more vulnerable. Keeping your hands warm is certainly a good idea. If you go from a warm studio out into the cold winter evening air while carrying a heavy guitar and case you are most likely to put the tendons and ligaments in your hands and forearms under sudden stress. Muscles, tendons and ligaments are very susceptible to temperature changes, so take steps to ensure that they are never exposed to sudden or extreme heat or cold.

There are some simple tests that may indicate CTS:

- Tingling in the thumb and fingers, but not the little finger, can suggest but not prove that the median nerve is being trapped in the carpal tunnel;

- Extreme bending of the wrist inwards with the thumb folded in towards the palm of the hand will cause a sharp pain to shoot up the arm. This is often known as *Phalen's signal*;

- Hold out your arm and tap your wrist on the palm side. If you feel a tingling like a small electric shock – what's known as *Tinel's sign* – this could indicate CTS.

Treatment Of CTS

Very often the best treatment is resting the hand for a few days or a week. In this time you should refrain from all playing. (Use it as an opportunity to brush up on some music theory or ear training!) In more serious cases the hand must be splinted in an extended position to allow the swelling of the carpal ligament to subside. In some cases the cause could be further back along the line at the shoulder or neck, in which case a chiropractor may be needed to release the trapped nerve.

Here are some of the possible causes of overuse injuries:

- A radical increase in the amount of playing/practising. Over the many years I've been teaching at guitar colleges, such as the Musicians' Institute, London, and the Academy of Contemporary Music, I have come to expect a small number of cases where students leave the school within the first month due to hand injuries. For many of these guitarists, they are moving up to fifth gear in their practice schedules too soon. Under pressure to compete with their classmates, they fail to follow the warm-up advice given in the first class. They change from playing guitar two to four hours a day to playing and practising for up to eight hours a day. This puts an increased stress on all the muscles, bones and tendons involved in guitar playing. In some cases, it can result in injury.

- Poor technique. One of the most common mistakes made by guitarists is to play with too much tension. It can be most common in the left hands of guitarists who grip the neck and fingerboard too tightly. Apart from impeding their movement, this over-squeezing of the hand and fingers can cause tendonitis. When the muscles are tight and weak, they are far more vulnerable to injury particularly through over use. Carpal-tunnel syndrome is relatively rare among guitarists, although some people seem to be more susceptible to CTS than others. Overbending of either wrist for prolonged periods can bring it on.

- Poor posture. We use our whole bodies to play the guitar. Our legs support the body. The neck and shoulders, via the guitar strap, support the instrument. Our arms and hands are involved in the selecting and generating of the sound. Our posture, whether it is standing or sitting, is critical for the effective action of our fingers and hands. Finding the appropriate posture for our own bodies is a search that too few guitarists consider. Consistency of posture is also important. Practising the guitar whilst sitting on the edge of bed mattress or slumped back into a sofa will not translate into the technique and posture that is necessary for standing up on stage. The guitar neck and hand positions during practice should be carried through to the performance situation. You should strive to keep a consistency of technique from practice through to performance (you will find that this is helpful in beginning to overcome stage fright – more about this in a later chapter).

- A sudden change in the style of instrument or style of music. There are so many varieties of instrument styles and musical styles that many guitarists will explore over many years. The string tension on a typical nylon-string classical guitar is far less than on a typical 12-string guitar. They require greatly different techniques and are generally used for very different styles of playing. A large 'Dreadnought'-style guitar will have a radically different shape and weight to a 'parlour' guitar. Switching from a classical-based fingerstyle technique to a heavier blues style, where the hand is required to bend lots of notes, can also translate as a sudden stress to the system.

- General health. A change in the health of the musician, or a genetic condition that predisposes to weak muscles or bones, can also be the cause of injury. Women are statistically more likely to develop osteoporosis (weakening of the bones). Poor diet can also lead to under-developed muscles and bones. Previous injuries, particularly those that haven't been correctly treated or possibly have been left untreated, will make the system more prone to further injury.

- Work and everyday life. Our activities outside of our guitar-playing lives, such as work and playing sports, can put particular strains on our arms and hands, bones and muscles. Frequent rest and proper procedures are key to ensuring that you are at the least degree of risk.

Symptoms

So, how do you know when you have incurred an overuse injury? There are various categories, classified according to the level of discomfort:

1 Pain is associated with playing and is in one place only (eg wrist, forearm and palm).

2 Pain is in a number of places, and again is only noticeable while playing the guitar.

3 Pain persists after you stop playing and includes some loss of mobility of the painful area.

4 Any of these three types of pain, as described here, but which are also brought on by everyday activity away from the instrument.

All of the above pains, and any activity with a specific muscle or area, causes disabling pain (that is, you are completely restricted in your use of that body part).

Effective Practice Plans

Your practice schedule will be particular to you. Your lifestyle, musical ability, goals and determination will each affect the regularity and pattern of your practice. Therefore it is impractical to create a generic practice plan that will suit everyone. For most people, time spent practising is at a premium and must be as effective as possible. These tips will help you to design the most effective practice session for you.

- Start your practice session with some warm-up and stretching exercises (see Example 1.10 below). As a rule of thumb you should warm up for five minutes of every hour you intend to practise. So, for example, if you intend to do a two-hour practice session then you should do some warm-up exercises for about ten minutes first.

- Have some goals in mind before you start. The goals need to be challenging yet achievable. A goal may be to play a certain scale at a certain speed by the end of the session. It may be to play the opening 16 bars of some challenging piece. It may be to perfect a certain technique or tone. Whatever your goal, keep it in mind as you practise.

- Ideally you should have some variety in your practice time. This can be achieved by setting goals in different aspects of your playing – technique, performance and repertoire, music theory and music reading.

- Your practice sessions need to connect with each other. Goals set and achieved in one session need to be followed through and built upon in a subsequent (though not necessarily the next) session. You may set yourself a goal to play a particular piece up to concert standard within two/four/six weeks/months/years(!).

- Don't confuse 'jamming' or rehearsal with practice. Often a guitarist will sit down to practise and immediately go over music that she can already play to a high standard. The practice session becomes a self-indulgent ego massage! (Incidentally I highly recommend this type of activity – it is healthy and fun and allows the musician to explore music in an expressive and free way. However, it is important that you do not include this in your end-of-year practising accounts!)

- Finish the practice session with a 'warm down', gently playing those exercises at a slower tempo than in your warm-up.

A friend of mine had a unique approach to his practice planning. It was entirely a repertoire-based practice schedule. He would select a 'piece of the week' – a piece of music perhaps a couple of pages long that he would

Example 1.10: A good left-hand position allows you to play more comfortably.

master each week. He would then move onto a new piece each week. At the same time he would work on a 'piece of the month', which would be a more challenging piece. Again he would move onto a new 'piece of the month' each month. Then as a challenge to himself he would set the goal of a 'piece of the year'. This piece was a guitar 'masterwork' that required dedicated practice and involved some challenging technical development. So at any one time he would be working simultaneously on three pieces and, in theory, was getting through 65 pieces a year. No mean feat! His technique now shows the results of that dedication and focus. I took his method and adapted it to composing, aiming to write a piece each month and a more developed and challenging composition once a year. However, composition does not seem to work on the same principles as practice!

Plateaus And Ruts

Many guitarists report of finding themselves in a rut or on a plateau of playing ability. No matter how much they practise, they feel that they cannot get out of this rut. As a beginner, you may find that you progress relatively rapidly – with a few chords and a few simple techniques you can play numerous songs and pieces. After a while your rate of improvement slows down until you eventually feel that you cannot improve at all, and may in fact be rolling back down the hill! Then, without warning, you find yourself moving uphill again with greater ease, only to find yourself in a rut again some time later. The general trend is upwards, but these plateaus would seem to get longer the further along the road you progress.

In my experience, there are a few things that spark off that new lease of life in your playing. A new teacher, a new artist, a new piece, a concert, a life event – any of these things can inspire your playing and kick-start you into the

next phase of your growth. My only advice to you is to stay focused on what you are doing right now and don't fall into the trap of comparing yourself to others and their progress (or lack thereof!). Everyone progresses at their own rate and they cannot be compared with each other. With each stage of development there will be a deeper understanding of music and the instrument, which will open your eyes and ears to deeper levels of problems and technicalities. It's rather like climbing to the top of a mountain only to face an easy run down and an even more difficult climb over a higher mountain! Just take solace from the fact that all guitarists face these plateaus and ruts. Always remain a student. Those who think they are masters are not.

Reading Tablature

All the examples in this book are presented on two staves, each containing either standard notation or tablature notation (tab). I expect that many of the readers have a basic understanding of traditional music notation (that is, the dots, lines and spaces). However, this book will also use tab notation for all of the exercises and examples.

The system of notating guitar music in tablature form has its origins in the notation of lute music in the Renaissance and Baroque periods (15th–18th centuries). As the lute went out of fashion, tab notation also fell out of use. It was all but dead when it was revived during the folk boom of the 1960s.

Thousands of guitar enthusiasts with little or no music-reading skills found the tab system easy and accessible. It has developed into a much more highly complex system, particularly since the 1980s, when there was an enormous explosion in popular guitar books and transcriptions.

While there are a number of variations of the basic system, the tablature notation system is based on a simple diagram – the *stave* – representing the six guitar strings:

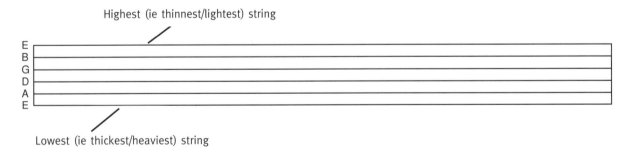

Highest (ie thinnest/lightest) string

Lowest (ie thickest/heaviest) string

Example 1.11: The tablature stave

The bottom line represents the lowest (in pitch) string of the guitar while the top line represents the highest (in pitch) string.

The tab 'clef' at the start of the stave is normally used to distinguish it from the very similar standard-notation stave:

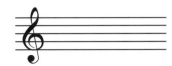

Example 1.12: Standard-notation stave with a treble clef

For the moment you should understand that, while guitarists and all other musicians can use standard notation, the tab system can be used only by guitarists, although there are related tab systems for other stringed instruments in the guitar family, such as the electric bass, banjo and mandolin.

This is certainly one of the tab system's greatest shortcomings – that it cannot be used universally by all musicians. (Try handing some tab to a piano player!)

We use numbers to indicate the guitar frets in the tab system. Here are the open strings:

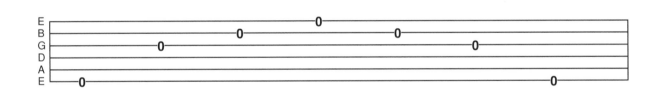

These numbers represent the open strings from lowest to highest. Here is a simple melody using the open strings:

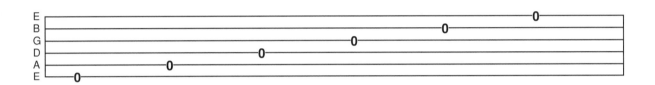

We can also represent the fretted notes with other numbers. Remember, the numbers represent the frets, not the fingers:

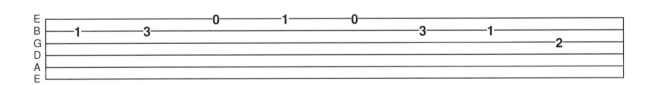

And a simple E major arpeggio:

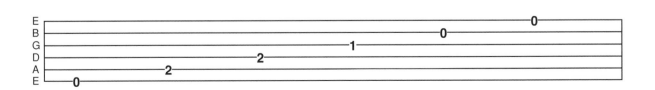

...and the notes of an A minor pentatonic scale (2 octaves):

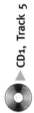
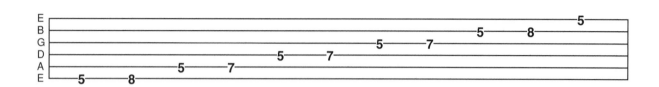

Here's the same scale played an octave higher:

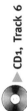
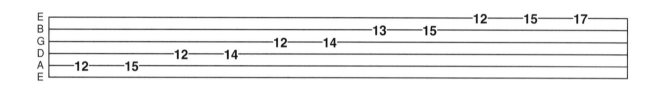

We can always play more than one note at a time. In fact, all of the chords that you play involve at least two notes and, often, up to six notes simultaneously. Fortunately, as there are only six strings on a guitar, guitar chords will never involve more than six notes!

Here are the notes of a simple D major chord. As you can see, the numbers are now written vertically, suggesting that they should be played together:

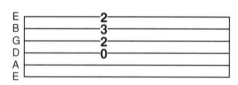

Here's a simple chord progression:

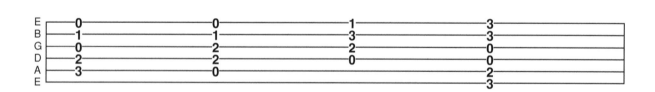

You will also see simple harmonies written in tab. Remember that the pairs of notes are played together:

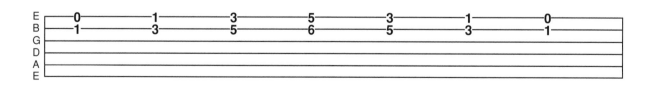

Some Warm-up Exercises

These first exercises are designed for the left (fretting) hand. The aim of these exercises is to achieve the following:

- Greater clarity of the notes through effective fretting
- Greater stretch between the left hand fingers
- Improvement of tone and wider tonal range
- Greater rhythmic accuracy
- Improved synchronisation between both hands
- Expanded dynamic control

...all with the minimum exertion of energy and the maximum efficiency of movement. The exercises that follow should all be practised with a metronome; each will have a recommended tempo or range of tempi indicated.

Longitudinal Exercises

In this first exercise, begin by holding your arms at full length parallel to the floor. Let your wrists and hands relax and fall towards the floor. Shake them loosely for a few moments and then try the exercise below.

Set your metronome to 70bpm. The fretting-hand fingers are lined up on adjacent strings and frets, as indicated in the notation below. Hold down the first four notes together to form a (quite dissonant!) chord (from the D diminished scale). You will find that the left-hand thumb needs to be approximately in the position suggested in the photograph on the left in Example 1.10 (pg. 23). The fingers should be arched and pressing the strings just behind the frets with the fingertips. The only points of the hand touching the guitar neck and fingerboard should be the pad of the thumb and the tips of the fingers.

Before you start the exercise, make yourself aware of the feeling in your forearm, hand and fingers. Are you able to hold the simple chord effortlessly? Is it possible to play the notes with less pressure? Is there any perceptible change in tone or sound quality if you do so? The pressure needs to be just enough that you can ensure that the note is steady in tone, volume and quality. By playing as close to the fret wire as possible, you should be able to reduce the pressure exerted by your fingers without compromising the sound. Many guitarists apply too much pressure to the neck; with light-gauge strings (.011 sets and less) the pressure applied is enough to bend the notes sharp (very useful when done intentionally!). This effect is usually undesirable, though, and you will find that you will have greater control of your hands

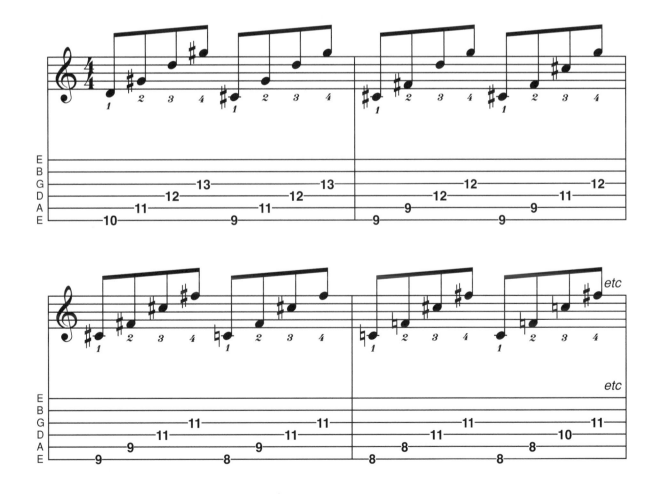

and sound when you apply less (but just enough) pressure. Think of it as the Goldilocks effect – not too much pressure, not too little, but just right. That 'just right' pressure varies with hand size, posture, string gauge, the camber of the neck, the action of the strings and the strength of your fingers.

At this point, many of the simple principles of yoga come into play. You need to develop a good relationship with yourself and your body. Learn to 'listen' to your body. Know where all your 'edges' are. Learn how to approach each edge and how to extend these 'barriers' so that you can do more, more easily.

Right Hand Warm-up Exercises

For these exercises we will concentrate on the right hand. Each finger has its own particular name and abbreviation.

Example 1.13 shows diagrams of the left and right hand fingering abbreviations. The left hand is numbered 1–4 with the thumb marked T and the right hand is lettered p, i, m, a and c, letters taken from the Spanish names of the fingers: *pulgar*, *indice*, *medio*, *anular* (ring) and *chico*.

The next exercise is a template for numerous other exercises in the book. The thumb plays the three bass strings,

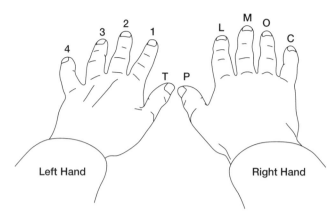

Example 1.13: Numbering system for left and right hands

the index finger plays the g string, the middle finger plays the b string, the ring finger plays the high e' string. The little finger (c) is less commonly used in fingerstyle playing. Play this exercise with a metronome. Aim for a steady, even rhythm, even tone and even dynamics. Try to keep all the notes at the same level of volume and quality of tone.

The exercise is based on a simple E major chord. You can shift the shape up one fret every four bars to give some more interesting sounds to a potentially monotonous sound.

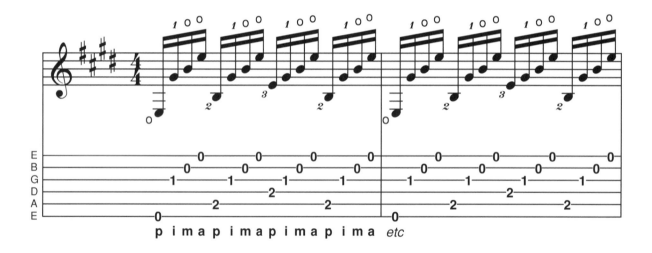

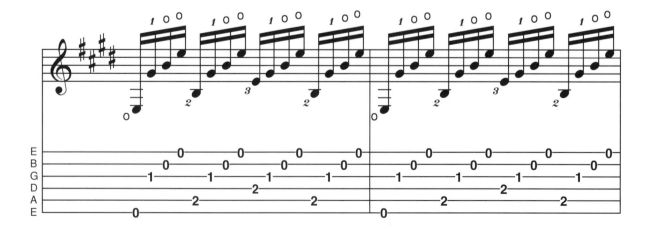

There are also some simple variations that you can try, such as...

...and:

Left And Right Hand Synchronisation Exercise

This exercise is designed to help the player create greater and deeper synchronisation of the left and right hands. Like the previous exercise, it should be played with a metronome. This exercise is written in eighth notes (that's two notes per metronome click). Start with the metronome at 80bpm and build up to 120bpm. Aim for clear and even tone, as before. The right hand fingers alternate index/middle, index/middle, etc:

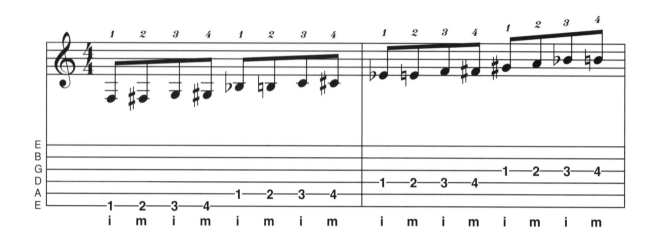

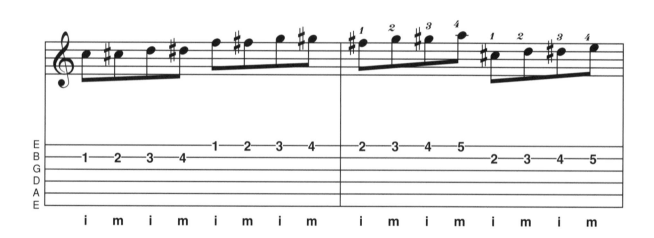

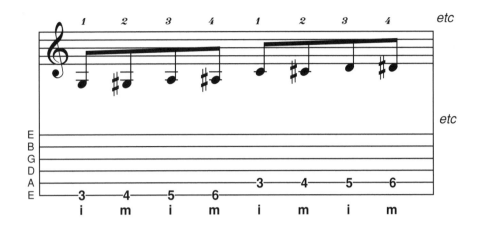

Try some of these variations for the right hand:

m	a	m	a		m	a	m	a
m	i	m	i		m	i	m	i
a	i	a	i		a	i	a	i

These exercises will appear in different forms later in the book so make sure that you become familiar with them.

2 THE WHOLE WORLD IN HIS HANDS

The Role Of Technique

'Technique lets you fly your kite!' – Tommy Emmanuel

Here's a simple equation:

TECHNIQUE = CONTROL

Without technique, you are powerless. Poor technique will not allow you to execute the notes, chords rhythms textures, and tone. that you are trying so hard to achieve. However, we all have some level of technique. The question is always:

How effective is my technique?

Ultimately, we have to adapt any technique to suit our particular situation. We all have different hand shapes, arm lengths, guitar necks, fingernail preferences and posture preferences. You can look to other players as a source or inspiration and information in our development of effective technique, but in the end the technique has to serve *you* and the music you are making. As we saw in the previous chapter, the warm-up exercises can expose deficiencies in our technique and point the way to improving it.

It is useful at this point to appreciate that it is music that has generated the techniques of music playing. Composers and players down through the millennia have built, adapted and struggled with instruments to create the music. Technique, that is *control*, arose from musical needs and problems. Just as music theory follows practice, so too does music technique. It is from this perspective that many of the great guitar innovators have emerged, players such as Chet Atkins, John Fahey, Michael Hedges, Joni Mitchell, etc, who have pushed the envelope of guitar technique and allowed the music to guide their technical innovations rather than vice versa. 'The music has generated all the techniques I use,' said jazz-guitar guru Pat Martino. In a world where we have endless guitar schools, guitar tuition videos, guitar tuition magazines and guitar instruction books, there is a danger that students

of the guitar will feel compelled to accumulate as much technique and as many varieties of techniques as possible. This approach of 'technique being an end in itself' has no place on the path to musicianship. Many student guitarists I meet are overly concerned with the 'how to do' questions rather than the 'what to do'. The question 'What should I play?', if reflected upon seriously, will guide you to the answer for 'How do I play it?'. This is not in any way meant to free you from the obligation to practise to the point where your technique allows you to play freely. However, many students stop listening to the sound they are creating at some point and continue single-mindedly on a journey into the stratosphere of technical prowess, leaving music behind in their jet stream!

> *Don't practise in order to master a particular technique, but instead practise so that the technique allows you to hear what music sounds like.*

The development of effective technique will allow you to control the myriad of parameters that make up a musical performance and experience. Effective technique will allow you to control the length, attack, decay, sustain, tone, volume, projection and the emotion of any note. Poor technique leaves many of these aspects of sound to chance. For certain styles of playing, this may not be the greatest crime, but in other styles it may result in an average or below-average execution. And before you assume that these parameters are only related to the right (plucking) hand, it is equally important to have an effective technique for the left hand. The correct fingering of a note or chord, placement of the fingers on the fingerboard and the position of the hand relative to the fingerboard are all matters that affect the quality of the sound.

In very broad terms, the hands can be classified as:

LEFT HAND = TONE SELECTOR
RIGHT HAND = TONE GENERATOR

The left hand will generally, though not always, select the notes that the right hand sounds. Immediately obvious exceptions to this description of 'division of labour' are left-hand *hammer-ons* and *pull-offs*. Here the left hand will both select the note and sound it. Another exception is where the right hand taps notes on the fingerboard, thereby selecting and sounding notes, or the case of *harp harmonics*, where again the right hand selects particular harmonics and also sounds them. All of these techniques and more will be discussed and demonstrated in subsequent chapters.

Practice Makes Perfect

But perfection is unattainable! So, again, in broad terms, the development of effective technique is equally important to each hand.

> 'Establish the possible and then move gradually towards the impossible.'
>
> – *Robert Fripp*

As some of the exercises in Chapter 1 demonstrated, when engaged in your practice you should start from 'the point where you are'. In other words, establish your present ability in terms of technical ability and move forward gradually in controlled steps. In this sense, the approach is very similar to yoga. The aim should be to do a little at a time, very often. All of the aspects of sound are measurable. Aspects such as speed, stretch, and finger independence are easily quantified, while matters such as tone, dynamics and emotion are audible but more subjectively determined.

The word *yoga* means 'to bind together'. In the spiritual sense the binding together is of the body, mind and spirit. In guitar terms we could bring together these three aspects:

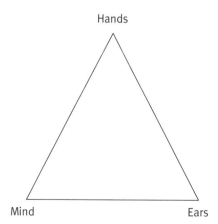

Hands
The hands are engaged with the techniques and physical aspects of music making. By themselves they are quite useless; they may be able to play all the correct notes in the correct order, but without the mind and ears, the notes will effectively be empty. The mind trains the hands (guided by the ears) to make the music, but the *musical intention* is a little further back along the chain of events.

Mind
The mind is engaged with the guidance of the hands but also processes the information coming back to it from the ears and other senses, including the hands. To varying degrees the mind is also analysing this information from musically theoretical point of view. In this sense the mind also needs training. By developing the mind's *inner* ear (not to be confused with the inner ear that forms part of the ear's construction) the musician can anticipate sounds before they occur. This also facilitates musical composition. This inner ear was so highly developed during his lifetime that Ludwig van Beethoven composed his final (and some say his greatest) works despite his deafness.

Ears
Hearing is the most important sense for a musician. It is followed closely by touch and sight. The ear sends the mind a constant flow of information about the music that is occurring around it. This gives the mind the tools it needs to make decisions about the quality of the sound and to execute any adjustments. Even with an intermediate-level player, this process takes place at lightning speed. Matters such as left-hand pressure, posture, tone, dynamics, tempo, right-hand position, context of the sound and placement of the sound in space are just some of the many pieces of information flowing to the brain and being minutely adjusted in 'real time' (effectively). The ear can also be trained to listen very critically to the sound coming into it. 'Ear training' programmes and classes are generally designed to train the mind to analyse and recognise musical sound. However, there is also an element of actual 'ear training' whereby the musicians learn how to move their heads and ears through space (as any good sound engineer does) to listen to the sound in different ways.

By developing this 'yoga' approach to your guitar playing you may begin to feel a shift from *guitarmanship* to *musicianship*. It is through the combination of these three aspects of musicianship that the guitarist can begin to 'zoom out' and see technique in the correct context – as a means to a musical end.

But now we need to develop our technique...

Technique

'All this discussion of musicianship, yoga, practice and kites is fine, but where are the technical-development exercises?' I hear you ask.

Let's keep these technical exercises as musical as possible. You didn't buy this book to have me show you lots of boring exercises and scale patterns.

The first exercise is based on a simple four-note/four-finger pattern for the right hand. The pattern is the same for each chord – the thumb plays the bass note of each chord on the down-beat and the other fingers play on the subsequent three 16th notes. Aim for even dynamics, tempo and tone:

CD1, Track 10

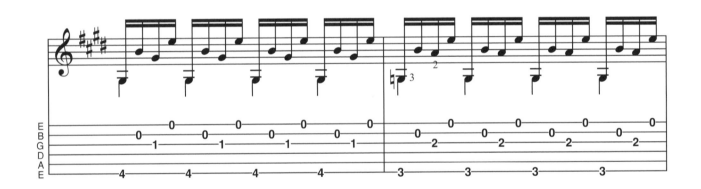

Example 2.1

Next is a similar example. Here the thumb moves across to other strings in the pattern. It gives the rhythm an interesting 'rolling' effect. Take note of the interesting chord voicings that the combination of fretted notes and open strings produces.

CD1, Track 11

p i p m p i p m etc

Example 2.2

Exercise 2.2 is in the key of D minor but moves through the natural and the harmonic minor (bar 8) versions of this key.

One of the greatest influences on fingerstyle guitar, and guitarists in general, was Merle Travis. Merle was born in Kentucky in 1917. He was inspired to switch from the 5-string banjo to the guitar by the playing of the local coal miner Ike Everly (whose sons Don and Phil went on to fame and fortune as The Everly Brothers). Merle took this inspiration and developed a new approach to guitar playing with his alternating bass lines:

CD1, Track 12

Example 2.3

In the example above you need to be aware of the independent bass line that the thumb plays. If you find Example 2.3 challenging, practise Example 2.4 first with a metronome. In this exercise, the right-hand thumb plays this bass line steadily. When you're confident, go back to Example 2.3.

CD1, Track 13

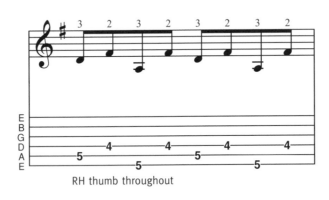

RH thumb throughout

Example 2.4

These bass lines alternate between the *root* and the *fifth* (more about these terms later). In Example 2.4, the fifth is below the root. In Example 2.5, at the top of the next page, the fifth is above the root.

In both Examples 2.3 and 2.5, the left-hand third finger is moving in time with the bass line – it must do so. If there is poor synchronisation between the left and right hands, the notes will sound either too short (if the left hand places the notes too soon) or indistinct (if the left hand lifts just before the right-hand thumb strikes the note). Practise the bass line in all these examples with a metronome and ensure that (for the moment) the notes are as long as possible. The left-hand third finger should be moving perfectly in time with the right-hand thumb.

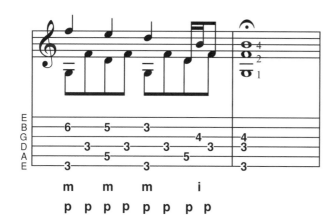

Example 2.5

Here is an example of a Travis-style lick in E blues:

Example 2.6

The thumb plays the notes with the down stems. In this example the guitar strings are slightly muted by the action of the right hand on the strings.

Paradoxically, by damping the bass notes you accent their rhythmic effect. Many of the overtones (as discussed in Chapter 1) are muted, and the fundamental tone, though slightly muffled, is more prominent.

Strumming

Many guitarists start their guitar journeys by strumming simple chords as accompaniment for vocal performances or playing along with records. Yet, as they progress in various other techniques, it is common for many guitarists to leave strumming and rhythm playing on the shelf. However, strumming is one of the unique characteristics of acoustic guitar. It produces a sound and texture that can't be emulated by other instruments.

Now let's take a look at a simple strumming pattern that should reveal any inadequacies that might be present in your technique:

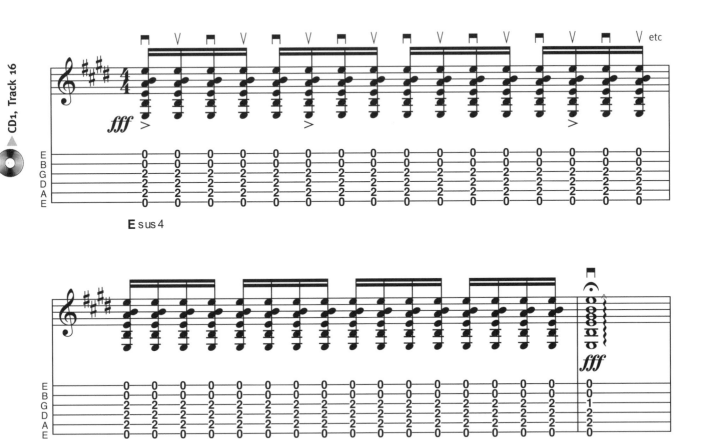

Example 2.7

In this next exercise, the simple E chord shape is played in a repeating rhythm. You can continue to shift the shape up the neck to produce different harmonic effects:

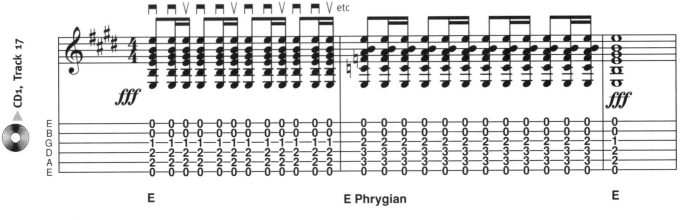

Example 2.8

The rhythm is simply 'down, down-up' ('dah, da-da') repeated. It is important that you keep the radius of the strumming stroke to a minimum. I suggest using the soundhole as a general reference; your right hand should not rise too far above or sink too far below it; if it strays too far from it, you'll have to wait until your hand is back over the strings to strum them. If you watch flamenco guitarists (and they know how to strum!) you will notice that their right hands are rarely far away from the strings. You needn't play over the soundhole, but you should use its diameter as a reference.

The right hand technique requires the right hand to play the downstroke with the fingernails and the upstroke with the back of the thumbnail. The transition from downstroke to upstroke is made through a twist of the wrist. The fingers also need to be left slightly loose yet firm enough to make the attack. The pad of the thumb is in constant, but moving, contact with the near side of the index finger; its motion through the strum cycle is not too dissimilar to the international hand symbol for counting money!

This technique can be adapted simply to work over smaller numbers of strings:

CD1, Track 18

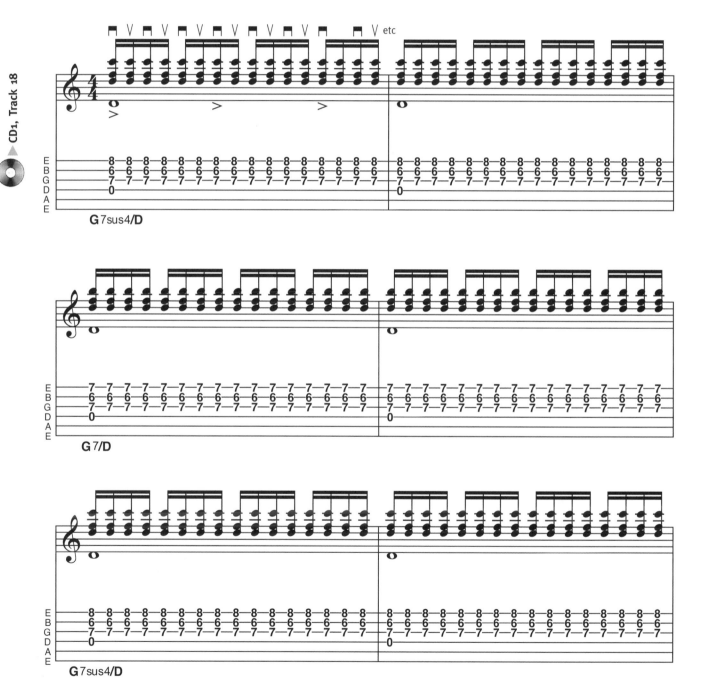

Example 2.9 (continues...)

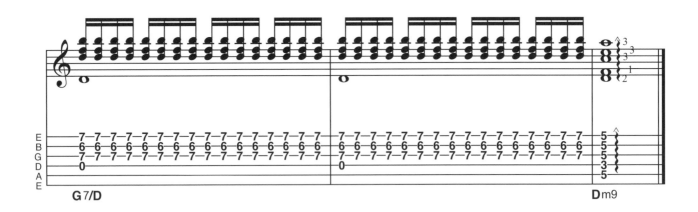

Example 2.9 continued

You can achieve a more contemporary sound using this approach in an example like this:

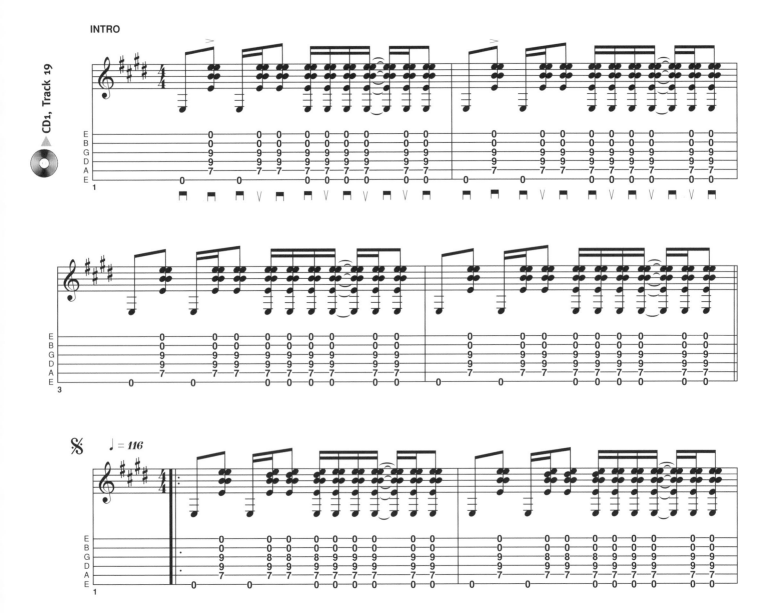

Example 2.10 (continues...)

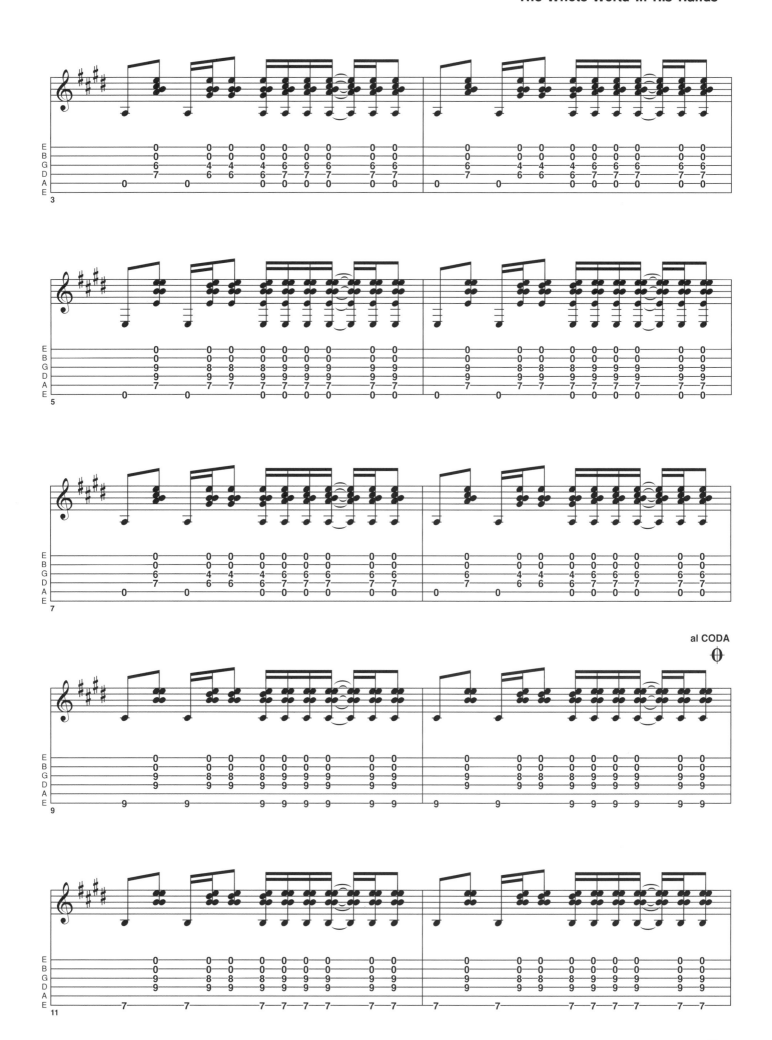

al CODA

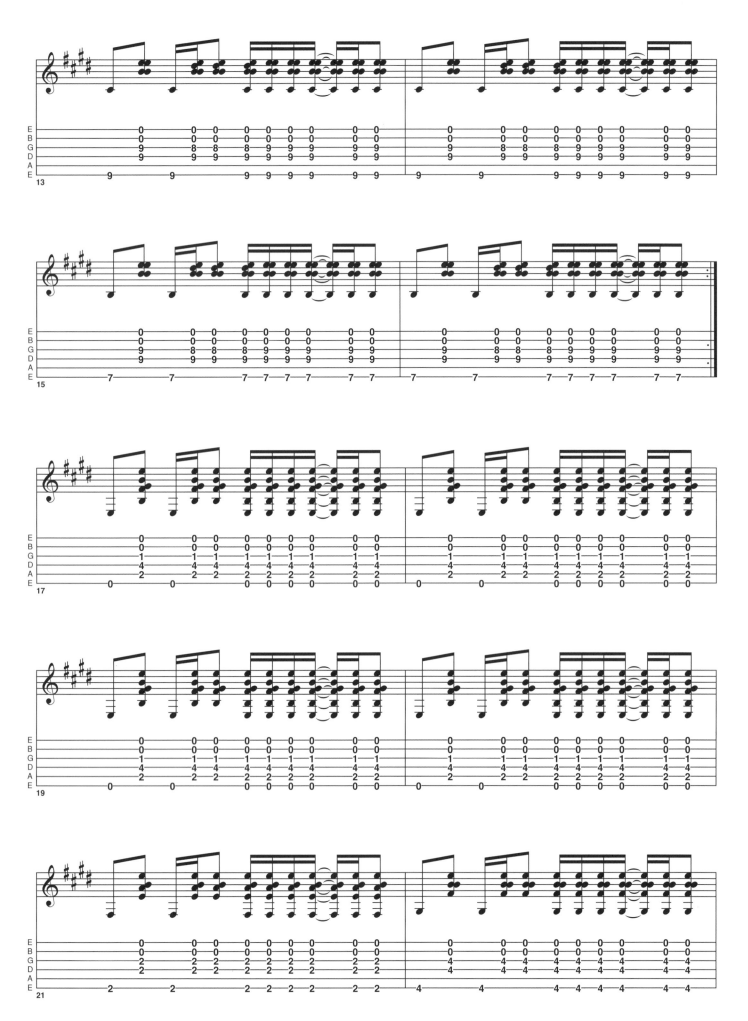

CODA

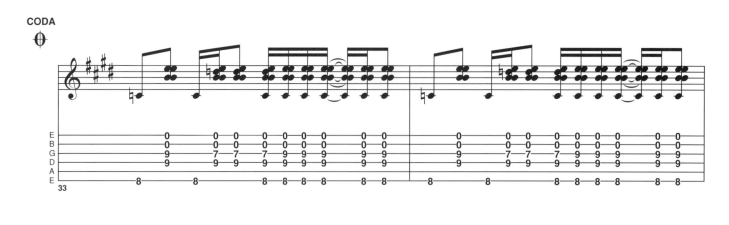

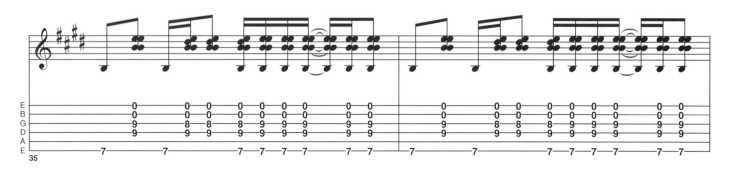

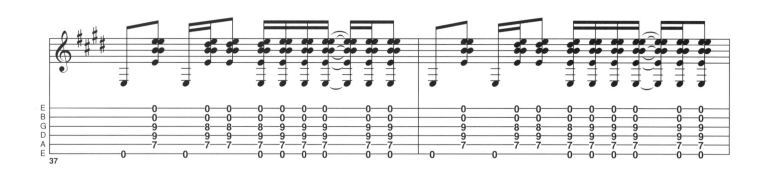

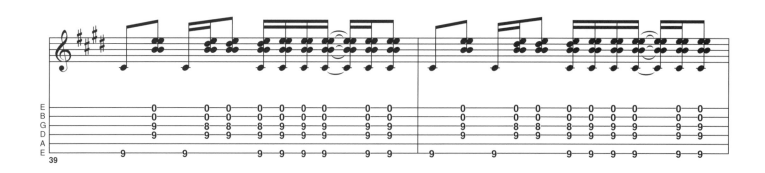

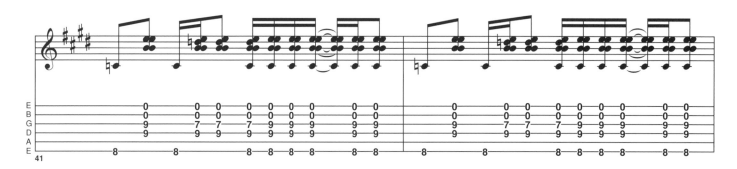

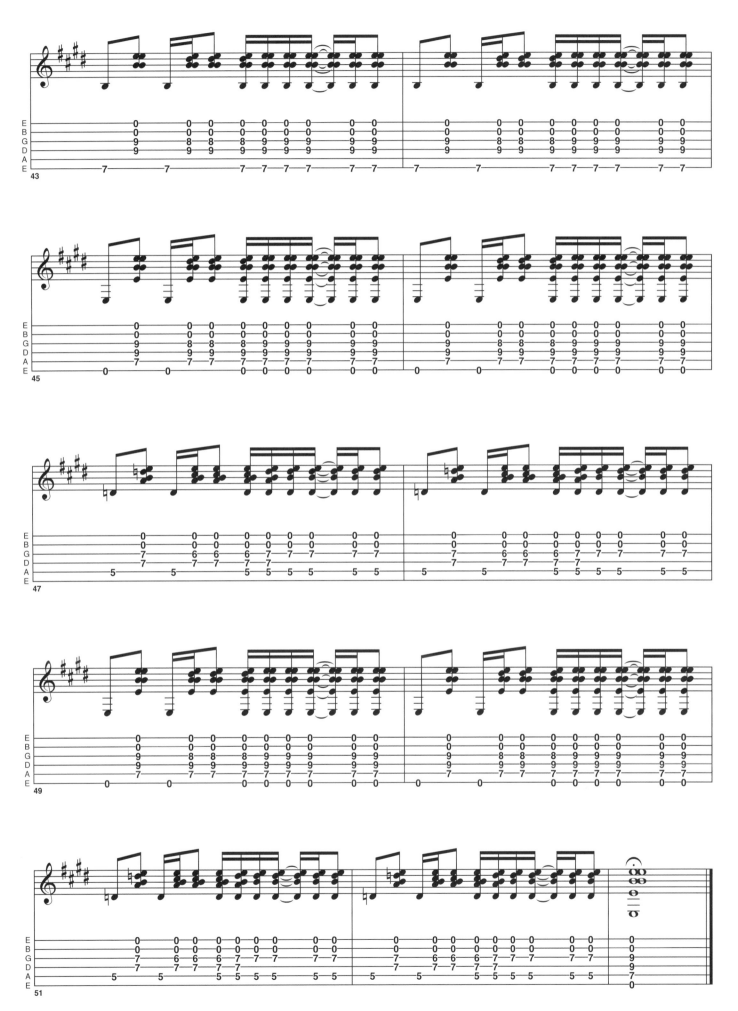

Here are the chord shapes. Why not use them to create your own examples?

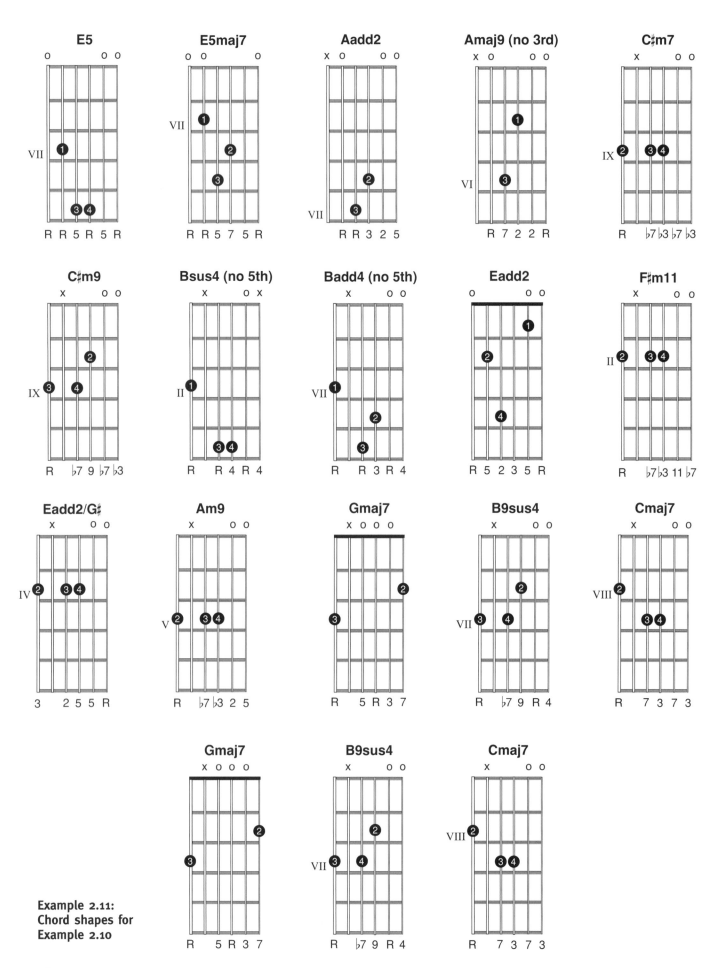

**Example 2.11:
Chord shapes for
Example 2.10**

Let's look at a more challenging example in 5/4 time. This one has a strong nuevo-flamenco flavour. Check out players like Ottmar Liebert for more examples. Count out a few bars of five time before you start. The accents are on beats 1 and 4 so you may find it more helpful to count **1** 2 3 **1** 2, **1** 2 3 **1** 2, and so on.

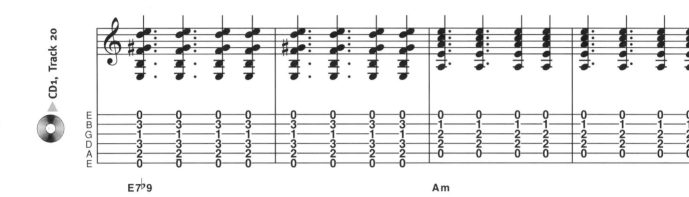

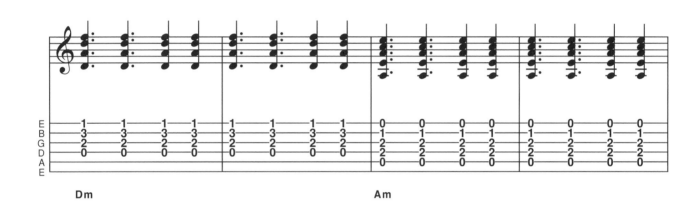

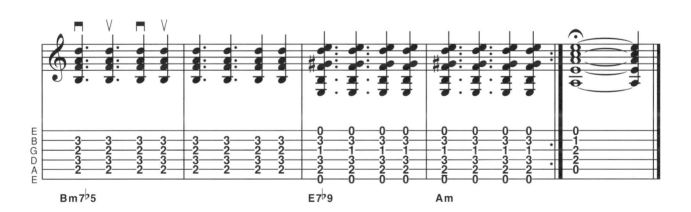

Example 2.12

Here's another example in the nuevo-flamenco style using similar chords but with some interesting voice-leading at the top of each chord. Check out the left-hand fingering carefully:

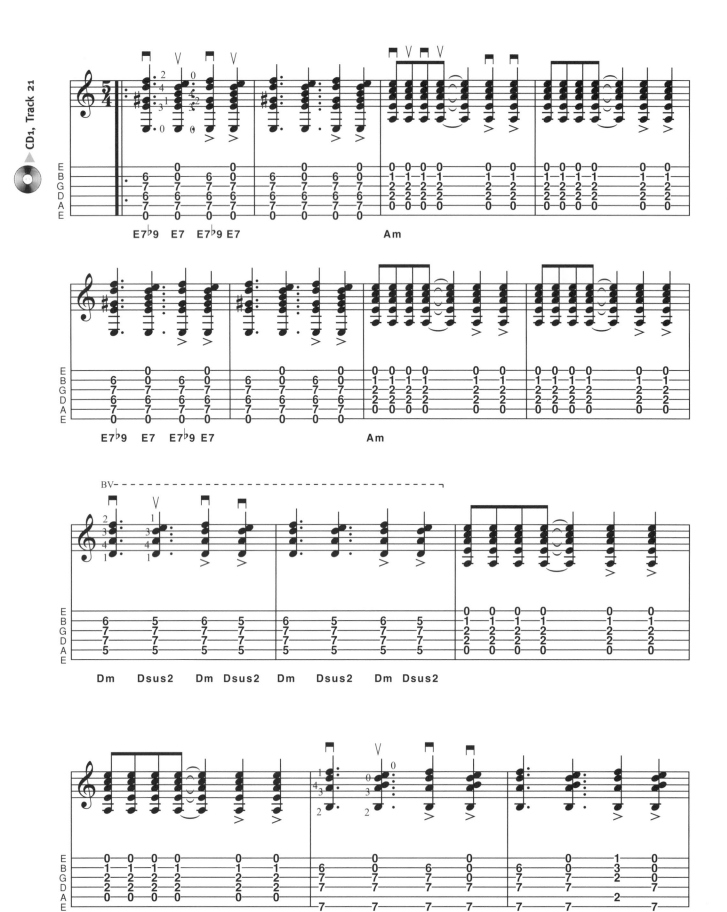

Example 2.13 (continues...)

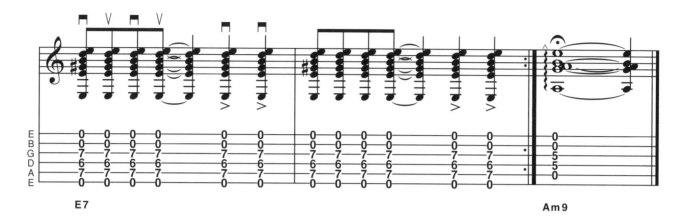

Example 2.13 continued

Fingerstyle Blues

The guitar is synonymous with the blues. The origin of the blues is difficult to pinpoint as it emerged from the lifestyle of a whole section of the US. It is certainly true that, by the early years of the 20th century, what we would now recognise as blues was being played.

Being a 'folk' music, many of the performers and composers of the style were not musically trained. The blues primarily was a vehicle for the lyrics and the instruments were used to support those melodies and words. Instrumental blues developed out of the singing tradition and, the guitar being a particularly accessible (and, more importantly, portable) instrument, it became the main tool of the bluesman. All of the legendary blues players were guitarists – or at least singer/guitarists. During the early decades of the 20th century a whole generation of guitar stars were born and went on to redefine the guitar and blues music. The names read like a Who's Who of blues: Blind (Arthur) Blake, Big Bill Broonzy, Reverend Gary Davis, Blind Boy Fuller, Son House, Mississippi John Hurt, Robert Johnson, Blind Lemon Jefferson, Leadbelly, Muddy Waters, Howlin' Wolf and, from New Orleans, Snooks Eaglin. This list is only a small section of a whole generation of great bluesmen who toured and recorded throughout the 1930s, '40s, '50s and beyond. Many of the recordings of these players are still available today and are well worth investigating. The very commercial '12-bar blues' was developed a little later on the recommendation of the record companies, who even back then wanted to standardise the style.

The style of many of the blues players listed above didn't conform to such strict standards and many of their recordings show examples of inconsistent bar lengths and form – one verse might be 8 bars while the following may be 11 bars long. At a whim they would regularly add or drop a beat if it suited the lyric or the moment. When the more educated jazz musicians took the blues form and used it as a format for improvisation, the chord sequences, bar lengths and form had to be more tightly tied down. Blues, ragtime and jazz each evolved at around the same period of time and there was a lot of common ground, culturally, between the musicians. There was also a lot of cross-fertilisation between the different styles, although of them all, ragtime remained the purest and experienced the least change.

Fingerstyle blues guitar comes in many shapes and forms. However, the original fingerstyle guitar blues were essentially contrapuntal – a bass line with a simple melodic line on top. This requires a certain amount of independence. The following examples should help you to develop a greater degree of independence between the fingers and thumb.

Let's look at a simple bass line with a standard fifth-to-sixth vamp:

The Acoustic Guitar Bible

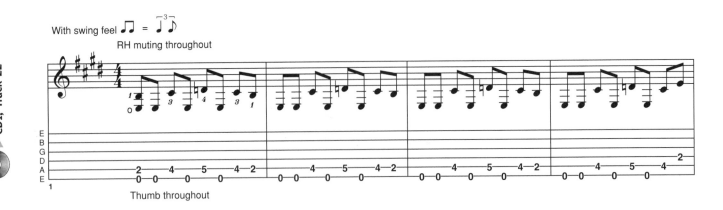

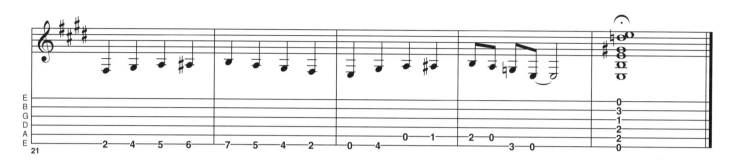

Example 2.14

Here the right hand mutes the strings with a simple technique – laying the flesh of the right hand down lightly on the strings near the bridge. This has the effect of muting many of the overtones so that you are left with a clearer fundamental and a much clearer rhythmic definition. Practise this exercise with the right-hand thumb only.

The next example is a simple development of this approach. In Exercise 2.15, a simple harmony in sixths is added. This fills out the harmony nicely and gives the chord progression greater depth and colour. When you get to bars 9 and 10, however, you might need to spend some extra time in the woodshed.

CD4, Track 23

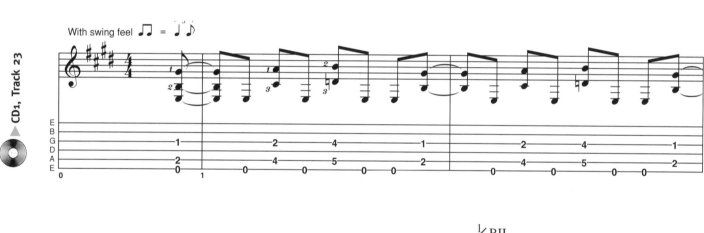

Example 2.15 (continues...)

Example 2.15 continued

The next example adds some melody over the chord changes and bass line. Listen to the audio example to get the correct feel for this one. On the second run-through from bar 13, there is distinct accent on the last off-beat of each bar. This type of syncopation is typical in blues and is a good method of developing a simple idea. The right hand uses a 'claw hammer' technique – the hand being held in a shape not too unlike a hammer. The a, m and i fingers move together in time to pluck the chords in syncopation with the bass line. The thumb, as usual, plays the bass line throughout.

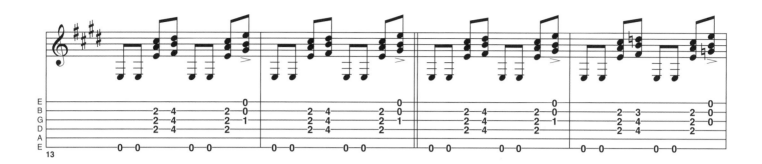

Example 2.16

This next example is the last in the series of fingerstyle blues examples. The techniques and sounds explored here are a combination of those that we have been developing over the last few pages. There is melody, bass lines and chords. In fact, for this example I added some very tasty chords from outside the key. These appear in bars 13–14 and again towards the end of the example. Don't worry about the names of these chords; we're going to study the complex world of chords and chord names in later chapters.

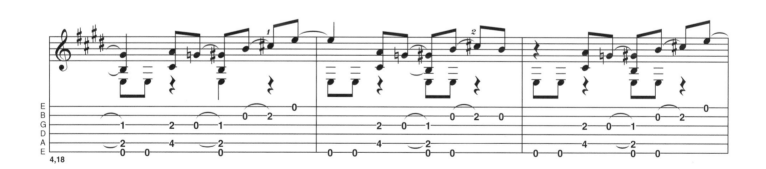

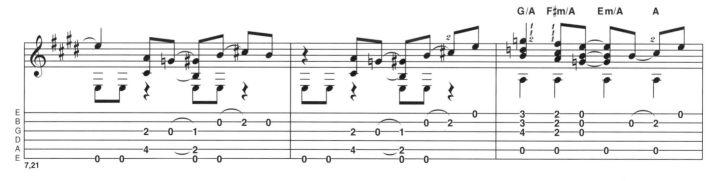

Example 2.17 (continues...)

Example 2.17 continued

Let's Get A Little Jazzy…

Earlier on I mentioned the links between jazz and blues. The jazz musicians took the blues form and standardised it so that it became a vehicle for improvisation. Many jazz composers wrote jazz blues, and even today it is still a common meeting ground for many musicians. We will look at the standard 12-bar jazz blues shortly. First, let's take a simple technique to create a type of walking jazz bass line:

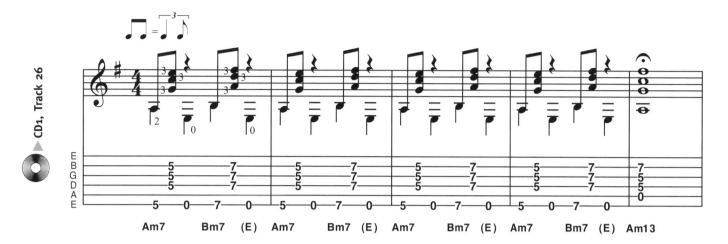

Am7   Bm7   (E)   Am7   Bm7   (E)   Am7   Bm7   (E)   Am7   Bm7   (E)   Am13

Example 2.18

This can be used as the basis for so many popular jazz/pop tunes, including 'Moondance', 'Fever' and 'Summertime'.

Let's develop this technique by working through a 12-bar blues. The following 12-bar sequence is in G:

4/4:   G7 C7 G7 G7 |
        C7 C7 G7 G7 |
        D7 C7 G7 D7 ||

With some simple chord-substitution tricks (discussed more fully in later chapters) and some standard jazz/blues changes, the chord sequence can be embellished in the following way:

4/4:   G7 C7 G7 Dm7/G7 |
        C7 C#°7 G7 E7 |
        A7 D7 G7/E7 A7/D7 ||

Now some measures have two chords. They share the four beats – two beats each. If some of these chords are a little unfamiliar, just work through the following jazz/blues arrangement to get a sense of how these chords can sound:

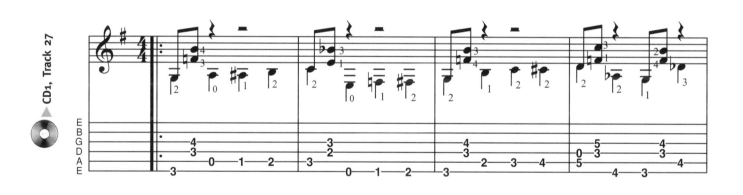

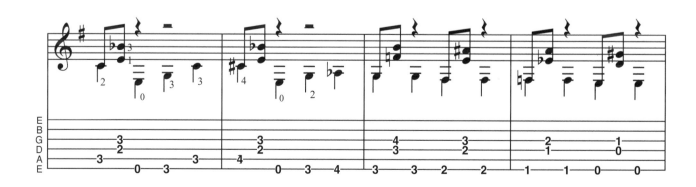

Example 2.19 (continues...)

Example 2.19 continued

Latin Jazz Style

The simple technique of alternating bass notes between the root and fifth of a chord is common to a number of styles of music. We already saw the use of 'root and fifth' bass lines in the Travis picking example. Latin music also uses this simple harmonic device to create tension and release in a chord. By placing the fifth degree of a chord in the bass, some harmonic tension is set up. This tension is released by placing the root of the chord also in the bass. By alternating between these two points you can add a little harmonic 'drama' to a chord. This simple *bossa nova* (a typical modern dance rhythm from Brazil) uses the alternating-bass approach. The bass line is played by the thumb and the chords are played claw-hammer style as in the example above. The bossa nova is a particularly precise rhythmic pattern and many of the chords have been imported from jazz. We will discuss these chords and harmony in more depth in the following chapters.

CD1, Track 28

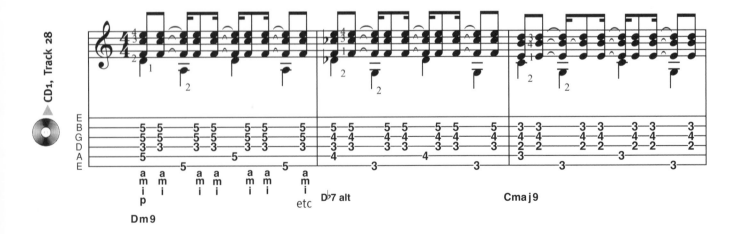

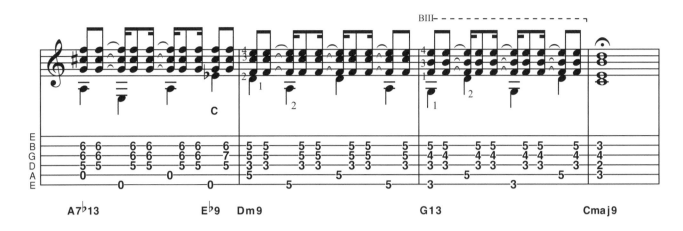

Example 2.20

In the above example the bass line is 'on the beat' – a straight 1, 2, 3, 4. However, in other Latin rhythms the bass line can be syncopated, with many of the bass notes being played *off* the beat. In Example 2.21 below, the bass line plays straight for the first four bars and is then syncopated with the chords from bar 5.

The chords in Example 2.21 require the left-hand thumb to reach over the neck to play various bass notes. This may require a bit of practice. I have marked the thumb in the transcription with a T.

CD1, Track 29

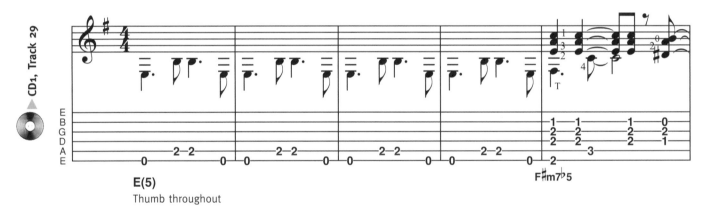

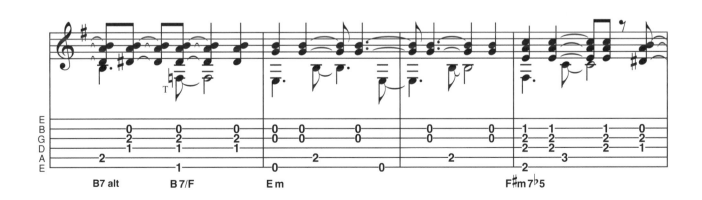

Example 2.21 (continues...)

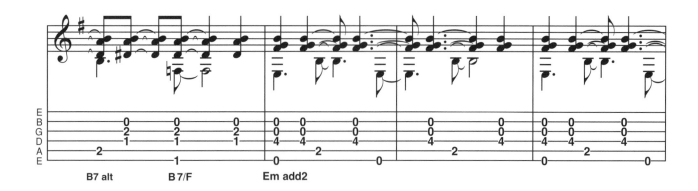

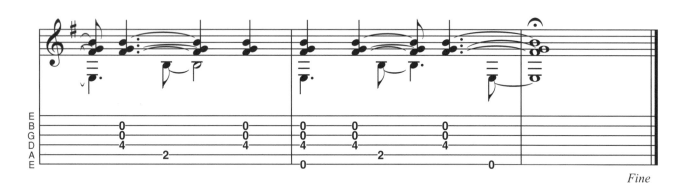

Fine

Example 2.21 continued

The alternating bass of the Latin style can be combined with a more contemporary funk feel to produce a more jazzy funk style. Once again, the important consideration here is the rhythmic alignment between the chords and the bass line. This independence is a very useful musical skill which you should strive to develop.

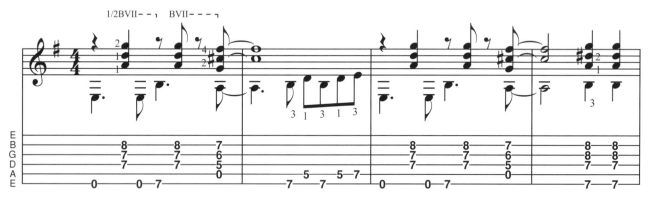

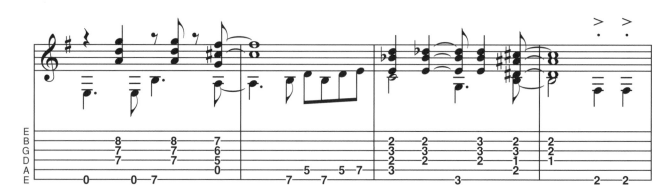

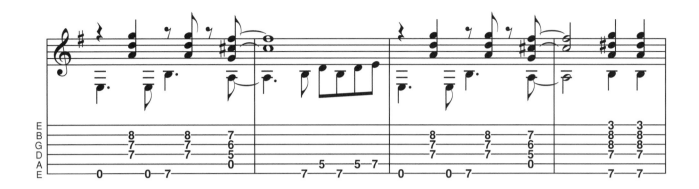

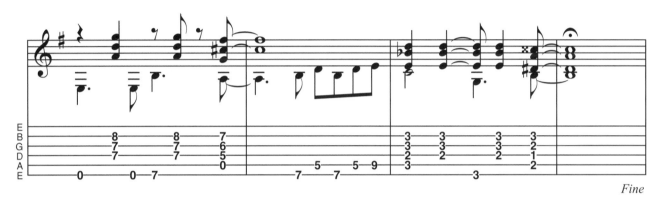

Fine

Example 2.22

Let's Go Back In Time

The following example, 'Study In A', is by one of the great classical guitarist/composers of the early 19th century. Matteo Carcassi (1792–1853) was one of a small, elite group of Italian guitarists who were instrumental (excuse the pun) in spreading the popularity of the guitar as a solo instrument. Until that time, the guitar had primarily been an accompanying instrument for singers and other instrumentalists. The instrument's poor projection and general lack of popularity had relegated it to the lower ranks in both the public's and the composers' minds. There was a minimal repertoire that guitarists could reach into. However, at the turn of the 19th century, Carcassi and a small number of his contemporaries began to standardise and codify a standard technique for the instrument. They also began to compose for the instrument and to widen the repertoire. Apart from these two noble activities, they also travelled all over Europe, giving concerts and recitals as well as teaching the instrument. Slowly, their efforts began to bear fruit. Many of their compositions came in the form of short studies for their students, who were often aristocrats and whose families who could afford to buy instruments and

pay tutors. Many of the pieces written at this time were dedicated to such patrons in return.

The following example is a complete transcription of one of Carcassi's studies. Each study was composed with a particular technique or musical point in mind. 'Study In A' is in 4/4 time with triplet eighth notes. Count it like this:

one-and-a, **two**-and-a, **three**-and-a, **four**-and-a

The melody line, while simple, is interesting for the fact that it uses a tension note on the second beat of each bar and resolves it on beat 4. Listen to the CD recording to hear the phrasing and tone required.

The right hand plays a repeating pattern, but the melody needs to be brought out above those arpeggios. It is useful to use a stronger stroke on those melodic notes on beats 2 and 4. Classical guitarists would use a rest stroke (also known as *apoyando*) to accent these notes, a technique that involves plucking a note with the finger and bringing it to rest firmly on the adjacent string as you follow through. This technique allows you to dig in to the string a little more firmly than the free stroke.

Study In A Major

Matteo Carcassi

CD1, Track 31

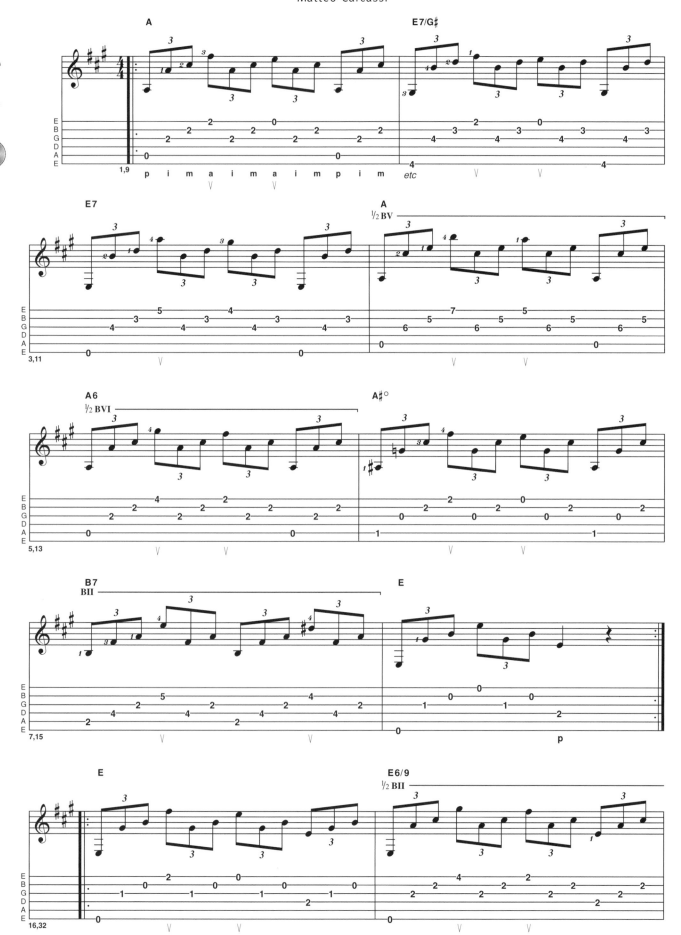

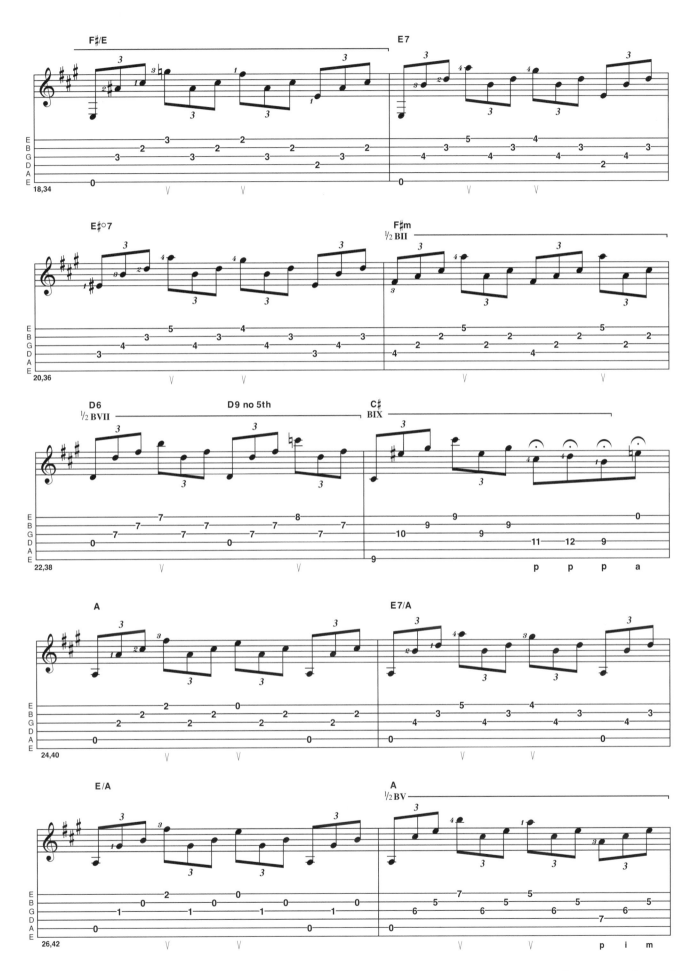

Example 2.23 (continues...)

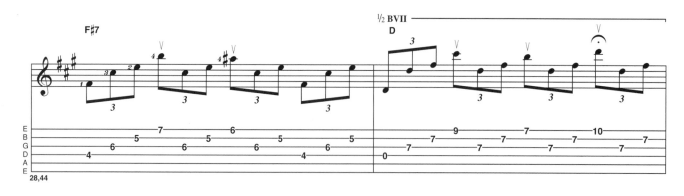

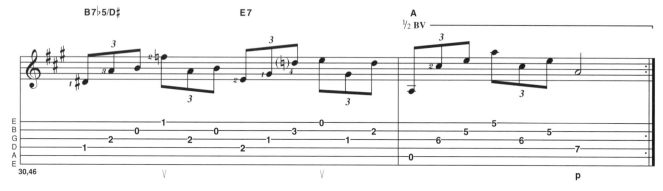

Example 2.23 continued

Simple Legato Exercises

Many guitarists associate the term *legato* with electric-guitar players and, in particular, rock-guitar players. While it is true that many electric-rock players have taken legato techniques to extreme levels of proficiency, the techniques themselves have many applications across all styles and genres of guitar music.

The legato techniques are primarily used for phrasing – although watching some players you would be forgiven for thinking that showmanship is a higher priority than musicality! Like any technique, if it is over-used, it can lose its effectiveness. The tasteful use of a simple legato technique can change a phrase from being bland and non-musical to being very effective and powerful.

The term *legato* comes from the Italian word meaning 'to bind together', and this is a good description of what legato techniques do – they bind two consecutive notes together. The techniques leave no gap between the notes and in theory should create a seamless transition from one note to the next. The opposite of legato is *staccato*, where the gap between notes is as long as rhythmically possible. (Or, if you prefer, the sound of a *staccato* note is as short as possible.)

There are various techniques for achieving legato on the guitar. The four main legato techniques are:

• Hammer-ons;

• Pull-offs;

• Slides;

• Taps (a close relation of hammer-ons).

We will look at note tapping in a later chapter, but for the moment we will look at the first three techniques.

Hammer-ons

Although the plural of 'hammer-on' is probably stretching the limits of good grammar, it seems more correct than 'hammers-on'! In any case, the technique is very common and easy to acquire.

The first exercise is based on a single string. For the moment, the technique is a left (fretting) -hand technique. It is important to set up the left hand correctly so that the four fingers are placed on the string simultaneously. For this first exercise I am starting with the index finger at the 10th fret. To get your hand into the correct position, line up the adjacent fingers on adjacent frets on the high e' string. You may need to make postural adjustments to seemingly unrelated parts of your body, such as your lower back, neck and shoulder – you may need to reposition the guitar so that the left hand can be in a comfortable playing position.

Once you're comfortable with this posture and hand position, make a mental note of how your fingers, hand, wrist, arm, elbow, shoulder, neck and spine are aligned. It is useful to develop a good sense of body awareness – knowing where the tensions and pressures are building up and learning how to release them both in practice and performance.

Now place the index finger at the 10th fret, high e' string. Pluck the e' string with the right-hand index finger. Hammer down sharply and suddenly with the left-hand middle finger on the same string at the 11th fret. Once you have struck the string, leave the fingers in place. Aim for a clear and sustained note. The technique does not necessarily require a great amount of force, but rather *quickness*. You should also imagine that you are hammering into the fretboard

through the string. You should strike the string with the fingertip, not the pad of the finger. The finger should be travelling perpendicular to the plane of the fretboard. Leave these two fingers in place and repeat the technique with the ring finger hammering into the same string at the 12th fret. Repeat the process with the one remaining finger at the 13th fret. You may find that the ring finger and little finger are weaker than the others, but with practice you will build up their strength and be able to play the notes loudly and clearly. Indeed, this exercise doubles as a good finger-strengthening exercise.

Repeat the steps above from the 9th fret, and so on

▲ CD1, Track 32

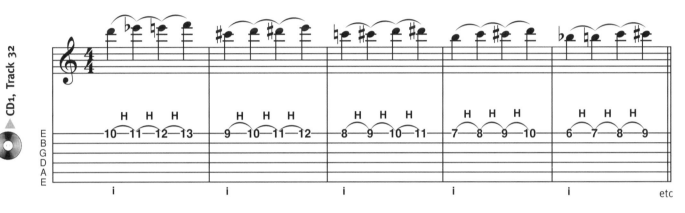

Example 2.24

down the neck to the 1st fret.

You will find it a little more challenging to execute this exercise on the inner strings, but you should include this in your practice schedule. Practise with a metronome. Start at 70bpm and build up to 120bpm and beyond.

You can focus this technique on one finger by practising the following exercise. Place the index finger at the 5th fret on the high e' string. Pluck the note and hammer down at the 6th fret with the middle finger. Aim for a clear and sustained note. Remove the middle finger and re-pluck the e' string at the 5th fret. Hammer down at the 7th fret. Again,

remove the middle finger, re-pluck the string and hammer down at the 8th fret. To complete the four-beat cycle, pluck the E string at the 5th fret and hammer down at the 7th fret. Repeat the cycle and then shift down a fret to the 4th and repeat the process. The frets are slightly wider at the 4th fret and give you an extra challenge. Continue on down the neck to the nut. If this exercise isn't challenging enough, why not try adding an extra fret to the stretch? Work with a metronome and increase the tempo gradually. There are numerous ways in which you can adapt any of these simple exercises and make them more challenging.

▲ CD1, Track 33

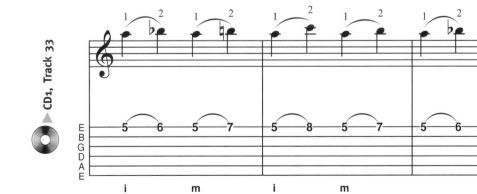

Example 2.25 (continues...)

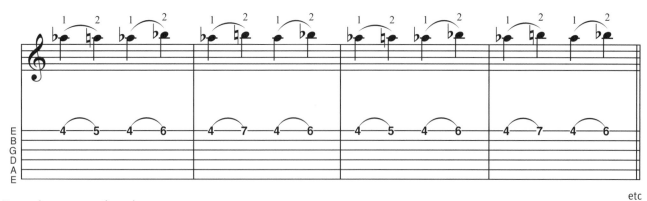

Example 2.25 continued

Develop the strength in each of your other fingers by playing through the previous exercise with the ring and little fingers:

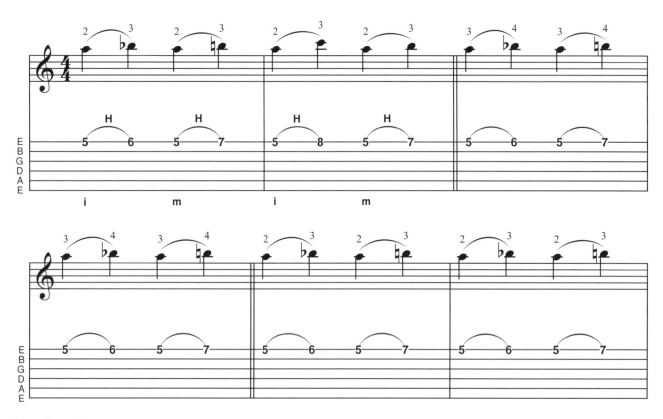

Example 2.26

Very often this technique will be used while other notes are being played or ringing. The following exercise is a good one for developing some left-hand finger independence:

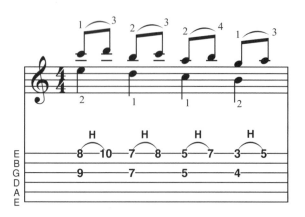

CD1, Track 34

Example 2.27

The following legato exercise is played across all six strings. Once again, play this exercise with a metronome. You should alternate your right-hand fingers (i,m,i,m) to continue developing your right-hand technique.

CD1, Track 35

Example 2.28

The following exercise is a scale exercise which incorporates the legato technique. Take the C major scale, starting at fifth position. I have written this exercise in 9/8 time to add a little rhythmic interest. You can then shift up a whole step to the D major scale and play the exercise again.

CD1, Track 36

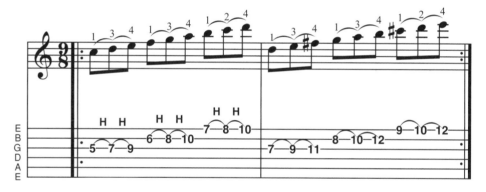

Example 2.29

The last of these hammering exercises is certainly the most challenging. Holding down two notes at a time, hammer two fingers at once to sound an interval. The shapes in the exercise move through the G major scale. The final double hammer-on will require some practice, I expect!

CD1, Track 37

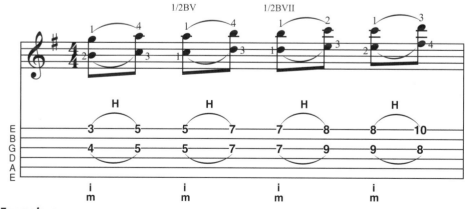

Example 2.30

Pull-offs

Another guitar term with a dubious plural form! The second legato technique, the pull-off is the opposite of the hammer-on. The term is somewhat incorrect as the technique is actually closer in motion to a 'pull-across' than a pull-off.

Any readers coming from the rock/electric school of guitar playing will have a very different approach to this technique. Electric guitarists, with their generally lighter string gauges, lower neck actions, high gain pre-amps and loud amplifiers, will be able to execute something resembling a pull-off with minimal effort. In fact, the simple act of lifting a finger off the string will produce a note. Not so with acoustic guitar. On acoustic (please feel free to read 'real' here!) guitar, the string needs to be driven to perform. Simply lifting your finger off a string will result in…well, nothing. A pull-off on an acoustic guitar has to drive a heavier string, through higher action, and also drive the soundboard so that the note can be heard. The more correct technique is pulling the left-hand finger *across* the string (as if you are plucking it).

The finger/hand/arm position is very similar to that for the hammer-on technique. (Please re-read the section about posture for legato techniques above if you are unsure.) Example 2.31 below is similar to the first hammer-on exercise except in reverse.

Place all four left hand fingers on the high e' string from frets 10–13. Pluck the string with the right-hand index finger, then with the left-hand small finger, and pull firmly downwards across the string, *away* from the neck. Aim for a clear and sustained note. If you use too much force in this technique, you could possibly pull the string out of tune, or even over the edge of the fingerboard. (More about strange and weird techniques in a later chapter!) The index, middle and ring fingers should be pressing directly and perpendicularly onto the fingerboard to steady the hand and the string. When the small finger executes the pull-off there should minimal movement in the string. If the index, middle and ring fingers press too hard then this may cause the string to go sharp. As always, find the balance of pressure required.

Continue with the ring and middle fingers to produce the next notes shown in the sequence. Then repeat the exercise from the 12th fret and so on down the fingerboard towards the nut.

CD1, Track 38

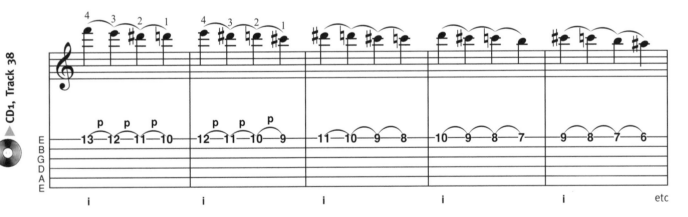

Example 2.31

The following exercise is good for strengthening the fingers, in particular the naturally weaker ring and little fingers. Anchor the left-hand index at the 7th fret and exercise each of the little, ring and middle fingers in turn. As before, shift the whole exercise down a fret towards the nut and continue until you reach it. Practise the exercise on the other inner strings:

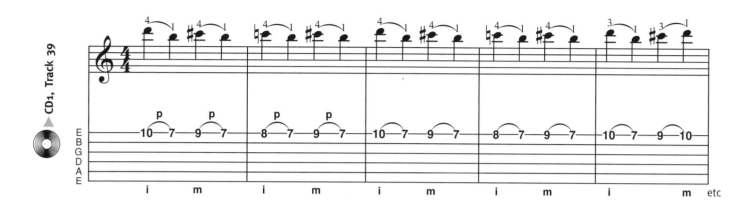

CD1, Track 39

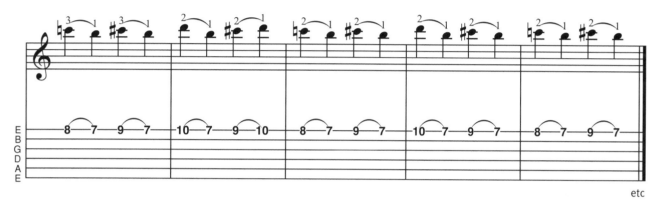

etc

Example 2.32

The following exercise is similar but more challenging. It will help you to develop strength and independence in your weaker fingers. Remember to aim for a clear and sustained tone. You should also aim for an even dynamic between the notes – keeping the plucked and legato notes at the same volume:

CD1, Track 40

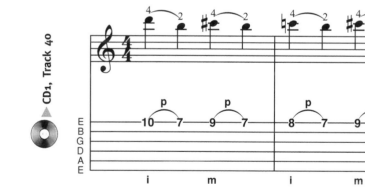

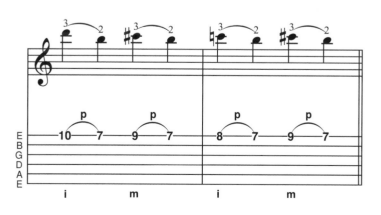

Example 2.33

The following exercise is more challenging and is based on simultaneous pull-offs on non-adjacent strings. Remember that the trick is to pull across the strings (in this case, two strings at once):

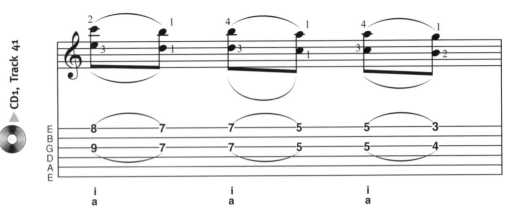

Example 2.34

The exercise below applies the technique across all six strings. Again, you can shift this exercise to different frets as required. Aim for consistent dynamics and tone on all strings and across the whole fretboard:

Example 2.35

Here is another scalar exercise to work through. Feel free to shift through different scales and to make up similar exercises for yourself:

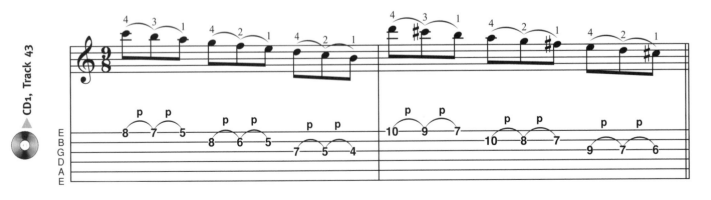

Example 2.36

While holding down another ringing note, you should be able to pull off on another string cleanly without disturbing the ringing note in any way:

CD1, Track 44

Example 2.37

Slides

The third legato technique is sliding between notes. This technique, as with the previous two, has a rhythmic element. Slides can be short and quick or long and slow. It is important to be rhythmically aware of the context of these techniques.

The slide has an advantage over the first two techniques in the sense that it can work in either of two directions. The pull-off only works downwards and the hammer-on upwards, whereas with the slide technique you can slide up to a note from below or down to a note from one above. When sliding over a distance greater than one fret, you will by default pass through any intervening notes. Obviously this cannot be avoided.

The slide technique requires, as with the previous legato techniques, a careful balance of pressure in the left hand. If you squeeze the string and fingerboard too hard, you may impede the slide, or even stop it altogether. If you don't apply enough pressure, you won't hear the intervening and target notes. It also requires careful control of force and speed in the lateral plane; if you slide too far or too short, you will miss the target note.

The following exercises are designed to help you to improve your slide technique. Remember that the acoustic-guitar string must be driven, and you may need to practise the technique as played on electric guitar even further in order to execute it properly on an acoustic guitar.

This first exercise is simply sliding up and down one fret. Take care not to over-do these exercises as you can quickly develop a blister!

CD1, Track 45

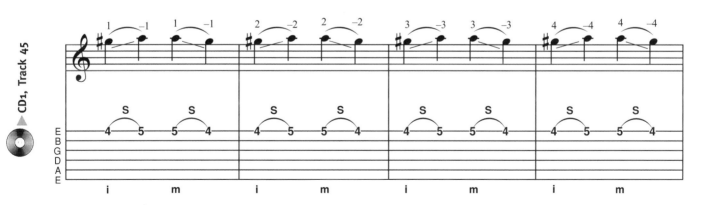

Example 2.38

This second slide exercise is interesting. Use consecutive fingers to slide into the same note:

CD1, Track 46

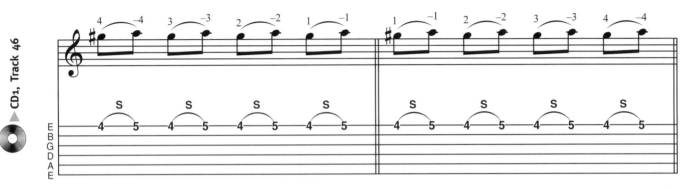

Example 2.39

Sometimes you may need to slide up to a note and slide back down to the original note (or indeed another note). Each set of three notes is played with one pluck:

CD1, Track 47

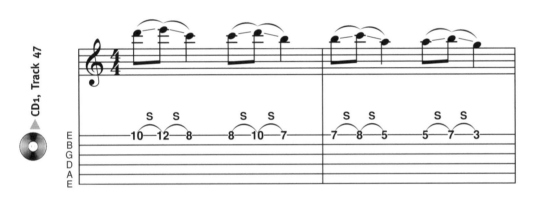

Example 2.40

Many slides are played over quite large intervals. Try some of these slides for size!

CD1, Track 48

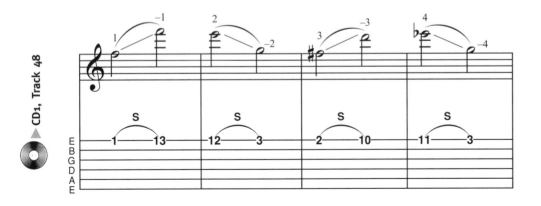

Example 2.41

It is sometimes necessary to change fingers during a slide. A slide may start off on one particular finger and end on another finger! In the following exercise, the G note is held by the little finger. Pluck and slide the note. At some point (around the 7th fret, for example) the second finger falls in behind the little finger and hitches a ride on the way up! When you get to the target note, lift the little finger and let the second finger do the work. This technique is mostly used when there are other chord tones or bass notes requiring particular fingers. It is well worth practising this technique.

The technique in reverse is much more difficult. It requires that you swap fingers at the very last possible moment as you enter the target note:

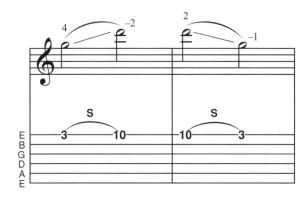

Example 2.42

It's possible to be quite creative with slides. The example below shows you how to slide into an A major chord one note at a time:

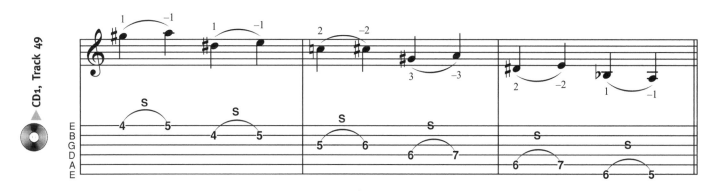

Example 2.43

And finally an example where you can slide chord shapes up and down the neck:

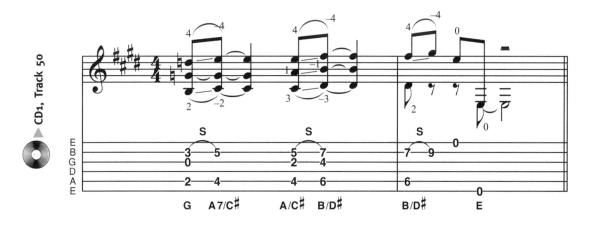

Example 2.44

71

The Acoustic Guitar Bible

Here is a example which incorporates all of these legato techniques in various contexts. Have fun working through it and use it as a launching pad for creating your own compositions.

CD1, Track 51

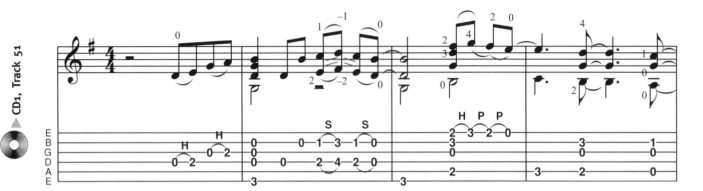

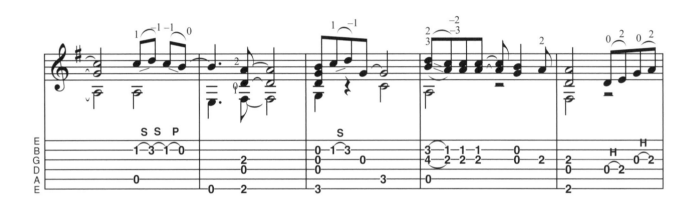

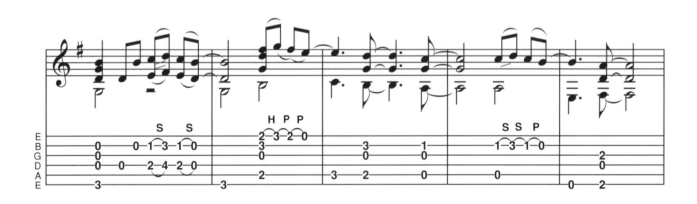

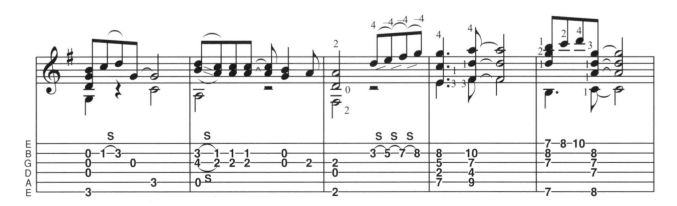

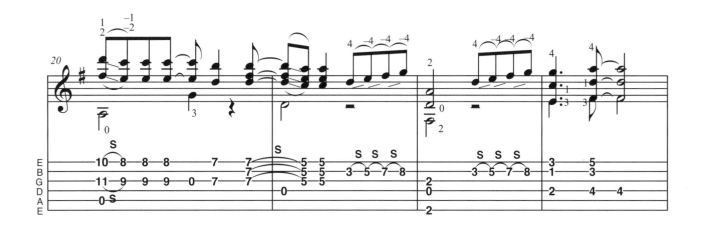

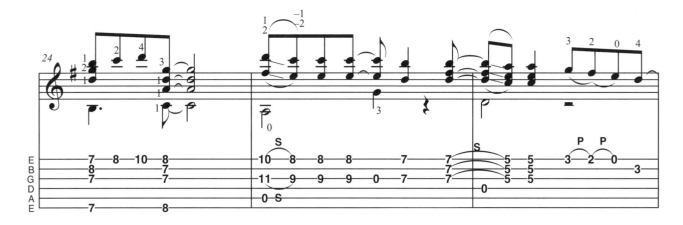

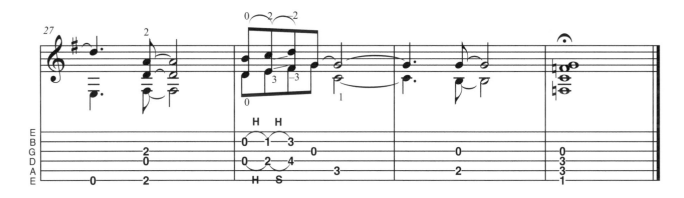

Example 2.45

3 ONE-MAN BAND

Arranging For Solo Fingerstyle Guitar – Part 1

'Music is nothing else but wild sounds civilised into time and tune.' – *Thomas Fuller*

Of all the instruments, the guitar has the widest variety of tonal colours. Where the piano has logic and a wide range of pitch, the guitar has a whole spectrum of timbre and expressions. Where the violin has the soaring projection and sustain required for melody, the guitar veers towards the harp with its cascades of arpeggios and expansive voicings. In short, the solo guitar is an orchestra all in itself. The guitarist has so many possibilities at his fingertips that very often the decisions one has to make are more about what to leave out. The left hand has six notes to choose from at any one time with its four fingers (and occasionally the thumb), and many of these same notes can be played at numerous points on the fingerboard. The right hand has six notes to choose from with its thumb and three fingers (and occasionally the little finger) and a whole panorama of tone with which to express each.

My personal approach to fingerstyle guitar and arranging for the instrument is to start from the point of 'there are no limits'. I like to work backwards from that point and enjoy working through the various problems and obstructions that the guitar naturally presents. Let's consider what the main aspects of any musical piece are.

Melody

Most pieces of music have a discernible melody or 'top line'. In most cases this melody can be played on the guitar. In certain situations the melody may need to be adapted – for example, it must change key, or be raised or lowered by an octave. It is important that you can capture the melody accurately. This will generally be the starting point for all arranging of music on the guitar. The phrasing of the melody is always a matter for the player to decide. Phrasing is one of the many ways a musician can put a piece of themselves into the arrangement. It is one way to put a personal stamp on an arrangement. All the other steps are there to support the melody. Melody is king!

Harmony

The harmony, or the chord changes ('changes' for short) as guitarists often call them, is something that underpins but also arises from the melody. The harmony, used to support a melody, can enhance the tune or detract from it. There are many different approaches to harmonisation and re-harmonisation; each player will have a personal preference for harmony. As with phrasing, the harmony you choose can be very personal and indicative of your style. The chord shapes, voicings and progressions that you choose will be particular to you and your style.

Bass Line Movement

Not all music will have a distinctive bass line. In some cases it will just take the form of the lowest note in the chord changes or even the simple root movement from chord to chord. In many cases it is possible to create a bass line and to devise bass-line steps between chord changes. Inverting chords (and we'll have more on this later in this chapter) will open up possibilities for you to create unique bass lines for your arrangements.

Rhythm

Rhythm is a very broad topic. In the context of this lesson alone there are various descriptions of rhythm, but ultimately:

Rhythm = sound + silence

It is at once simple and complex. It is events occurring and ceasing. It is the sound and the gaps between the sounds. It is on–off, up–down, in–out, back–forth, around-and-around…

There is melodic rhythm – the rhythm of melody – which you can play with in your exploration of phrasing. There is harmonic rhythm – the rate and placement of chord changes. There is also percussive rhythm, which has neither a melodic nor harmonic quality but still encompasses a range of sounds and timbres which can loosely described as pitch (the sound of the bass drum is lower in pitch that the cowbell, while the snare drum falls somewhere in between).

Tone

We tend to describe tone in either very visual terms (bright or dull, dark or light) or in very tactile terms (hard, soft, sharp, round, cold, warm or flat). We also describe tone in quantitative terms, such as full, empty, high and low. The relationship between the frequencies of coloured light and pitch have been well documented, and some composers have gone as far as to make a definite correlation between particular keys and particular colours. It would appear that this is entirely subjective, although that doesn't make it any less real for those who feel a strong link.

The tone of a particular note can be varied widely on the guitar, as discussed in Chapter 1. In short, the tone is affected by such factors as string gauge, the attack of the right hand, and the position of the note on the fingerboard. (See Chapter 1 for a more detailed discussion.) The tone of a note or phrase or complete composition can also be compared with *emotional tone* (as can be easily demonstrated with the voice).

As a young beginner on guitar I was always amazed at the difference between two of my early guitar heroes, Rory Gallagher and Mark Knopfler. They each played a vintage Stratocaster, yet I could tell which one was playing from a *single* note! These players were just two examples of musicians with a distinctive voice and tone on the guitar. Years later I realised that everyone has this – it's just at different stages of development. Pat Metheny always sounds like Pat Metheny, Larry Carlton like Larry Carlton, Neil Young like Neil Young, Julian Bream like Julian Bream, and Pierre Bensusan like Pierre Bensusan. Finding your own tone is an exciting voyage of self-discovery. Very often we need to find another player's tone first and, in the process, learn to listen to ourselves.

> *There are different ways of listening to music. There is a technical state, when a person who is developing technique and has learnt to appreciate better music feels disturbed by a lower grade of music. But there is also a spiritual way, which has nothing to do with technique. It is simply to tune oneself to the music.*
> – Inayat Khan, Sufi master

Texture/Orchestration

This aspect of arranging is another broad topic and one that encompasses harmony, tone and rhythm. The texture of our arrangement can be light and airy, with lots of space and room to allow for further development. Conversely, the texture can be heavy, dense, rich or dark. (I personally cannot help drawing analogies here with painting and cooking!) All of these descriptions carry over into other disciplines. The chord voicings we choose, the positions we choose for them, the tone we apply, the rhythms and tempi that we select – all of these criteria affect the texture of an arrangement. If we consider the orchestra analogy, the various zones of the guitar fingerboard can be likened to different sections of the orchestra – strings, bass, woodwind, percussion – each playing an independent part but coming together in a symphony.

Dynamics

The dynamics of a piece of music work on many different planes at once. There are overall dynamics, where an arrangement is played loudly or quietly, but dynamics can also be more specific, where certain sections or phrases are played louder or quieter than others to create the impression of a 'dynamic curve' in the music. This enhances the shape of the arrangement. Dynamics can also be highly specific and work on a particular note or set of notes. These dynamics are part of the phrasing choices that are open to the musician.

We will discuss these points in more detail with specific arranging examples over the following pages.

Some Music Theory For Guitar Arrangers

Guitar music is notated on the standard five-line stave using the treble clef (also known as the G clef):

Example 3.1

Example 3.1 shows a treble clef, followed by some sharp symbols which make up a *key signature*. These are finally followed by a *time signature*. The time signature tells us about the number of beats in the bar and the type of beat in the music. Most music scores will open with some similar arrangement of symbols. Each line and space represents a different pitch:

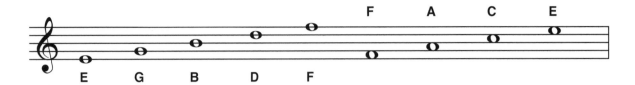

Example 3.2

The lines are E G B D F (easily remembered as Every Good Boy Deserves Favours), while the notes in the spaces spell FACE. By placing a note symbol on any line or space we can indicate any pitch. As you move from each letter to the following letter, you go up in pitch.

Here are the notes in ascending order:

Example 3.3

Here are the same notes written on the stave with a tablature stave added:

CD1, Track 52

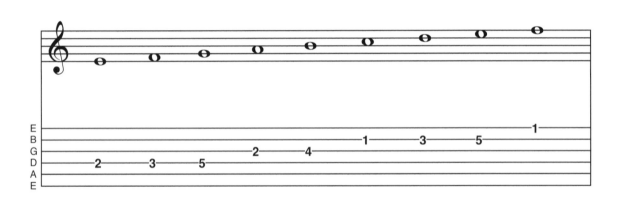

Example 3.4

This stave isn't wide enough to represent all the notes on a guitar fingerboard. The bass notes descend an octave lower, while the notes above the stave will extend for over one and a half octaves. By adding extra leger lines we can get notes such as these:

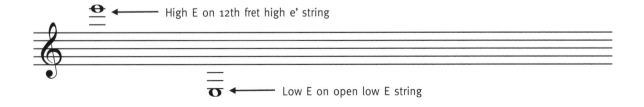

Example 3.5

Here are the notes found on the open strings of a standard-tuned guitar:

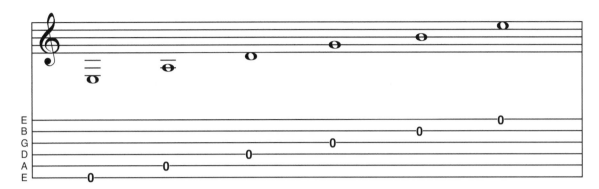

Example 3.6

They are E, A, D, G, B and E from the low pitch to the high pitch.

The Music Alphabet

At this point you may have noticed that the only letters that are used in notating pitch are the first seven letters of the alphabet:

A B C D E F G

One of the main units of measurement in pitch is the *octave*, the difference in pitch between one note and its next occurrence, up or down the register. The higher note vibrates at twice the speed of the lower note. Play these two notes consecutively and then simultaneously:

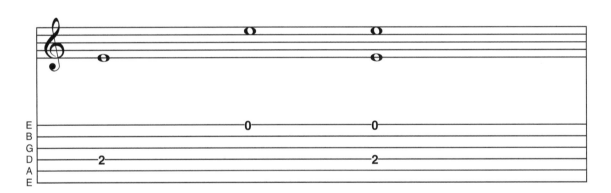

Example 3.7

If your instrument is in tune you will hear that the notes are very complementary, to the point that it is difficult to hear a difference between them. This simple ratio of frequencies – 2:1 – is reflected in the *consonance* (a subjective term suggesting a sound that is without tension) of the resulting sound. Certainly, if you compare it with this interval...

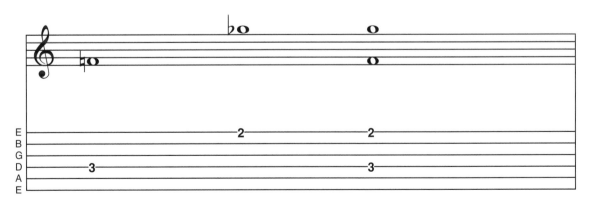

Example 3.8

...you will agree that they possess two very different qualities of sound. One sounds relatively at rest while the other sounds relatively tense. We will discuss these intervals and others shortly.

The octave can be divided up into 12 equal (theoretically, at least) steps. These steps are each called a *semitone* or a *half-step*. The semitone is the smallest notable difference in pitch between two neighbouring notes in Western music. There are numerous other intervals smaller than that in other cultures (which often have to struggle to survive against the imposition of Western pop) and even in blues music, where many of the bends on certain notes fall between these semitone steps. For the moment, though, you needn't concern yourself with these.

The Chromatic Scale

If we arrange all 12 notes in an octave in ascending order, they look like this:

Example 3.9

Starting on A, the next step is A♯ ('A sharp'). The following note is a semitone step above that and is called B.

The 12 steps are named alphabetically:

A A♯ B C C♯ D D♯ E F F♯ G G♯ A

The 12 semitone steps take us back to A, one octave higher. Here is the same series of notes written in tablature:

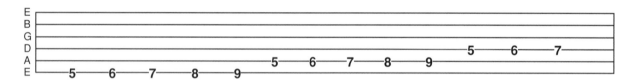

Example 3.10

As I mentioned earlier, each of these notes is a semitone above and below the notes before and after it respectively. So for example D♯ is a semitone above D and a semitone below E. Similarly A♯ is a semitone above A and a semitone below B. You will notice that any note with a ♯ ('sharp') sign is a semitone above a note of the same letter. The sharp sign increases the pitch of a note by one semitone (or by one fret, in guitar terms). You will notice two obvious exceptions to this rule: B and C are a semitone apart, and E and F are a semitone apart

There is no note between B and C, or between E and F. Well, in fact, that's not strictly true – there are an infinite number of notes in those gaps, all incredibly close (infinitely close, in fact, Captain Kirk!), but we have no way of notating them. Also, on the guitar, we could say that B♯ is the same pitch as C and that E♯ is the same as F.

The Chromatic Scale – Continued

If we arrange the same 12 notes in descending order, they can be renamed as follows:

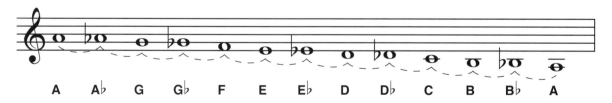

A A♭ G G♭ F E E♭ D D♭ C B B♭ A

Example 3.11

And in tab:

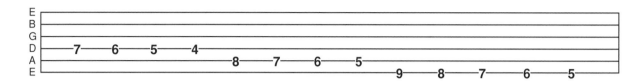

Example 3.12

In this case each note is *lower* than the note before it and a semitone *above* each note that follows. The ♭ (flat) symbol decreases the pitch of a note by a semitone.

As in the ascending form of this scale, there is no pitch between the pairs B-C and E-F. You could in fact say that C♭ is the same pitch as B and that F♭ is the same as E.

Enharmonic Notes

By comparing the two forms of the scale we can say that any sharp note can be rewritten as a flat note, and vice versa. Look at the following chart:

A♯ = B♭
C♯ = D♭
D♯ = E♭
F♯ = G♭
G♯ = A♭

Depending on the situation (usually the key), you will choose one note name over another. In one case B♭ will be the correct choice of note name while in another piece of music it may be the A♯ that is more accurate.

We can apply this concept of *enharmonic* (a word derived from the Greek for 'sharing the same sound') notes a little further and say that:

C♯♯ = D

By 'sharping' (somehow sharpening doesn't seem like the right word!) the C note *twice* we arrive a whole tone above at D. In notation, this 'C double sharp' has its own symbol:

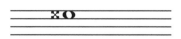

Example 3.13

You will see this symbol from time to time, although it is quite rare.

There is also a 'double flat' symbol in music:

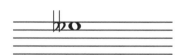

Example 3.14

This lowers a note by a whole tone (ie two semitones). In Example 3.14, the 'E double flat' is the same pitch as a D natural.

The 'natural' symbol looks like this:

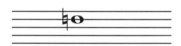

Example 3.15

The double sharp and double flat are very rare and are usually rewritten (very often wrongly, in terms of theory!) for ease of reading. Become familiar with all note names and their positions on the guitar fingerboard.

The Major Scale

Now that we have a good understanding of note names and the simple intervals – tones and semitones – we can start to look at scales and chords. By far the most important scale in Western music is the *major scale*. Here is a C major scale:

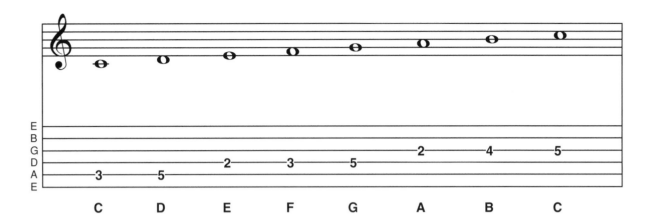

Example 3.16

You will notice that the notes are not all the same distance apart like the chromatic scale. This major scale is made up of two intervals, the tone and semitone. These intervals are sequenced in a strict order:

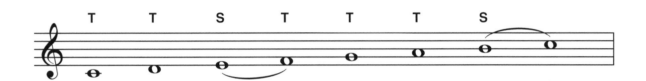

Example 3.17

The semitone intervals always occur between the third and fourth notes and between the seventh and eighth notes in the scale. This C major scale is one octave in length. It starts and finishes on a C note.

A good way to practise is to take a major scale and play it in different positions. Here are some suggestions:

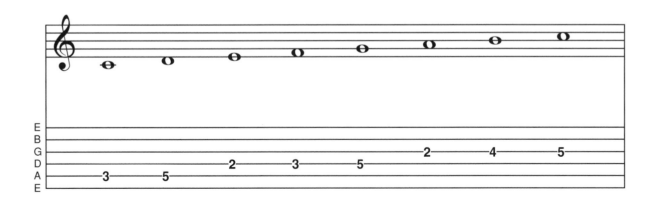

Example 3.18

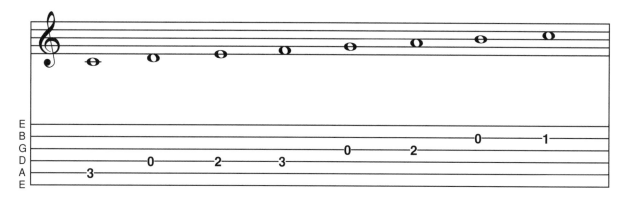

Example 3.19

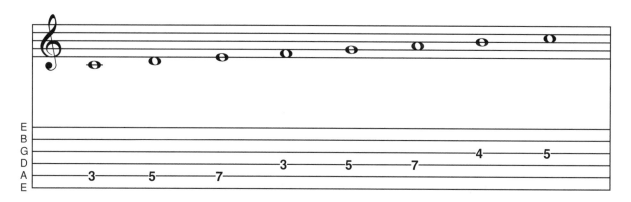

Example 3.20

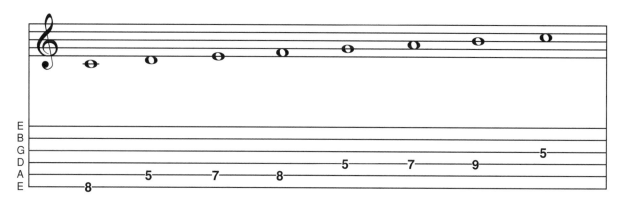

Example 3.21

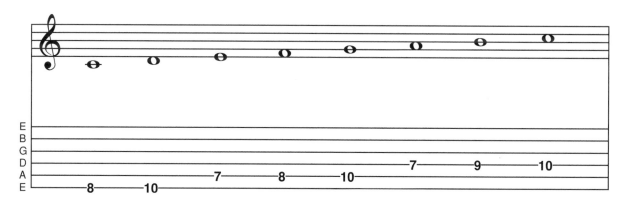

Example 3.22

Of course these are all one-octave scales. Let's try some two-octave patterns:

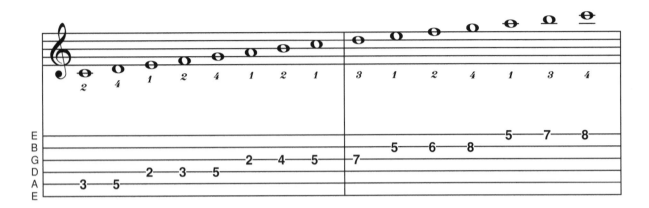

Example 3.23

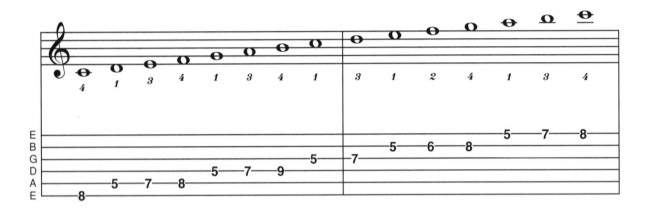

Example 3.24

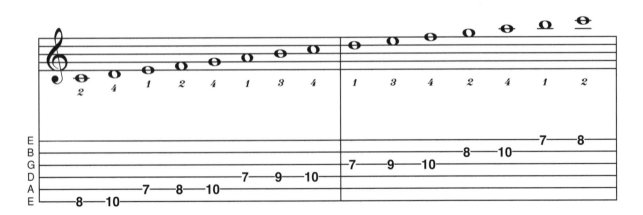

Example 3.25

You can practise these scales with various combinations of right-hand fingerings. As discussed in Chapter 1, try some of the following combinations:

im im im im (etc)

mi mi mi mi (etc)

ma ma ma ma (etc)

Also try this:

pi pi pi pi (etc)

No doubt the sound of this scale is very familiar to you. This scale and its various modes have been in use for thousands of years, and its origins date back to the mathematical investigations of Pythagoras and friends.

The first note of the scale – the *tonic* (or *tonal centre*) – gives the scale, or *key*, its grounding. It's possible to have any note from the chromatic scale as a tonic note. In other words, there are 12 keys in music (with five of those having an enharmonic equivalent – such as the keys of E♭ and D♯).

With only 12 different note names to choose from, many of these keys have a lot in common. For each tonic note we choose there will be a unique sequence of notes for its major scale – for example, the key of G major will have to include an F♯ to fit the major-scale formula of T(one) T S(emitone) T T T S:

Example 3.26

Check out the intervals between these notes:

G A B C D E F♯ G

You will see that they indeed fit the correct pattern.

The following sequence of notes, while having the correct sound and pattern, is not the correct set of note names:

G A B C D E G♭ G

There are obviously two types of G note in this scale: the G natural and G♭. It also gives the impression that there is no F♯ note in the scale. This can lead to confusion when analysing note sequences in melodies and chords.

The two simple rules in major-scale nomenclature are:

1   Use all seven letters of the musical alphabet;
2   Use each letter only once.

Take the various fingerboard patterns for the C major scale above in Examples 3.18–25 and move them to a G starting note. Some will have to move up the neck, some down the neck. Use the scale patterns explored above to 'shift' these patterns into a G major scale. For example the pattern in Ex 3.21 would shift down the neck to the 3rd fret.

Connect the technique of playing the scale pattern with the sound you are hearing via your understanding of the theory.

The 12 keys of music are playable with these patterns all over the guitar fingerboard. Take care to follow the correct fingering. Very often there are alternatives for fingering scales and chords, but usually there will be one fingering that is most logical. However, every situation is unique, so be open to the possibilities of fingering notes, scales, phrases and chords in new ways.

The movable patterns each begin on the relevant tonic note. As you move through successive octaves or *registers*, you will cross the tonic note again. I often imagine these patterns are like a spiral staircase rather than a straight line or ladder. Although the note names repeat again and again, you move on to higher and higher (or lower and lower as you descend) levels. With practice you can jump a few steps at a time without falling and move forwards or backwards at will. With a little more practice you'll find that you can perform these athletic feats with ease at great speeds.

There is an order to the 12 keys. Understanding this order is useful when you're trying to decipher a melody or chord sequence. The key in which a particular song or melody is written is not always so obvious; not all tunes start on the tonic. In fact, tunes will more often start on one of the other *diatonic* notes (notes in the scale) or *scale steps*. Very occasionally a tune will start on a note outside the key – a chromatic note. These notes can be very misleading unless you understand the various scales and keys.

The Cycle Of Fifths

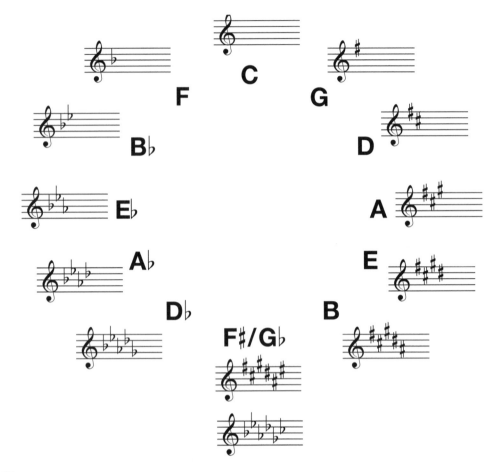

Example 3.27

The cycle of fifths is based on a very simple principle: start at the '12 noon' position and move clockwise around the wheel. Starting at the key of C and moving clockwise, the first stop is G, the fifth:

```
C D E F G A B C
        G A B C D E F♯ G
```

Rewrite the C scale starting on G, then add a sharp to the seventh note. As we saw earlier, this sequence of notes fits our major-scale formula perfectly.

You can follow the same procedure for each step:

```
G A B C D E F♯ G (go up a fifth)
        D E F♯ G A B C♯ D (sharp the
                                seventh)
```

The simple rule is 'up a fifth, then raise the seventh'.

At each point on the cycle we are adding another sharp note. After seven steps we arrive at a point with seven sharp signs – every note in the scale is sharp:

```
C♯  D♯  E♯  F♯  G♯  A♯  B♯  C♯
```

This scale fits the pattern of T T S T T T S like every major scale. It includes the unusual note names of E♯ and B♯. For this reason, the scale is more often renamed the D♭ major scale.

All the keys on the right-hand side of the cycle are 'sharp' keys. If we continued clockwise past the key of F♯, through the key of C♯ we would get to the key of G♯. Here we would need to include an F double sharp. At this point it is more practical to discuss keys with flats rather than double sharps.

The Flat Keys

Return to the top of the wheel to the key of C. The key of C has no sharps (or flats).

We are going to move anticlockwise around the circle in fifths. Instead of moving up a fifth, we move down a fifth through the descending C major scale:

```
C B A G F E D C
        F G A B♭ C D E F
```

Moving down a fifth from C brings us to F. Rewrite the notes of the scale beginning on F and flatten the fourth note, B♭.

As well as thinking of this as moving down a fifth, you can also think of it as moving up a fourth:

C D E **F** G A B C
   F G A B♭ C D E F

So the simple rule for moving anticlockwise through the cycle of fifths and the flat keys is 'up a fourth, then flatten the fourth'.

The next anticlockwise step on the cycle of fifths is as follows:

F G A **B♭** C D E F (go up a fourth)
B♭ C D E♭ F G A B♭ (flatten the fourth)

Practise this by following through the next few steps by yourself.

Key Signatures

The particular sharps or flats in a scale form a unique key signature for each key. The accidentals always follow the particular order, as shown in Example 3.27.

The trick is to remember the order of sharps or flats and to be able to create an image of the cycle of fifths in your mind when you need it. With time and practice you will start to memorise these key signatures.

Here are some simple mnemonics (wordplay exercises to aid memory) for memorising the order of the keys in the cycle of fifths:

For the sharp keys moving clockwise from C:

(Charles) **G**oes **D**own **A**nd **E**nds **B**attle **F**ighting

For the flat keys moving anti-clockwise from F:

Fierce **B**attle **E**nds **A**nd **D**own **G**oes **C**harles

A similar mnemonic can help you to memorise the order of sharps and flats. The sharps follow the order:

Father **C**harles **G**oes **D**own **A**nd **E**nds **B**attle

Just reverse that and the flats follow the order:

Battle **E**nds **A**nd **D**own **G**oes **C**harles' **F**ather

Some Interesting Observations

- Keys that are next to each other on the cycle of fifths have the closest relationship (ie notes in common). For example the keys of C and G have only one note in the difference between them (F/ F♯) as have the keys of C and F (B/B♭).

- Keys that are directly opposite each other have far fewer notes in common. For example the keys of A and E♭.

- Keys a semitone apart have the fewest notes in common (for example the keys of E and F).

- Every note in the chromatic scale appears in seven different keys.

The notes in every key are summarised below in this table:

KEY	I	ii	iii	IV	V	vi	vii
C	C	D	E	F	G	A	B
G	G	A	B	C	D	E	F♯
D	D	E	F♯	G♯	A	B	C♯
E	E	F♯	G♯	A	B	C♯	D♯
B	B	C♯	D♯	E	F♯	G♯	A♯
F♯	F♯	G♯	A♯	B	C♯	D♯	E♯
C♯	C♯	D♯	E♯	F♯	G♯	A♯	B♯
F	F	G	A	B♭	C	D	E
B♭	B♭	C	D	E♭	F	G	A
E♭	E♭	F	G	A♭	B♭	C	D
A♭	A♭	B♭	C	D♭	E♭	F	G
D♭	D♭	E♭	F	G♭	A♭	B♭	C
G♭	G♭	A♭	B♭	C♭	D♭	E♭	F
C♭	C♭	D♭	E♭	F♭	G♭	A♭	B♭

Example 3.28

You need to be familiar with these notes and their relationships to each other from many different angles:

- Memorise the notes in every scale

- Recite note names as you play through the scales

- Recognise the similarity between the keys

- Memorise the various positions of every note on the fingerboard

- Learn which note is a fifth above and a fifth below each note

Intervals

An *interval* is the distance between any two pitches. That distance can be large (eg many octaves), very small (eg a semitone), medium (eg a fifth) or nothing (unison). The intervals that occur in the major scale are used as the reference point for all other intervals and their names. The intervals in the major scale are known as *diatonic intervals*.

Notes	Size	Names
C–C	Zero	Unison
C–D	1 Tone / 2 Semitones	Major Second
C–E	2 Tones / 4 Semitones	Major Third
C–F	2.5 Tones / 5 Semitones	Perfect Fourth
C–G	3.5 Tones / 7 Semitones	Perfect Fifth
C–A	4.5 Tones / 9 Semitones	Major Sixth
C–B	5.5 Tones / 11 Semitones	Major Seventh
C–C	6 Tones / 12 Semitones	Octave

Example 3.29: Diatonic Intervals

All major scales follow the same interval pattern and therefore have these *diatonic* intervals. Of course there are other intervals – all of which turn up between various notes of the major scale. They are divided simply into two categories:

- **Perfect Intervals** – Unison, octave, perfect fourth and perfect fifth

- **Major Intervals** – major second, major third, major sixth, major seventh.

Interval Shapes On The Fingerboard

Some examples of unison intervals on the guitar fingerboard:

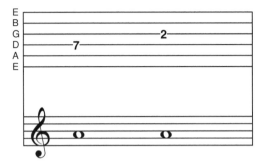

CD1, Track 53

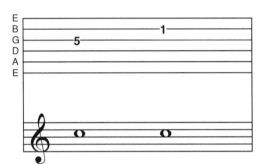

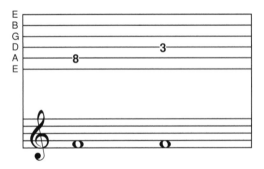

Example 3.30: Diatonic Intervals

Some examples of major second intervals on the guitar fingerboard:

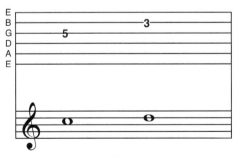

CD1, Track 54

Example 3.31 (continues...)

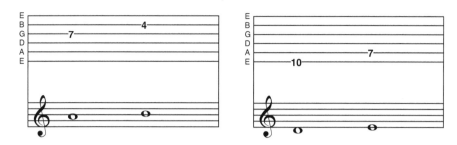

Example 3.31 (continued)

Some examples of a major third interval on the guitar fingerboard:

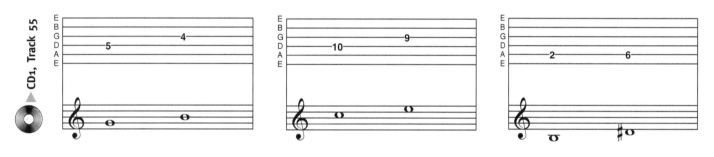

Example 3.32

Some examples of a perfect fourth on the guitar fingerboard:

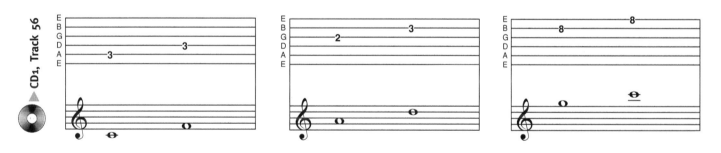

Example 3.33

Some examples of a perfect fifth on the guitar fingerboard:

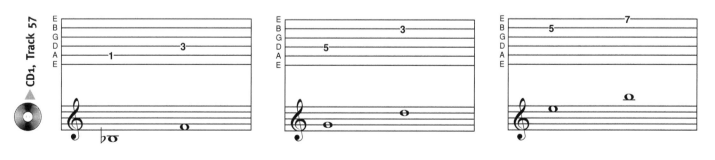

Example 3.34

Some examples of a major sixth interval on the guitar fingerboard:

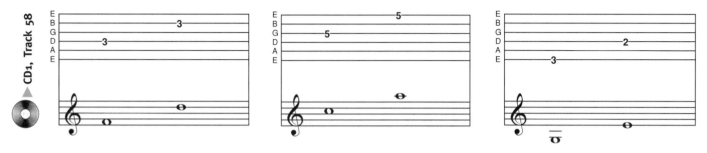

CD1, Track 58

Example 3.35

Some examples of a major seventh interval on the guitar fingerboard:

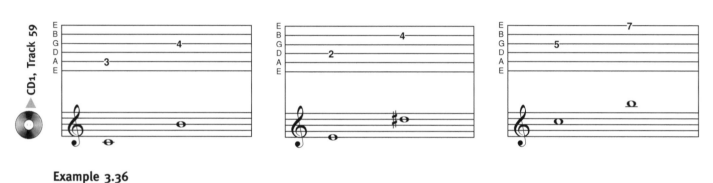

CD1, Track 59

Example 3.36

Some examples of an octave interval on the guitar fingerboard:

CD1, Track 60

Example 3.37

Be familiar with these shapes. Start to memorise the characteristic sound that each has. Find other shapes around the fingerboard using various pairs of strings. Always remember to connect the technique with the sound via your understanding of the theory.

Chromatic Intervals

The remaining intervals in music are the five enharmonic pairs that we discussed earlier in the chapter. Each interval will have two names. Which name you choose will depend on the note names involved.

Notes	Size	Names	
C–C♯	1 Semitone	Augmented Prime	
C–D♭	1 Semitone	Minor Second	
C–D♯	1.5 Tones/3 Semitones	Augmented Second	
C–E♭	1.5 Tones/3 Semitones	Minor Third	
C–F♯	3 Tones/6 Semitones	Augmented Fourth	⎫ Tritone
C–G♭	3 Tones/6 Semitones	Diminished Fifth	⎭
C–A♯	5 Tones/10 Semitones	Augmented Sixth	
C–B♭	5 Tones/10 Semitones	Minor Seventh	

Example 3.38

Here are some shapes for these intervals. First off, some examples of a minor second interval on the guitar fingerboard:

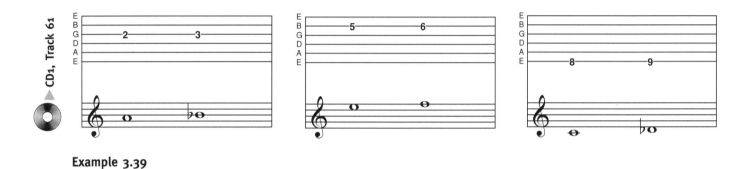

Example 3.39

Next, some examples of a minor third interval on the guitar fingerboard:

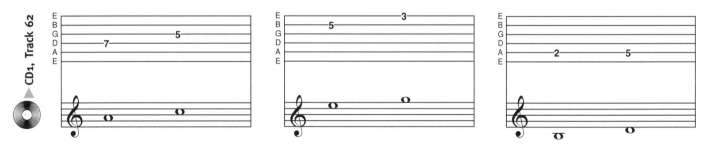

Example 3.40

Some examples of tritone intervals on the fingerboard. Can you see which one(s) are augmented fourths or diminished fifths?

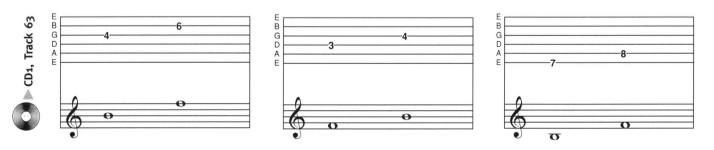

Example 3.41

Some augmented fifth and minor sixth intervals on the fingerboard. Can you tell which is which? Look at the note names.

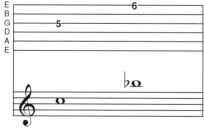
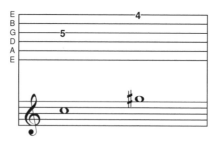
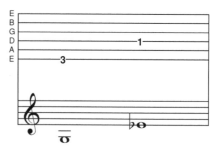

Example 3.42

Some minor seventh intervals on the fingerboard. The augmented sixth has the same sound but rarely, if ever, occurs.

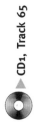
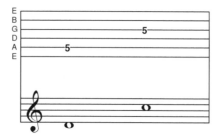
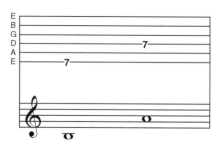

Example 3.43

The Easy Guide To Naming Intervals

With all these intervals and so many possibilities of note names and note combinations, it is useful to have a couple of rules to help you name these intervals.

Rule 1

To decide what the basic nature of the interval is – *count* the inclusive letters from the lower note to the higher note. This will give you the quantitative aspect of the interval (such as a seventh, a fourth, or a second). For example the interval between the following two notes:

Example 3.44

These can be counted by starting at the lower note D and counting the inclusive letters up to the top note (C):

D E F G A B C

The D is counted as '1' and C is counted as '7'. So the interval is some type of *seventh*.

The inclusion of sharps or flats doesn't have any bearing on this stage of the process. Here's a type of third:

Example 3.45

Count the alphabetical letters from the F to the A (3: F G A). This tells us that it is some kind of *third*. The next stage in the process will give the rest of the detail.

Rule 2

To decide on the quality of the interval (that is, if the interval is major, minor or augmented) you should count the number of tones or semitones. In the case of this seventh:

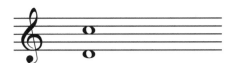

Example 3.46

There are *five* tones between the two notes. We can therefore pinpoint the interval as a *minor* seventh. (Remember the chromatic interval table.)

The interval in Rule 1, the third...

Example 3.47

...is *two* whole tones so we can name it specifically as a *major* third. (See diatonic interval table.)

So, in summary, to identify and name an interval:

- Count the letters
- Count the tones
- Name the interval

Hear Ye! Hear Ye! Now Listen Up...

One simple way to start memorising the sounds of these intervals is to record yourself playing them at random. Perhaps play each interval twice or three times. Why not start with a select few – for example the perfect intervals. Play back the recording and try to identify each interval.

You can start to relate the sounds to the opening notes of popular tunes and songs. This will help you to recognise the intervals more quickly. Here is a list of some suggestions:

- **Unison** – The same note played twice
- **Minor Second** – The 'cello motif in *Jaws*
- **Major Second** – 'Happy Birthday'
- **Minor Third** – 'Georgia'
- **Major Third** – 'When the Saints Come Marching In'
- **Perfect Forth** – 'Here Comes the Bride'
- **Tritone** – 'Maria' (from *West Side Story*)
- **Perfect Fifth** – 'Twinkle Twinkle'
- **Minor Sixth** – Theme from *Love Story*
- **Major Sixth** – 'My Bonnie Lies Over The Ocean'
- **Minor Seventh** – 'Everybody Hurts' (REM)

- **Major Seventh** – The second motif in the *Superman* theme
- **Octave** – 'Somewhere Over the Rainbow'

One of the most effective ways to train your ear is to sing these intervals while visualising the name of them. Through regular repetition you will start to train your mind and ear to recognise these sounds in various contexts.

Here endeth the ear-training lesson!

Harmony

The combination of sounds produces harmony. The study of music theory and in particular the study of harmony is the study of how musical sounds have been organised. I say 'have been' because harmony is constantly developing. What was acceptable 200 years ago can seem passé and unadventurous today. What is taken as 'standard practice' would have broken all the rules 300 years ago. What works in a blues guitar solo doesn't necessarily work in a typical string quartet. What is useful in jazz may not be suitable for a Top 40 hit. Harmony takes its context from the style, the times and the instrument. You can never say what is 'good' or 'bad' in harmony without taking the context into account. Because of this retrospective nature of teaching harmony, I often introduce harmony classes and workshops as a lesson in 'music history'!

In this section we are concerned with 'common practice' harmony. From that viewpoint you can move into all the other areas of harmony.

Harmony in popular music (which covers huge swathes of classical music, folk music, pop, rock and jazz music) is based on the harmony of the major scale. Combining notes from the major scale produces many of the standard chords and chord sequences. Other scales such as the various minor scales and modes are usually explained as deviations of the major scale as is the harmony taken from them.

After many centuries of experimenting with very stark and colourless harmonies in fourths and fifths, composers gradually shifted to a system of *harmony in thirds*. These explorations were initially restricted by a reluctance to try something new as well as certain organisations, in particular the Church, banning certain types of harmony.

Eventually the system that follows became standard practice.

Thirds

The scale below is a C major scale harmonised in *diatonic* thirds:

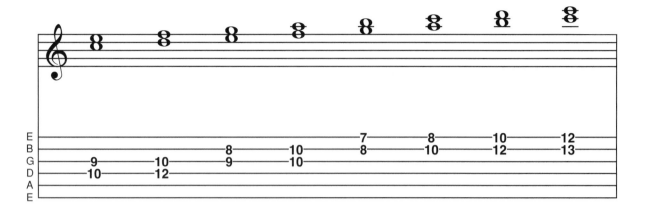

Example 3.48

Listen to it on the CD. Notice how it sounds very full, even with such a simple harmony. Let's look at the same harmony an octave lower:

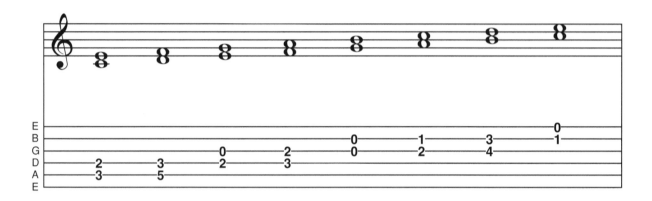

Example 3.49

The C major scale is harmonised a third above. These thirds are diatonic – that is, the notes used to produce the intervals are exclusively from the C major scale. If we were working in the key of A major there would three sharp notes – every F, C and G note would be preceded by a sharp:

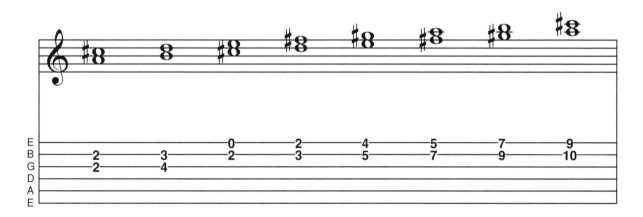

Example 3.50

These thirds are diatonic in the key of A. The more efficient way of writing the above example would be to include the correct key signature for A major from our cycle of fifths:

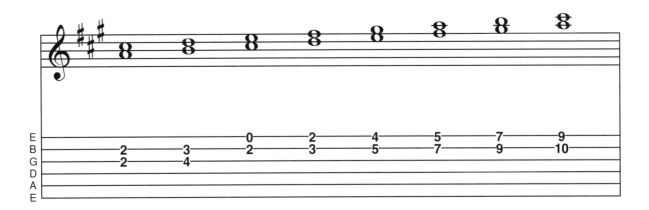

Example 3.51

The key signature tells you that every F, C and G that follows is in fact F♯, C♯ and G♯ (unless otherwise indicated).

A useful exercise would be for you to take the cycle of fifths and write out the major scale, harmonised in diatonic thirds, in each key with and without the key signature as above.

Triads

The thirds that result from harmonising in diatonic thirds

Example 3.52

In the diagram above you see a C note linked with its diatonic third, E which in turn is linked to *its* diatonic third, G. These three notes are stacked at the start of the scale to produce a *Triad*. The 'third of the third' is in fact the *fifth* note of the scale. We say that the triad has a *root* (C), a *third* (E) and a *fifth* (G).

The intervals produced from the root note are: root, *major* third and perfect fifth. This is often written in 'chord formula shorthand' as shown on the right:

follow a set pattern. As you know there are *two* types of 'third' interval in music – major and minor. The thirds in these harmonised scales follow the pattern:

major • minor • minor • major • major • minor • minor • major

The process of harmony in thirds continue by harmonising the 'thirds' in *thirds*.

R   3   5

The intervals of triads are normally calculated upwards from the root note at the bottom. In the case of this C triad the series of intervals produces a major triad (or major chord).

The process of harmonising in thirds is like playing a simple game of leap frog on each scale step. If we start from the D note and leap frog through the scale in thirds we get the following series of notes:

Example 3.53

The notes are root (D), third (F) and fifth (A). In this case the precise intervals produced from the root note are: root, *minor* third and perfect fifth. This is often written in chord formula shorthand as:

R ♭3 5

This triad, with this particular series of intervals is known as a minor triad (or minor chord). The only note that distinguishes the major chord from the minor chord is the middle note – the third.

I often draw an analogy between the strong but bare relationship of the root and fifth and the two pieces of bread in a sandwich. The real musical flavour is brought by putting different flavours of the third in between these two notes.

The thirds in these two chords are only a semitone apart in size. A major third interval is two tones distance while a minor third is one and a half tones. To simply turn a major chord into a minor chord we can 'flatten' the third of the major chord by one semitone (very often by simply moving that note down one fret).

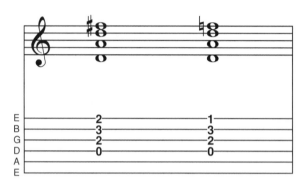

Example 3.54

In practice these two chord types are played in a wide variety of ways. The notes can be doubled up or more. The third can be on top with the fifth in the middle, or any of the three chord tones can be put at the bottom (in the *bass*). Take some standard major chord shapes and look at how the fit the theory:

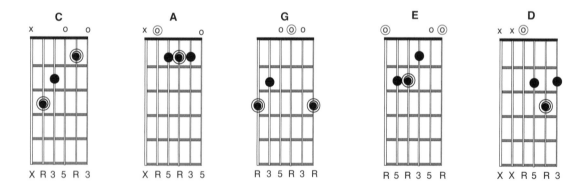

Example 3.55

For example, the standard open C major shape has a C in the bass on the A string, a third, a fifth followed by another C root note and topped with another third (high E). The E major chord however has six notes following the pattern:

R 5 R 3 5 R

Each shape has a particular sequence of the correct chord tones (R,3,5) that gives a characteristic *voicing*. Of these five shapes, the D has the narrowest band of pitch. It is a comparatively tight, highly pitched voicing, quite different from the deep, expansive voicing of the E shape.

These major triad shapes have one characteristic in common – they each have their root note as the *lowest* note, often referred to as 'root in the bass'. There are many voicings, or shapes for these chords that feature the third or fifth in the bass, but we will investigate these later.

The shifting of the minor third down a semitone in these five shapes will turn them to minor chords. You need to know which of the notes in each shape is the major third and how to lower it by a semitone. In the case of D major, this is quite simple – the major third is on the 1st string, 2nd fret. Just drop that major third (F♯) down one fret to F natural and *voilà*! Instant D minor.

Not so easy with C major. The standard voicing has two E notes in different registers, each of which must be adjusted downwards and replaced by an E♭ note (the minor third). One difficulty is that the higher of these E notes is an open string which can't be lowered without retuning. This isn't practical – who wants to re-tune for one chord each time?! Below are the five standard minor chord shapes.

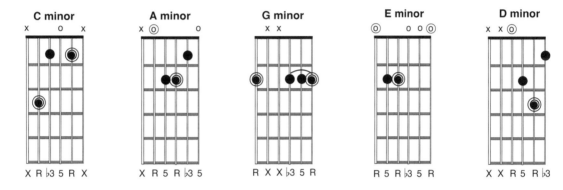

Example 3.56

Play through them and look for their relationships with their major counterparts. Continuing the process of harmonising in triads on the remaining scale steps, we get the following sequence:

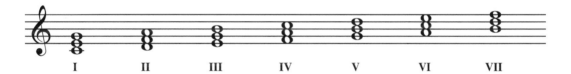

Example 3.57

The triads all fall neatly onto adjacent lines or spaces. If you analyse the intervals you will find that they all (except chord VII) fall into either the major or minor category. Chord VII (B-D-F) is known as a diminished chord and has the following interval pattern:

Root • Minor Third • Diminished Fifth

This is very often rewritten as:

R ♭3 ♭5

Of the three chord types in the major scale, this is most dissonant and the least stable. This is because of the dissonance in the diminished fifth interval. You may notice the diminished chord is in fact made up of two minor third intervals stacked on top of each other. This symmetry will be useful later in the book.

The order of chord types in the major scale is the same for every major scale (since all major scales have the same formula T T S T T T S). The order is:

Major • Minor • Minor • Major • Major • Minor • Diminished • Major

The chords in the key of C major therefore are

C major • D minor • E minor • F major • G major • A minor • B diminished

These are often written in chord name shorthand as:

C Dm Em F G Am B°

They are numbered with Roman numerals which is standard practice when so many aspects of music – rhythm, fingerings, time signatures, frequencies and intervals – are numerical in nature. The roman numerals help to distinguish chords or triads from one another in a particular key.

These scale steps also have another set of more formal names. Although it's true that they're less common in popular music, they nonetheless turn up. Here is a table showing the various ways in which the notes of a scale can be classified.

Roman	Formal	Key of C	Sol-Fa	Major Scale Triad		Interval with Tonic
I	Tonic	C	Doh	Major	Δ	Unison
II	Supertonic	D	Re	Minor	-	Major Second
III	Mediant	E	Me	Minor	-	Major Third
IV	Sub-Dominant	F	Fah	Major	Δ	Perfect Fourth
V	Dominant	G	Soh	Major	Δ	Perfect Fifth
VI	Sub-Mediant	A	Lah	Minor	-	Major Sixth
VII	Leading Note	B	Te	Diminished	°	Major Seventh

Example 3.58

These names and symbols are often used interchangeably, so it is important to become familiar with them. And don't forget to relate them to the sound of each scale step and the intervals between them.

The chords of every key in the cycle of fifths are presented in the following table. Become very familiar with them!

KEY	I	II	III	IV	V	VI	VII
C	C maj	D m	E m	F maj	G maj	A m	B°
G	G maj	A m	B m	C maj	D maj	E m	F#°
D	D maj	E m	F# m	G maj	A maj	B m	C#°
A	A maj	B m	C# m	D maj	E maj	F# m	G#°
E	E maj	F# m	G# m	A maj	B maj	C# m	D#°
B	B maj	C# m	D# m	E maj	F# maj	G# m	A#°
F#	F#maj	G# m	A# m	B maj	C# maj	D# m	E#°
C#	C#maj	D# m	E# m	F#maj	G# maj	A# m	B#°
F	F maj	G m	A m	B♭ maj	C maj	D m	E°
B♭	B♭ maj	C m	D m	E♭ maj	F maj	G m	A°
E♭	E♭ maj	F m	G m	A♭ maj	B♭ maj	C m	D°
A♭	A♭ maj	B♭ m	C m	D♭ maj	E♭ maj	F m	G°
D♭	D♭ maj	E♭ m	F m	G♭maj	A♭ maj	B♭ m	C°
G♭	G♭maj	A♭ m	B♭ m	C♭ maj	D♭ maj	E♭ m	F°
C♭	C♭ maj	D♭ m	E♭ m7	F♭ maj	G♭ maj	A♭ m	B♭°

Example 3.59

To really apply this knowledge of music theory in a practical way you should:

• Learn which notes and triads are in each key

• Notice which chords are in common between the keys

• Be able to recognise which keys any one chord comes from

From this table you will notice that:

- The I, IV and V chords are always *major*

- The II, III and VI chords are always *minor*

- The VII chord is always *diminished*

You should aspire to being familiar with every chord in every key.

Triads On The Guitar Fingerboard

There are some standard shapes for triads on the fingerboard. I've organised them into different 'string sets'. I've also circled the root note in each shape. These shapes are all closed (*no open strings*) and fully movable to all other keys. Don't forget to listen to them played on the accompanying CD!

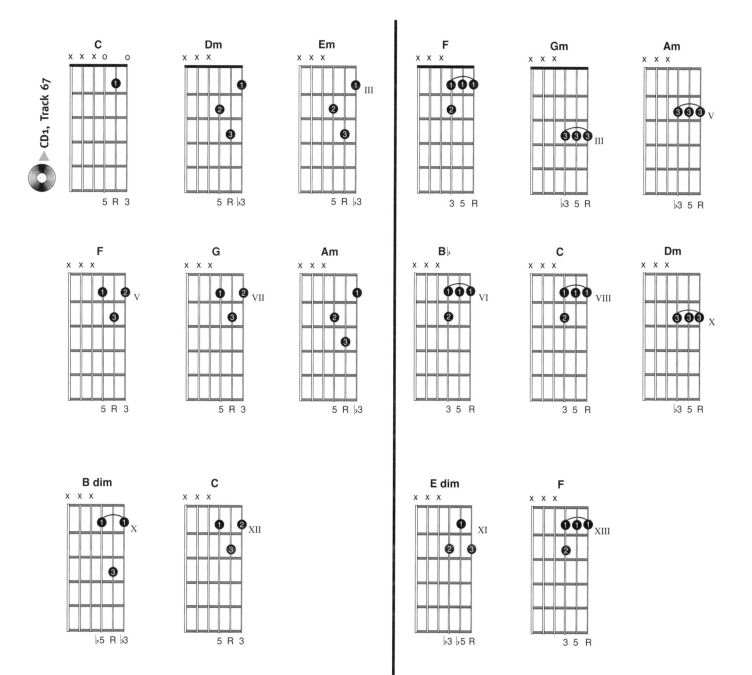

Example 3.60

Example 3.61

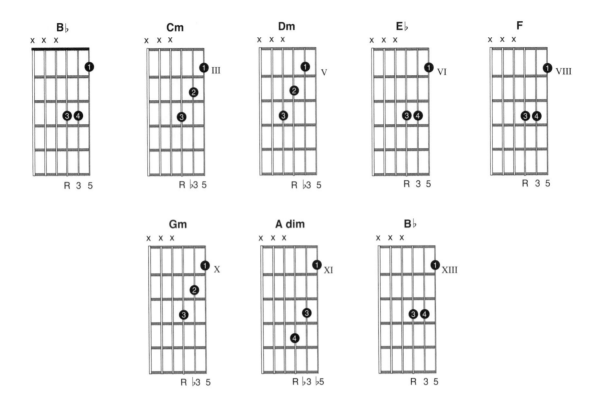

Example 3.62

On the recording I have played these first as 'single strokes', and then as simple arpeggios. They are played over a tonic drone. I have de-tuned my low E string to C to create this drone note for set 1, the low E string up to F for set 2 and the A string up to Bb for set 3.

CD1, Track 68

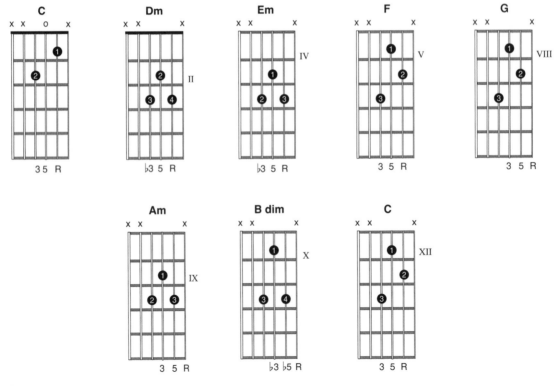

Example 3.63

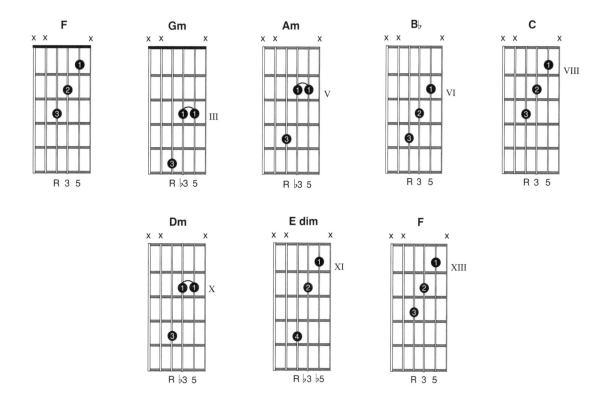

Example 3.64

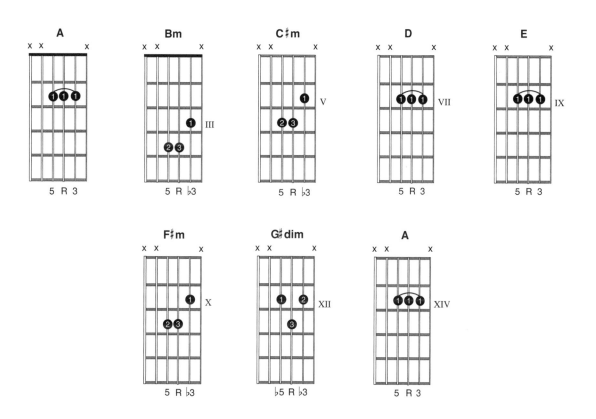

Example 3.65

Remember that all these shapes are movable to any key.

▲ CD1, Track 69

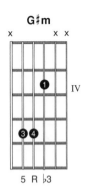

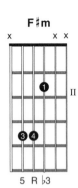

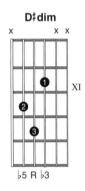

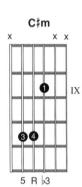

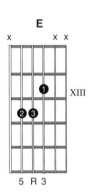

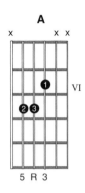

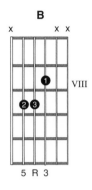

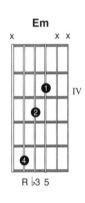

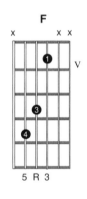

Example 3.66

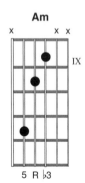

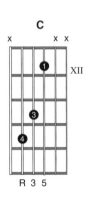

Example 3.67

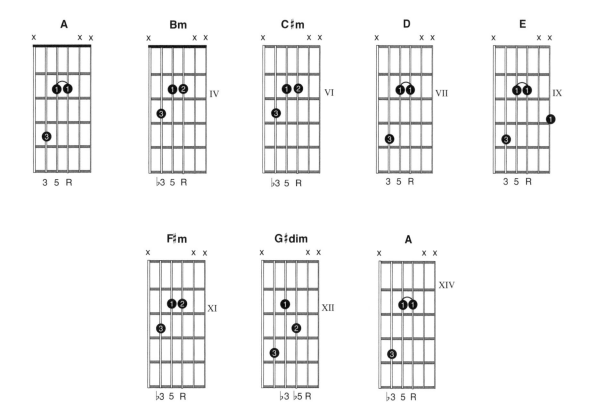

Example 3.68

These last three patterns for string set 3 work in the same way on the last string set – the D, A and low E string. From all these shapes we can arrange the various chord types. Here are the major triads. On the CD they're played over a tonic drone – C.

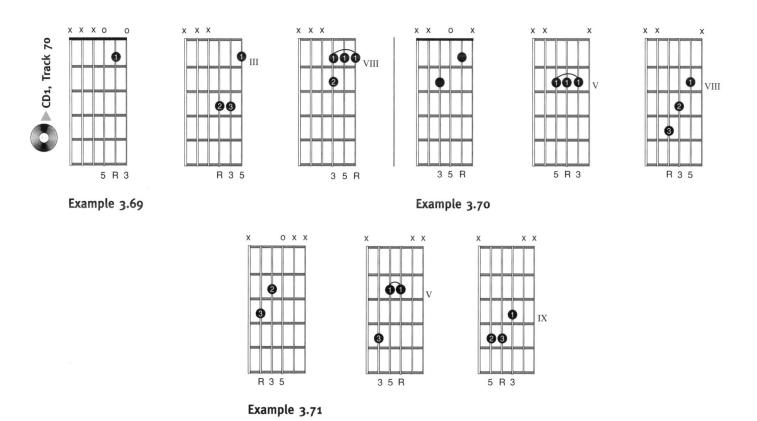

Example 3.69

Example 3.70

Example 3.71

Here are all the minor triad shapes. On the CD they're played over a tonic drone – A:

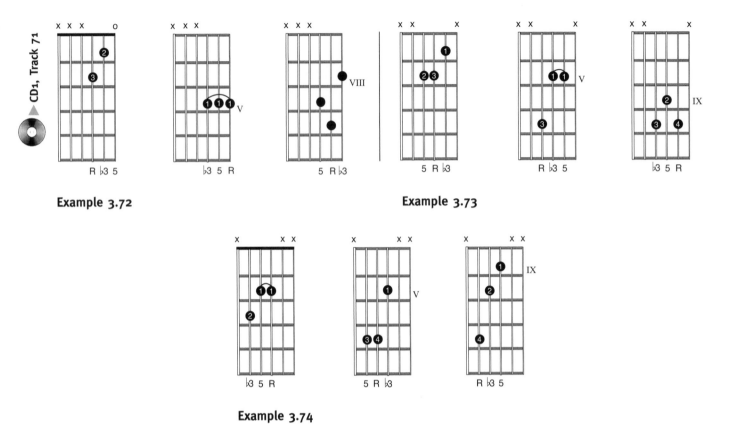

Example 3.72   Example 3.73

Example 3.74

The diminished triads from these sets also have three shapes per set. The harmony of the diminished triad is closely linked to that of the dominant seventh chord (more about that later). Here are some shapes for B diminished:

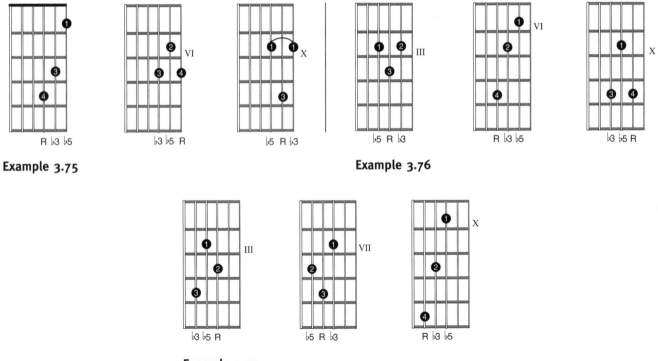

Example 3.75   Example 3.76

Example 3.77

Triads On Non-Adjacent Strings

The notes of a triad can be arranged in a wide variety of string combinations. Here is some simple mathematics:

On a standard guitar fingerboard there are 22 frets giving 23 different pitches (including the open string) per string. Any one note (for example, G) can be played in at least ten different places, in various registers, on the fingerboard:

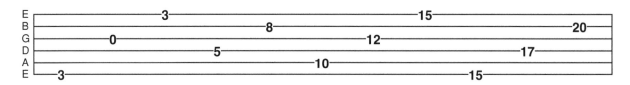

Example 3.78

This is true for all the other notes of the chromatic scale. A triad (say G major – with the chord tones G B and D) can be voiced in (approximately) 10 x 10 x 10 = 1000 different ways on the fingerboard! Obviously in practice that would include physically impossible shapes (or are they?) like these:

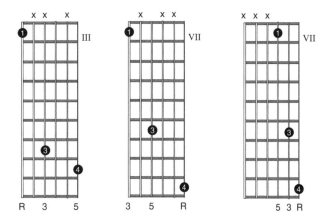

Example 3.79

I would suggest, conservatively, that of these 1000 shapes for G major triads there are about 100 practical and playable shapes. A good exercise in fingerboard knowledge is to select a region of the fingerboard – for example, frets 2 to 5 inclusive – and try to find as many voicings for the G major triad as you can. The order of notes isn't important for the moment. You can have any of the notes in the bottom, middle or top voices. Each voicing will have a characteristic sound depending on the arrangement of the notes, the strings they are played on, and the position on the fingerboard.

Here are some examples:

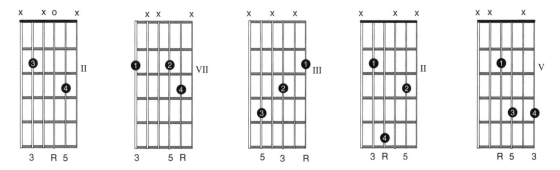

Example 3.80 (continues...)

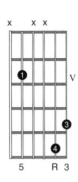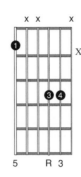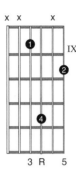

Example 3.80 (continued)

This process works for *all* triads and should be explored. This approach to creating chord shapes is based on two simple steps:

1 Know the position of all the notes on the fingerboard

2 Know the notes of every basic triad

If we take this mathematical process one more stage and look at chord *progressions*...

G Em C D

I could have chosen any four (or more) chords. If there are approximately 100 playable shapes for any triad, then the above chord progression can be played 100 x 100 x 100 x 100 ways! That's 100 million possible combinations of the various triad shapes!

Of these 10 million variations on the progression, I would again conservatively suggest that the 0.1% are practical – that's 100,000 ways to play the above chord progression using simple triad shapes.

In practice, we rarely play strict triads. We double up notes, maybe even triple them. Take for example the familiar E major chord shape:

Example 3.81

The root note E is played three times with two 'fifths' and a single 'third'. Including all these possibilities makes for a massive increase in the number of possible chord shape combinations.

Take the first four frets and look at the huge number of possibilities of playing the notes of an E major triad with a minimum of three different notes and a maximum of six notes (with all combinations of the notes allowed). Lots of choice! Take a listen to track 72 on the CD, which features an E drone with various voicings for E major played over it.

Inversions

The order in which the notes of a triad are arranged creates various harmonic effects. Which note occupies the lowest position (often referred to as the 'bass') in the chord can change the function of the chord. As there are only three notes in a triad, there are only three possible notes for this highly potent role.

Root In The Bass ('Root Position')

With the root in the bass position, the chord is in its most stable voicing. Regardless of how the remaining notes are arranged above that, the root in the bass gives the harmony a solid grounding, and each of the other chord tones can form a strong intervallic relationship with this root. This voicing is rarely referred to as an inversion. It is most often called 'root position'.

Third In The Bass ('First Inversion')

By putting the third in the bass the chord becomes a little less stable. The intervals formed with the bass are now a third and a sixth:

CD4, Track 72

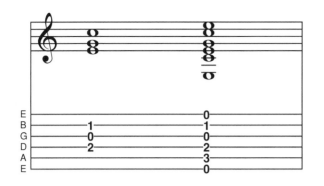

Example 3.82

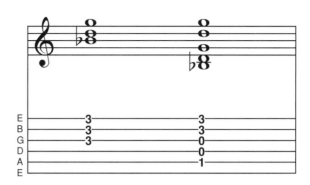

Example 3.83

The major triad has a minor third interval and a minor sixth while the minor triad, first inversion, has a major third and major sixth (a voicing often heard as a major sixth chord).

The first inversions of major chords are more unstable than their minor counterparts. The first inversion major chord is often used as a passing chord:

CD1, Track 73

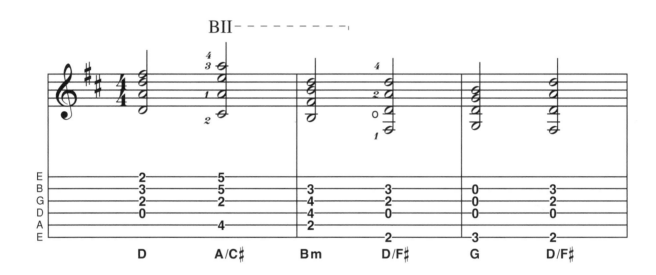

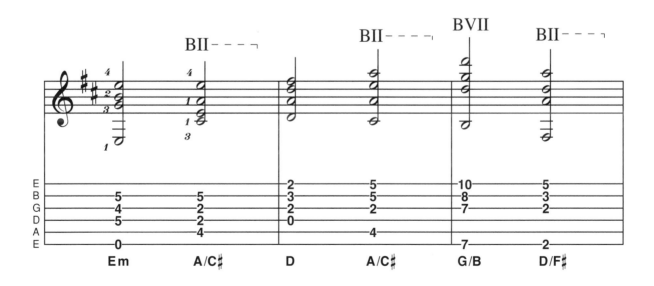

Example 3.84: Chord progression in D major using root-position and first-inversion voicings (continues...)

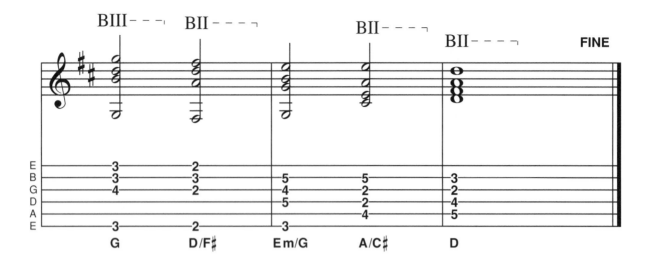

Example 3.84 continued

This typical chord progression has a bass line that is moving in simple step pattern. The various inversions create a sense of movement that wouldn't be conveyed by a series of root position voicings. The first inversion chords add *tension* to the harmony. Tension in music will eventually need *resolving*, and that is what is happening to greater and lesser degrees in the above example, as the chords move from one to the next, eventually coming home to resolve on the tonic chord.

Fifth In The Bass ('Second Inversion')

When you put the fifth as the lowest chord tone, the chord becomes more unstable. The intervals formed with the bass are a fourth and a sixth:

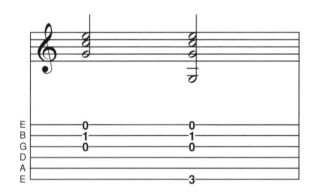

Example 3.85

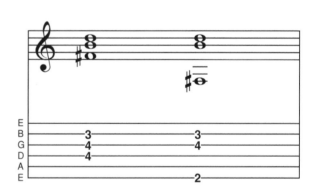

Example 3.86

This 'second inversion' voicing is the basis of all those 'root and fifth' bass lines used in so many styles, including country music and Latin music.

Example 3.87: Country-style progression with root/fifth line morphing to Latin-style progression.

The tension of the major chord in second inversion arises mainly from the interval of a perfect fourth. Although it is perfect, it actually creates tension in chords. (Notice the tension of a suspended fourth chord – the sus 4 – more about that later!)

A classic 'church choir' type chord movement would be as follows:

CD1, Track 75

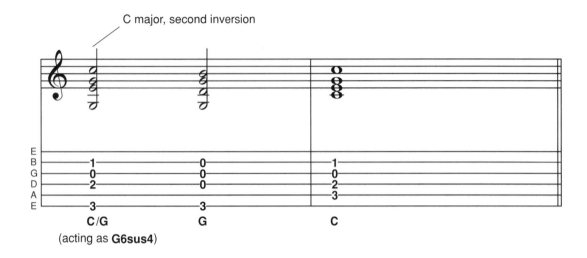

Example 3.88: 'Amen' progression in C

The tension created by the second inversion of C major is resolved by the G major chord which in turn resolves to the key centre of C.

The tasteful use of inversions can transform an otherwise standard chord progression. In 'Inside Out', the chord progression is primarily in E major. Many of the chords are inversions and written in the form of *slash chords.* The slash chord (for example, in bar 1) has two elements – the chord and a bass note. In the case of E/G# the E major chord is played *over* a G# bass note. However not all slash chords are inversions of triads. Look through 'Inside Out' to find some examples.

'Inside Out' also modulates (changes key) in a few places. It eventually comes to rest in the final bar outside the original key. However with the use of the inversion in bar 1, the chord progression can 'turn around', that is, the final bar can lead us back to the first chord. On the example on the CD, I slow down slightly (*rallentando* – an Italian musical direction meaning to slow down gradually) to create a greater sense of finality. Although not as strong as the dominant chord (in this case a B chord) leading back to the tonic (E major), it is nonetheless effective.

As the recording demonstrates the inversions of chords can create a more sophisticated and slightly less stable harmony that sets up more effective resolutions. Experiment with inversions in your own arrangements and compositions.

Inside Out

CD1, Track 76

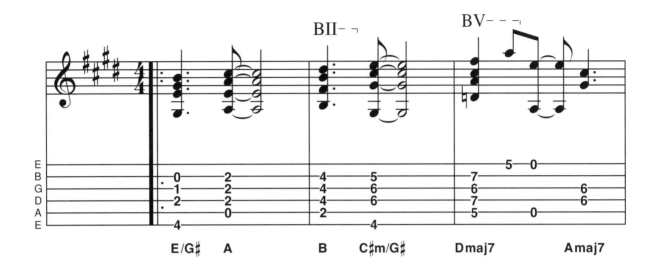

E/G♯   A   B   C♯m/G♯   Dmaj7   Amaj7

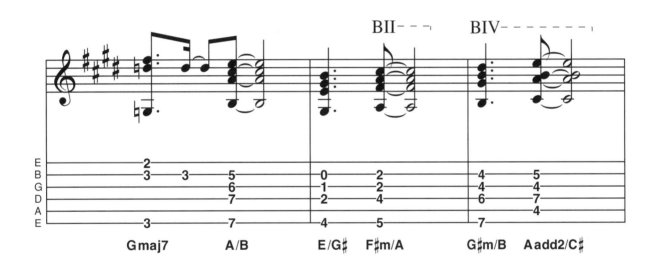

Gmaj7   A/B   E/G♯   F♯m/A   G♯m/B   Aadd2/C♯

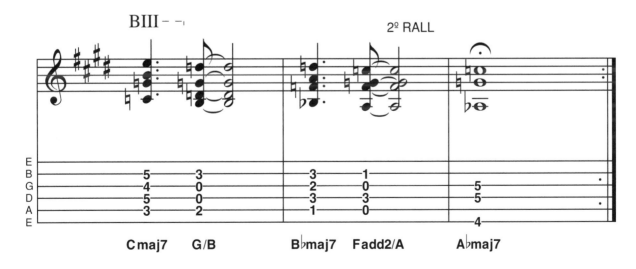

Cmaj7   G/B   B♭maj7   Fadd2/A   A♭maj7

Example 3.89: 16-bar progression in E using lots of inversions

109

4 EXPLORING THE FINGERBOARD

Arranging For Solo Fingerstyle Guitar – Part 2

*'I try to be prepared for the moment, through understanding and being warmed up, knowing
all about chords and scales, so I don't even have to think and I can get right to what it is I
want to say.' – Pat Metheney*

Now that we have a grounding in the basics of western harmony, we can start applying it to some practical examples. Take a simple tune like 'Twinkle Twinkle Little Star' for instance:

 CD2, Track 1

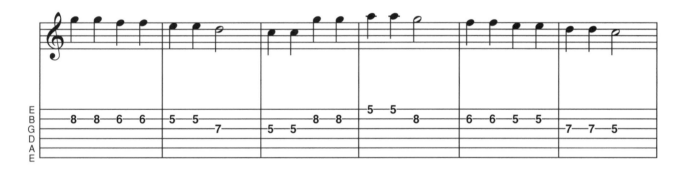

Example 4.1

Here is the same melody harmonised with the three primary triads. Underneath each chord change I have included the roman numerals – I, IV and V.

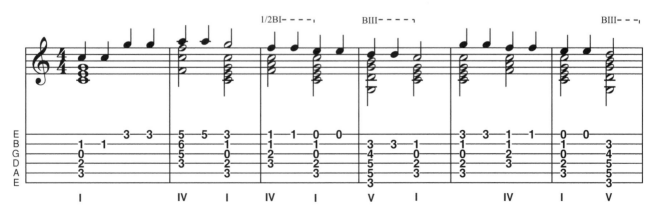

CD2, Track 2

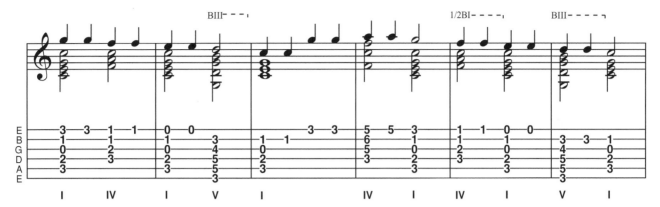

Example 4.2

The Three-Chord Trick

The above harmonisation is an example of the 'three-chord trick'. The 'three-chord trick' is often mentioned but rarely explained. Here's how it works.

The primary chords of any key are the tonic, subdominant and dominant chords (in short, chords I, IV and V). As we learnt earlier, these three triads or chords are always major in a major scale.

If you are working with a major diatonic melody (that is a melody whose notes, excluding passing notes or decorations, are exclusively from the same scale), then the melody can be harmonised using the primary chords of the key, shown on the left. This is true because any note from the melody will belong to at least one of the primary chords:

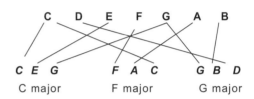

C major   F major   G major

Here you can see that each of the notes of the C major scale belongs to at least one of the C, F or G major triads.

So, any melody note can be accompanied or supported by at least one of the primary chords.

Check out this example where the melody is played with the 'three-chord trick' changes over a static tonic note (C):

CD2, Track 3

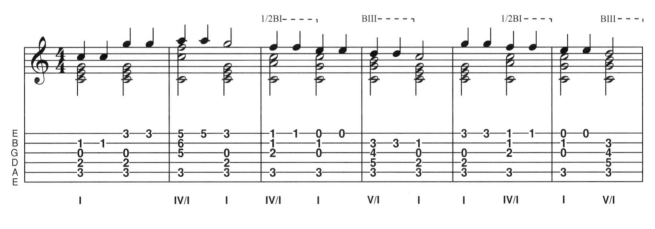

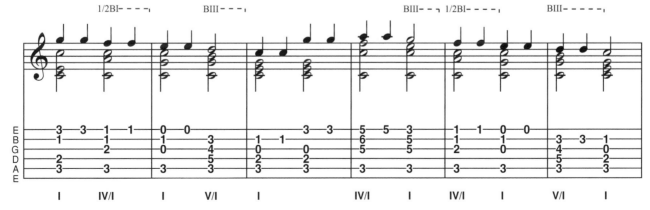

Example 4.3

A quite different harmonic effect can be achieved by playing all these chords with the melody over a static dominant note (G):

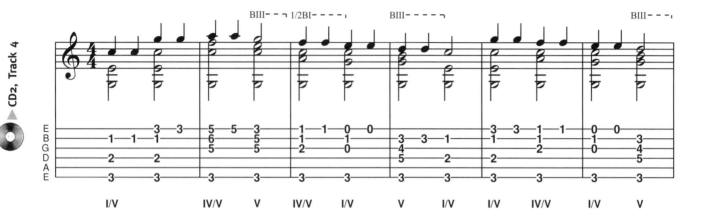

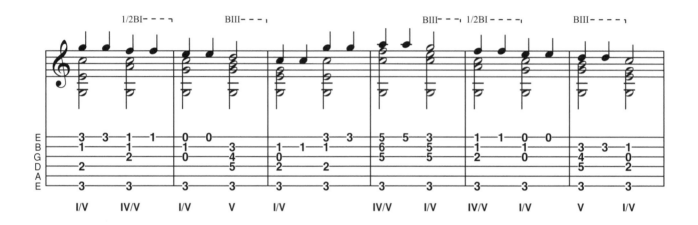

Example 4.4

The Three-Chord Trick: A Minor Variation

Excuse the pun! The three minor chords in any key (the 'secondary chords' – that is, chords II, III and VI) also contain all the notes of the parent major scale:

The same melody we have been working with can also be harmonised exclusively with this set of chords.

Listen to the following harmonisation with the three minor chords:

C major scale

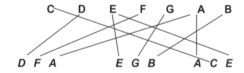

CD2, Track 5

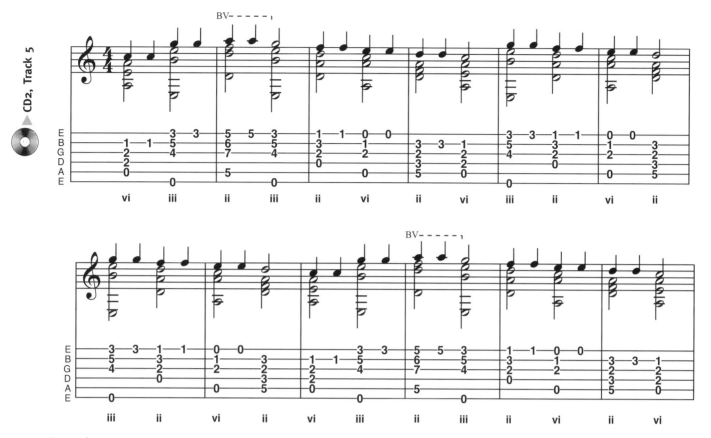

Example 4.5

The same melody has a very different 'appearance' when played with that harmony. Common practice would be to harmonise the melody with a variety of major and minor triads. We can even include the diminished triad.

CD2, Track 6

Example 4.6

Seventh Chords
Expanding Our Harmonic Palette

The process of harmonising in thirds can continue beyond the fifth of the triad. Adding a fourth note a diatonic third above the fifth will give us a series of chords with some very distinctive harmonic colours. The major scale will produce four types of seventh chords. Let's look at each in turn.

Major Seventh Chords

If we leapfrog from the fifth of the tonic chord, up a diatonic third we arrive at the seventh degree of the scale:

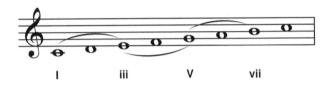

Example 4.7

Putting these four notes C, E, G and B together produces a seventh chord. The formula for this 'major seventh' chord is:

$$R \quad 3 \quad 5 \quad 7$$

The intervals of major third, perfect fifth and major seventh are the harmonic 'flavours' that produce this chord. Here are some common shapes for the major seventh chord:

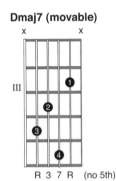
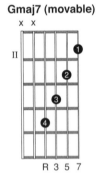

Example 4.8

There are many other ways to play these major seventh chords. As with the triads, you need to know the position of the chord tones on the fingerboard. Explore the fingerboard by trying to find the notes of C major 7 in as many combinations as possible. Remember that the various inversions have different harmonic tensions. For example, placing the major seventh – B – in the bass, will create a tension that needs resolving down to possibly an A minor chord or back up to the C major chord in root position. Using each of the first five shapes – the CAGED shapes, with a barré – you can shape shift to any major seventh chord.

Minor Seventh Chords

If we follow the same process on the second note – D – we get another seventh chord.

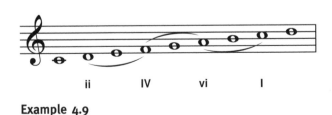

Example 4.9

This time the notes D, F, A and C form the following intervals:

R   m3   5   m7

Once again there are many ways to voice these four notes all over the fingerboard. Using each of the first five shapes – the CAGED shapes, with a barré – you can shape shift to any minor seventh chord.

Cm7
R ♭3 ♭7 R

Am7
R 5 ♭7 ♭3 5

Gm7
R ♭7 ♭3 5

    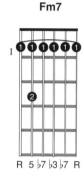 

Em7
R 5 ♭7 ♭3 5 R

Dm7
R 5 ♭7 ♭3

Dm7
R ♭3 ♭7 ♭3   (no 5th)

Gm7
R   ♭3 5 ♭7

Fm7
R 5 ♭7 ♭3 ♭7 R

Am7
R 5 ♭7 ♭3 ♭7

Example 4.10

The seventh chord formed on the third (mediant) note of the major scale also produces a minor seventh chord. The fourth note when harmonised in diatonic thirds produces a major seventh chord (just like the tonic chord). The next note – the dominant – will give us the next seventh chord.

Dominant Seventh Chords

The chord formed on the fifth note of the scale is a dominant seventh chord:

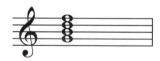

Example 4.11

The intervals in this chord have the following formula:

R   3   5   m7

This chord type is unique to the fifth degree of the scale. Very often a dominant seventh chord is a good pointer to the key centre, as every major scale has only one dominant seventh chord. Using each of the first five shapes – the CAGED shapes, with a barré – you can shape shift to any dominant seventh chord. Here are some common shapes:

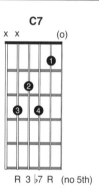  

C7
R 3 ♭7 R   (no 5th)

A7
R 5 ♭7 3 5

G7
R 3 5 R 3 ♭7

  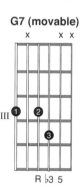

E7
R 3 5

D7
R 3 5

G7 (movable)
R ♭3 5

  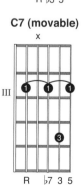

A7
R 5 R 3 ♭7

B7
R 3 ♭7 R 5

C7 (movable)
R   ♭7 3 5

Example 4.12

The next chord, formed on the sixth degree is the same chord type as the second and third chords – a minor seventh. The final type of seventh chord in the major scale is formed on the leading note.

Half-Diminished Seventh Chords (also known as Minor Seventh Flat Five chords)

Here, applying the same harmonic process to the seventh note of the scale creates the following chord shown on the right. The notes B, D, F and A form a minor seventh chord with a lowered, or flattened fifth. This chord is often written as Bm7♭5.

Example 4.13

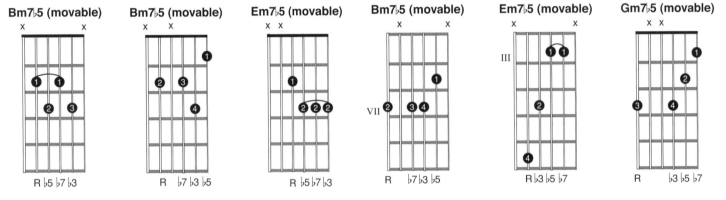

Example 4.14

This chord is the least stable of the four diatonic seventh chords and is almost always used as a passing chord between other chords. It is rarely used as a point of resolution. The flattened fifth means that the chord will never sound 'settled'. This in-built tension is useful for creating harmonic movement. The pattern of seventh chords in any major scale always follows a set pattern:

maj7 • min7 • min7 • maj7 • 7 • min7 • min7♭5

From our chart of diatonic triads, we can now construct a chord chart showing all the seventh chords in every key:

KEY	I	II	III	IV	V	VI	VII
C	C maj7	D m7	E m7	F maj7	G7	A m7	B m7♭5
G	G maj7	A m7	B m7	C maj7	D7	E m7	F♯ m7♭5
D	D maj7	E m7	F♯ m7	G maj7	A7	B m7	C♯ m7♭5
A	A maj7	B m7	C♯ m7	D maj7	E7	F♯ m7	G♯ m7♭5
E	E maj7	F♯ m7	G♯ m7	A maj7	B7	C♯ m7	D♯ m7♭5
B	B maj7	C♯ m7	D♯ m7	E maj7	F♯7	G♯ m7	A♯ m7♭5
F♯	F♯maj7	G♯ m7	A♯ m7	B maj7	C♯7	D♯ m7	E♯ m7♭5
C♯	C♯maj7	D♯ m7	E♯ m7	F♯maj7	G♯7	A♯ m7	B♯ m7♭5
F	F maj7	G m7	A m7	B♭ maj7	C7	D m7	E m7♭5
B♭	B♭ maj7	C m7	D m7	E♭ maj7	F7	G m7	A m7♭5
E♭	E♭ maj7	F m7	G m7	A♭ maj7	B♭7	C m7	D m7♭5
A♭	A♭ maj7	B♭ m7	C m7	D♭ maj7	E♭7	F m7	G m7♭5
D♭	D♭ maj7	E♭ m7	F m7	G♭maj7	A♭7	B♭ m7	C m7♭5
G♭	G♭maj7	A♭ m7	B♭ m7	C♭ maj7	D♭7	E♭ m7	F m7♭5
C♭	C♭ maj7	D♭ m7	E♭ m7	F♭ maj7	G♭7	A♭ m7	B♭ m7♭5

Each key has seven diatonic seventh chords. Apart from the V and VII chords, no seventh chord is unique to any one key. This is especially true of minor seventh chords, any of which belongs to three different keys.

Harmonising A Melody With Seventh Chords

The melody 'Twinkle Twinkle Little Star' can be harmonised with diatonic seventh chords. Play through the following example, which can also to be heard on the CD.

CD2, Track 7

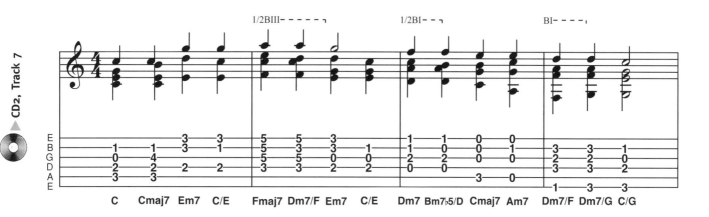

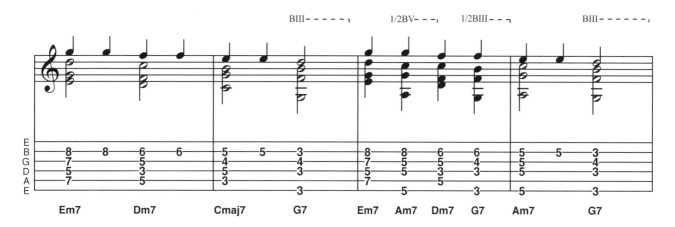

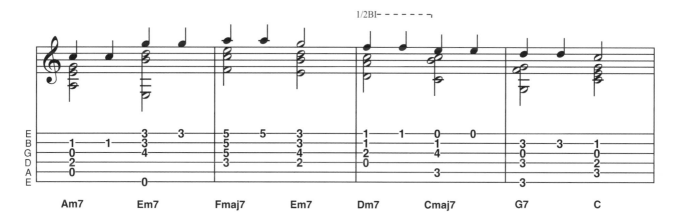

Example 4.15

Notice how the harmony is very different to the original simple triad harmony initially suggested. This is not suggesting that one is better than the other, but rather that the process of adding extra harmony lets you explore and experience different harmonic textures and

movement. Ultimately you have to choose your own chords and voicings. The best way to apply this knowledge is to try it out with other simple tunes (stick to tunes in a single key, or *diatonic* melodies, at first) or your own compositions.

Some More Chord Types

By adding or substituting notes in these triads and seventh chords we can embellish the harmony in subtle and dramatic ways.

Add 2 Chords

Add a note a tone above the root (the major second) to a major or minor chord and the result is an 'add 2' chord. Listen to the following progression of 'add 2' chords:

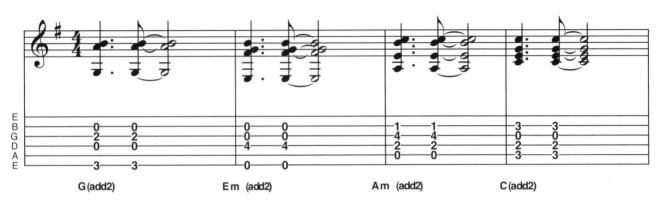

G (add2)   Em (add2)   Am (add2)   C (add2)

Example 4.16

Generally the 'add 2' note is most effective 'inside' the chord, not at its extremes (as the top note or bottom note). It is also quite effective when it is juxtaposed with the 'third' of the chord. In the A minor add 2 chord above, there is only a semitone between the minor third and the major second. This interval should theoretically produce a harsh dissonance, but the B note (the major second) also forms a strong interval with the E note which counteracts that dissonance. Placing the minor third on top with the second lower down in the chord can be a little 'grating' on the ear:

The use of 'add 2' (also called 'add 9' because the 9 is an octave above the 2) can add a subtle yet effective colour to a chord. The chord remains major or minor unless you replace the third with the second, in which case you create:

Sus 2 Chords

The 'sus 2' chord is a chord with a root, major second and perfect fifth. The absence of any third gives the chord a useful ambiguity which allows it to be used with major and minor melodies. The 'sus' is short for 'suspended' – the suspension created by the absence of the third. The chord is actually quite consonant and is commonly used as a substitute for major and minor chords.

Here are some standard shapes for it:

Example 4.17

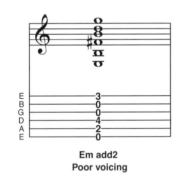

Em add2
Poor voicing

Compare that voicing to this much smoother voicing:

Example 4.18

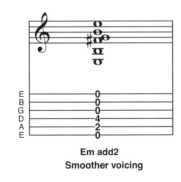

Em add2
Smoother voicing

Csus2

R 2 5 R

Asus2

R 5 R 2 5

Gsus2

R   5 2 5

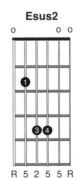

Esus2

R 5 2 5 5 R

Dsus2

R 5 R 2

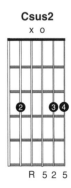

Csus2

R   5 2 5

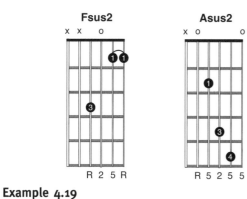

Example 4.19

Sus 4 Chords

Like the sus 2 chord, the sus 4 chord has no third. The interval of a perfect fourth above the root replaces the third and as above, creates an ambiguous chord. However, in this case, the fourth is heard as a downward tension that needs resolution. Listen to the following progression and hear the 'tension and release' as the sus 4 chord resolves to both major and minor chords.

Example 4.20

The tension towards the major chord is stronger than the tension that resolves to the minor. This is because of the smaller interval (a semitone) that exists between the major third and perfect fourth. The attraction from the minor third to the fourth is a whole tone and as a result is slightly weaker. A useful analogy is that of a pair of magnets. If the two magnets are brought together with their opposite poles (opposites attract) pointing towards each other, there will be a magnetic pull (tension) to complete the attraction (resolution). The closer the poles are brought together (think of intervals) the greater the attraction becomes. If you hold the two poles as close together as possible, without allowing them to touch, the magnets will shake to resolve the tension between them.

The next example shows some standard shapes for the sus 4 chord:

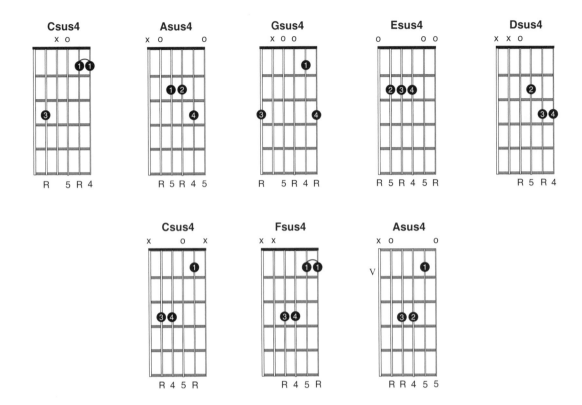

Example 4.21

The following rearrangement in the key of E major shows how these chords can be used effectively to add some tension and release to the music:

CD2, Track 13

Example 4.22

Inversions Of Seventh Chords

Just like triads, we can also invert seventh chords. The added seventh note creates the possibility of a *third* inversion. These third inversions are generally more unstable than the first and second inversions and they are used extensively as *passing* chords – chords that will bridge the transition from one functional chord to another. For example the following progression from A to D can be enriched with the inclusion of a passing third inversion of A7:

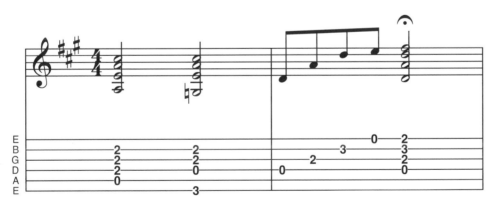

Example 4.23

The third inversion of a seventh chord will often be described as a 'slash chord'. In this case the A7 third inversion could be written as:

A/G

With A being the chord and G being the flattened seventh degree of A. This is usually referred to as 'A over G'. The progression shown in the following Example uses a variety of third inversions:

Example 4.24

Secondary Dominant Chords

A good way to enhance a chord progression is to add secondary dominants. These are dominant seventh chords built on each note of the scale. As we have seen, only one of these – the dominant built on the fifth note of the scale – is a true diatonic dominant seventh chord. Any dominant seventh chord built on any other note of the scale will feature at least one chromatic note (from outside the key).

Staying with the ever-friendly key of C major, the following dominant seventh chords would result:

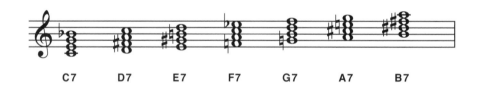

C7   D7   E7   F7   G7   A7   B7

Example 4.25

These secondary dominants (as distinct from the true 'primary' dominant of chord V) each resolve to a chord from the key of C. For example, the C7 will have a tension that is resolved by going to F major (or F major 7). The C7 would be referred to as the 'V7 of IV' or dominant seventh of the sub-dominant to give them their technical names. The D7 would go to G (or G7, true dominant chord of the key of C). A7 would go to Dm – the II chord – and would be described as the 'V7 of II'. The IV7 chord is explained in more detail below. Let's look at an example of a chord progression which incorporates secondary dominants. Let's take a simple chord progression such as a I VI II V in C major:

C Am Dm G

We can approach each of these chords through its dominant chord and create this type of progression:

C E7 Am A7 Dm D7 G G7 C

Each of the dominant chords is behaving as a secondary dominant. It resolves to the diatonic chord which follows it. The E7 is the V7 chord of A minor (just count up a perfect fifth – three and half tones – from A), the A7 is the V7 of

D, the D7 is the V7 of G and the G7 is the primary dominant of the C major key. Listen to the effect that these chords have on the harmony of the simple progression.

Here is a more contemporary example of secondary dominants in the key of B♭. Try to see the connection between the diatonic chords and the secondary dominants.

B♭maj7   B♭7   E♭maj7   D7   Gm7   C7

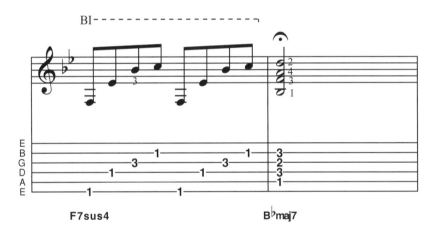

F7sus4   B♭maj7

Example 4.26

The IV7 chord (F7) is in fact a substitute for the B7 chord and could resolve to the E minor (III) chord also. This type of substitution is known as a *tritone substitution* (given the tritone interval between the root notes of those chords). The two chords B7 and F7 share the same third and flattened seventh notes, although they swap 'function': The D♯/E♭ is the major third of the B7, while it is the flattened seventh of the F7. Conversely, the A natural note is the major third of F7, and also is the flattened seventh note of B7. The fact that these two notes are *also* a tritone apart is no coincidence!

A simple rule for tritone substitution can be applied initially to dominant seventh chords.

Other Dominant Seventh Chords

It's also possible to substitute dominant chords whose root notes are a tritone apart. For example, in the following II, V, I progression (known as a 'two five one'), the V chord moves logically and smoothly to the tonic chord:

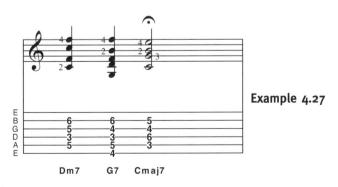

Example 4.27

Dm7   G7   Cmaj7

Here is the same progression with tritone substitution in place of the G7 chord:

CD2, Track 17

Listen to the CD to hear the harmonic effect that this creates.

The following example demonstrates a harmonisation of the simple nursery melody using all of these particular harmonic devices:

- Triads
- Seventh Chords
- 'Add' and 'Sus' Chords
- Pedal Bass Tones
- Inversions
- Secondary Dominants
- Tritone Substitution

Example 4.28

CD2, Track 18

Cmaj7

Example 4.29

These theoretical approaches and chord types are all applicable to modern song accompaniment. Here's an example of a contemporary pop chord progression incorporating many of the harmonic devices that we looked at above:

CD2, Track 19

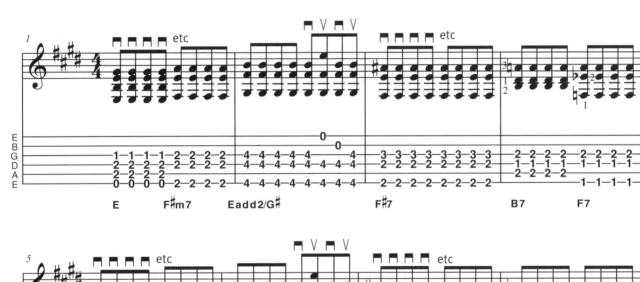

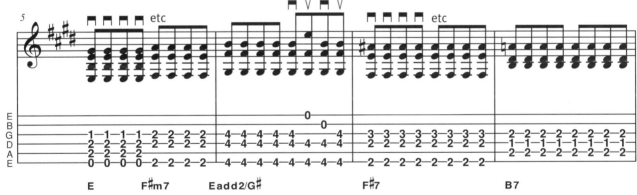

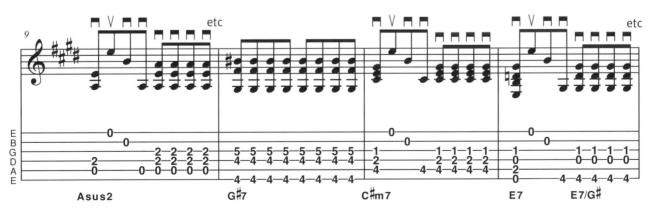

Example 4.30 (continues...)

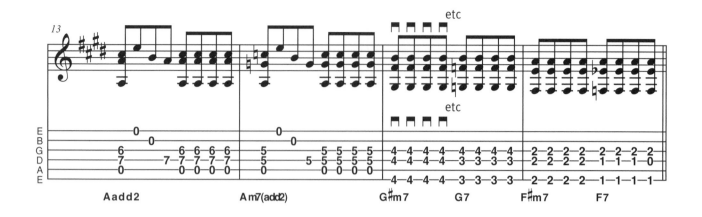

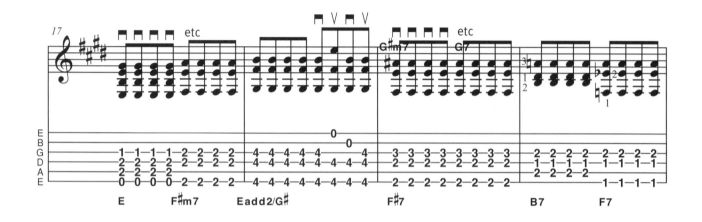

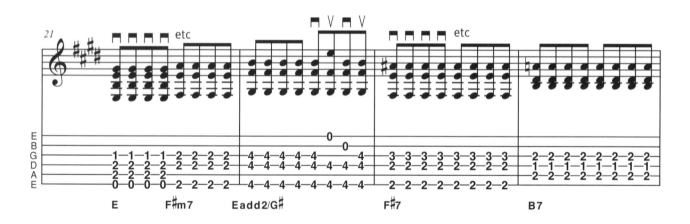

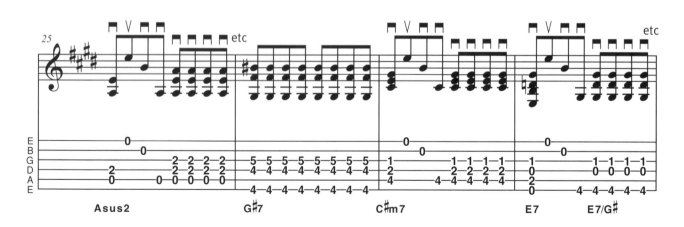

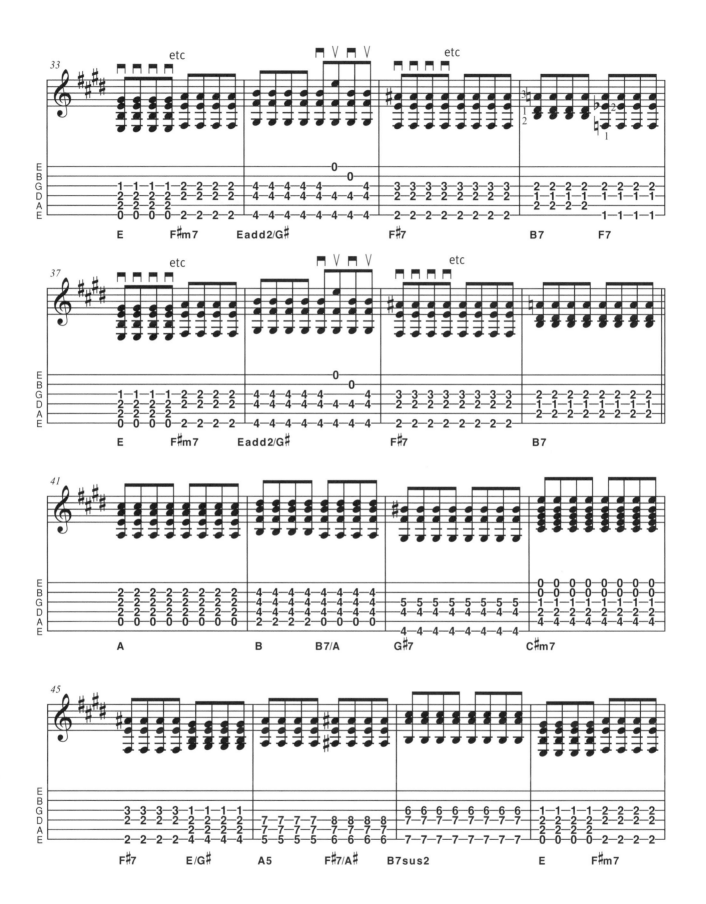

Example 4.30 (continues...)

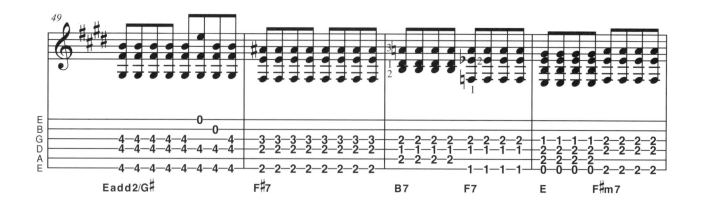

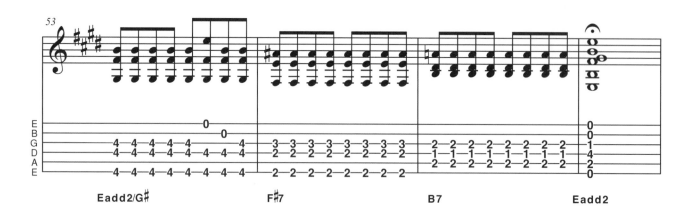

Example 4.30 continued

Extended Chords

So far in this book we have restricted our harmony to a maximum of four notes. The chords have been made up of a root note, some type of third, a fifth of some type and a seventh degree. Some chords replaced the third with another note, while other chords added a note to the basic triad (such as add 2 and add 6 chords). However, we can continue to add notes to a chord to create a whole array of 'extended chords'. Before we look at these, we need to extend our understanding of intervals.

Compound Intervals

In a previous chapter we looked at the intervals of the chromatic scale. The largest interval of these was the octave – a whole six tones in size. However, there are far bigger intervals possible. In the greater scheme of things, the range of intervals on the guitar fingerboard only represents a part of the enormous spectrum of intervals available to us on a keyboard or across the instruments of an orchestra.

Intervals of an octave or less are referred to as *simple* intervals, while the intervals greater than an octave are referred to as *compound* intervals.

Here is a diagram showing a two octave major scale:

Example 4.31

In short, if you add an octave to a simple interval you get a compound one. The interval from the low C tonic to the D note over an octave is a *ninth*. The interval from the low C tonic to the F note over an octave is an *eleventh*. The interval from the low C tonic to the A note over an octave is a *thirteenth*. The following table summarises this:

Simple Intervals	Compound Intervals
Major Second	Major Ninth
Major Third	(Major Third)
Perfect Fourth	Perfect Eleventh
Perfect Fifth	(Perfect Fifth)
Major Sixth	Major Thirteenth
Major Seventh	(Major Seventh)

You will see that the intervals of a third, fifth and seventh remain as thirds, fifths and sevenths, regardless of the register in which they appear in. These intervals comprise the basic chord tones and retain their name and function in each octave.

The extended intervals and their names follow the same rules and patterns as their simple interval counterparts. For example, when extended by an octave, the minor second interval becomes a minor ninth interval, augmented fourth intervals become augmented elevenths and so on. Now let's take a look at each of the intervals listed here in a bit more detail.

Ninths

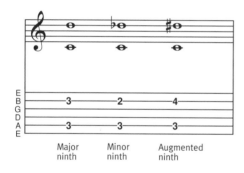

Example 4.32

The first interval here, a major ninth, is similar in nature to the major second. The next interval, the minor ninth (often called a 'flat nine'), is one of the more dissonant intervals in music. The third example is the augmented (or 'sharp') ninth. This interval is similar in nature to a minor third, but usually appears in chords and scales where there is also a major third. In such situations the major third takes precedence and causes the weaker minor third to be re-named as an augmented ninth. It is usual for such a chord to also contain a flattened seventh note. As an exercise in deepening your understanding of these intervals, you should take random root notes and practise identifying the various compound intervals built on that root.

Elevenths

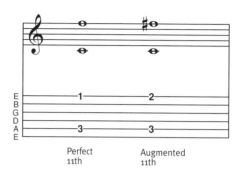

Example 4.33

There are only two eleventh intervals in common use in music – the perfect eleventh and augmented (or 'sharp') eleventh. In the absence of a third, the eleventh can be analysed as a fourth. The augmented eleventh might be better interpreted as flattened fifth in the presence of a minor third and absence of a perfect fifth. These various harmonic formations will be explored in the section on extended chords below.

Thirteenths

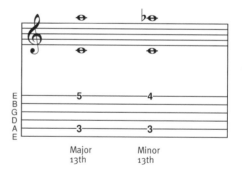

Example 4.34

The major sixth and minor sixth intervals produce major and minor thirteenth intervals respectively. These intervals have similar characteristics to their simple relatives.

Building Extended Chords

Extended chords are seventh chords with the addition of at least one compound interval. Let's first look at the various ninth chords that are diatonic to the major scale. These chords are generally formed by a root, a major or minor third, a perfect or in some cases a diminished fifth and a major or minor seventh. It is useful to become familiar with the construction of these chords. This information will allow you to construct your own shapes on the fingerboard.

Ninth Chords

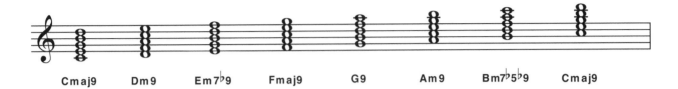

Cmaj9   Dm9   Em7♭9   Fmaj9   G9   Am9   Bm7♭5♭9   Cmaj9

Example 4.35

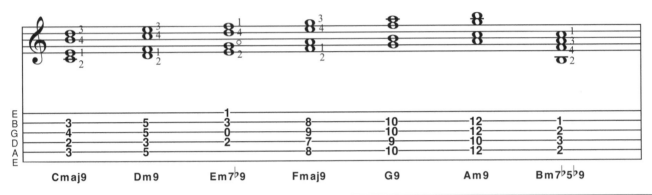

Cmaj9   Dm9   Em7♭9   Fmaj9   G9   Am9   Bm7♭5♭9

Example 4.36

The shapes indicated in the tablature stave are more practical shapes that are commonly played. Each of them (apart from the B minor seventh flat five flat nine, where I choose to leave out the third) leaves off the fifth. Very often the fifth of a chord (unless it is altered in the case of augmented and diminished chords) is disposable. The ear often 'imagines' the fifth and allows us to include the other chord tones. As we learned in our exploration of the overtone series, the perfect fifth has a subtle presence within every note played. The fingerings and shapes for extended chords are often made easier by the removal of the fifth.

When the major scale is harmonised in ninth chords, the following pattern of chords emerges:

C major ninth • D minor ninth • E minor seventh
flattened ninth • F major ninth • G ninth •
A minor ninth • B minor seventh flattened fifth,
flattened ninth

These chords are normally shortened to the following abbreviations:

Cmaj9 • Dm9 • Em7♭9 • Fmaj9 • G9 • Am9 • Bm7♭5♭9

Example 4.37 shows some standard shapes for these chords:

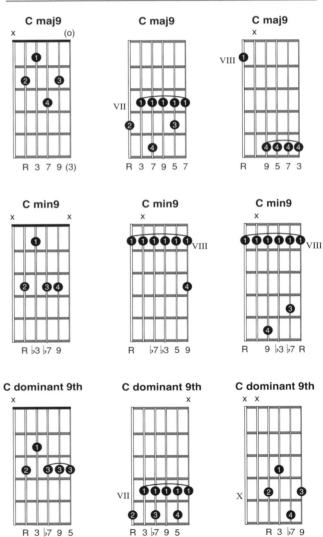

Example 4.37

The formulae for the main chord types are:

- Major ninth: R   3   5   7   9
- Minor ninth: R   ♭3   5   ♭7   9
- Ninth (ie dominant ninth): R   3   5   ♭7   9

Eleventh Chords

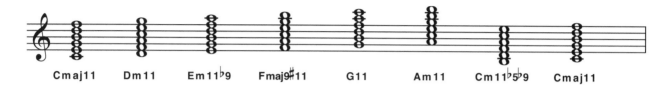

Cmaj11   Dm11   Em11♭9   Fmaj9♯11   G11   Am11   Cm11♭5♭9   Cmaj11

Example 4.38

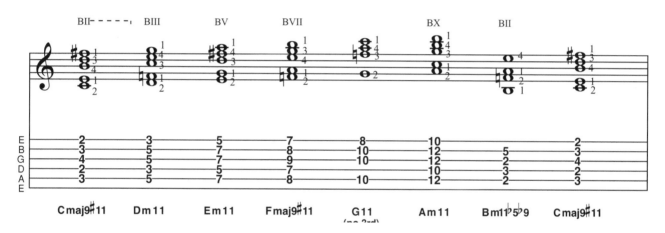

Cmaj9♯11   Dm11   Em11   Fmaj9♯11   G11 (no 3rd)   Am11   Bm11♭5♭9   Cmaj9♯11

Example 4.39

The shapes indicated in the tablature stave are more practical shapes that are commonly played. Each of them leaves out one or two other degrees. In general you should include the root, third, seventh and the highest extension – in this case the eleventh. These eleventh chords have six chord tones, which means all six strings are required. This is not ideal when you need to voice chords with a variety of textures and densities. You may not want to include six different notes in your chord shapes. Consider removing the fifth and possibly the ninth degrees to create more 'air' in the harmony. Conversely you may want to include all the notes to create a full and dense sound. As always, each situation will have different requirements. Being familiar with the construction of these chords will allow you to have a choice for each situation. Here is the C major scale harmonised in eleventh chords.

The chord names are:

C major eleventh • D minor eleventh • E minor eleventh flattened ninth • F major ninth sharpened eleventh • G eleventh • A minor eleventh • B minor eleventh flattened fifth, flattened ninth

These chords are normally shortened to the following abbreviations:

Cmaj11 • Dm11 • Em11♭9 • Fmaj9♯11 • G11 • Am11 • Bm11♭5♭9

It is common practice to alter the major eleventh chord on the tonic degree and the minor eleventh flat nine chord of the mediant degree. In the tonic chord, C major eleventh, the interval between the major third – E – and the eleventh – F – forms an interval of a minor ninth, which produces quite a dissonant sound. Listen to this voicing on the CD:

◢ CD2, Track 20

◢ CD2, Track 21

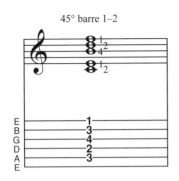

Example 4.40

Example 4.41

By raising the eleventh a semitone to a sharpened eleventh the dissonance is diluted significantly.

The same dissonance occurs in Em11 flat 9. By raising the ninth a half step, the dissonance is diluted. Below are some standard shapes for these eleventh chords:

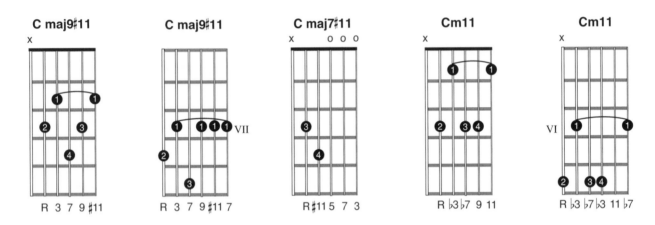

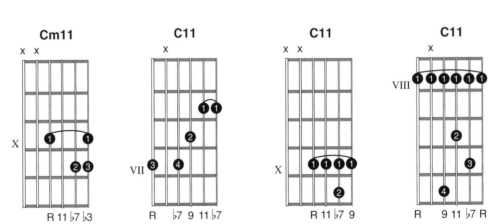

Example 4.42

The formulae for the main chord types are:

- Major eleventh: R 3 5 7 9 11
- Major ninth sharp eleventh: R 3 5 7 9 ♯11

- Minor eleventh: R ♭3 5 ♭7 9 11
- Ninth (ie dominant ninth): R 3 5 ♭7 9 11

132

Thirteenth Chords

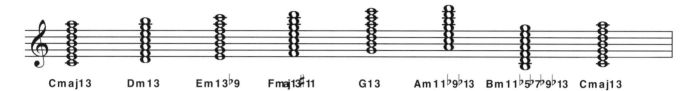

Cmaj13   Dm13   Em13♭9   Fmaj13♯11   G13   Am11♭9♭13   Bm11♭5♭7♭9♭13   Cmaj13

Example 4.43

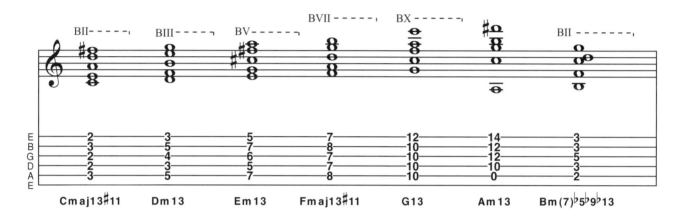

Cmaj13♯11   Dm13   Em13   Fmaj13♯11   G13   Am13   Bm(7)♭5♭9♭13

Example 4.44

The shapes indicated in the tablature stave are more practical shapes that are commonly played. Each of them leaves out one or two other degrees. In general you should include the root, third, seventh and the highest extension – in this case the thirteenth. These thirteenth chords have seven chord tones, so you will have to leave out at least one chord tone. The thirteenth chord can be used in all styles of playing, although it is very often thinned out to make room for the more important chord tones.

The chord names are:

C major thirteenth • D minor thirteenth • E minor eleventh flattened ninth, flattened thirteenth • F major thirteenth sharpened eleventh • G thirteenth • A minor eleventh flattened thirteenth • B minor eleventh flattened fifth, flattened ninth, flattened thirteenth

These chords are normally abbreviated thus:

Cmaj13 • Dm13 • Em11♭9♭13 • Fmaj13♯11 • G13 • Am11♭13 • Bm11♭5♭9♭13

It is common practice to alter the major thirteenth chord, as we do with the major eleventh chord. The chord is normally changed to a major thirteenth sharp eleventh chord:

Example 4.45

On the next page, Example 4.46 shows some standard shapes for these thirteenth chords. The formulae for the main chord types are:

- Major thirteenth: R 3 5 7 9 11 13
- Major thirteenth sharp eleventh: R 3 5 7 9 ♯11 13
- Minor thirteenth: R ♭3 5 ♭7 9 11 13
- Thirteenth (dominant): R 3 5 ♭7 9 11 13
- Minor eleventh flattened thirteenth: R ♭3 5 7 9 11 ♭13

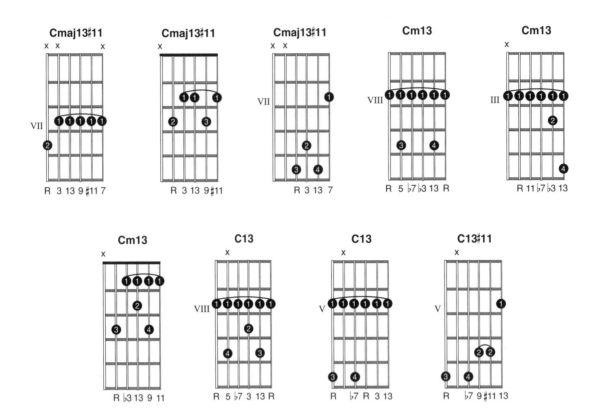

Example 4.46

Too Many Notes Spoil The Chord

Once we get to the family of thirteenth chords we can observe a very interesting fact. Look at the chords in diagram 4.46 above. These chords all have the same notes! In fact, it is quite correct to consider them as inversions of each other. Who is to say that Em11♭9♭13 is not just the first inversion of C major 13? Or that Bm11♭5♭9♭13 is not the second inversion of Em11♭9♭13? Of course, when you start thinking like that, you have moved out of the realm of music and firmly into the world of mathematics and arithmetic. From a guitarist's point of view, it is impossible to play these voicings fully, and even if it were possible with an extra string, who would want to play such dense, crowded and heavy voicings for more than a few moments? '*Just because you can doesn't mean you should*' as the old saying goes. From a pianist's or orchestra's point of view, it is far easier to voice these chords in a huge variety of ways. The notes can be spread out over many registers to create just the right tone and feeling. On a guitar fingerboard the chords have to be re-considered and adjusted to suit the instrument. Rather than thinking of this as a failing of the instrument, why not consider it a challenge for the musician?

Here are some simple tips for approaching the complicated world of chord voicings:

- If playing alone, try to include the root of the chord. It doesn't necessarily have to be at the bottom of your voicing. When working with a bass player you may find that he/she will cover the root and other chord tones. This releases you from having to 'ground' the chord and gives you more scope to bring out other combinations of chord tones.

- Try always to include the *functional* notes of the chord – the third and the seventh. These, more than any other notes, define the nature of the chord.

- Include the highest extension of the chord. For example, if you are trying to create a shape for E major 13, then include the 13th degree – C♯. You don't necessarily need to include the lower extensions, the 9th and the 11th, unless, as we see in the next point, they are altered.

- Finally, include any alterations where possible. If the chord is E major 13 ♯11, then look for a way to place the A♯ in the chord. So, for example, the chord E major 13 ♯11 should contain at least:

$$E \quad G\sharp \quad D\sharp \quad A\sharp \quad C\sharp$$

Ultimately your ear must be the judge. If the chord is too difficult too play or just sounds wrong, then look at the alternatives. Very often a chord will work in one shape for one particular situation and not in another.

Chords Inside Chords Inside Chords

Once the harmony moves into seventh chords and beyond there are numerous opportunities to look at chords from another angle. For example, a C maj 7 chord has four chord tones:

C E G B

You can see that the last three notes form an E minor triad. The chord can be thought of as a Em/C chord. From a voicing point of view, this is very useful. Look at the Em triad voicings in the previous chapter and play a C note underneath them. Similarly a Dm7 chord is:

D F A C

And can be thought of as F major/D (or simply F/D). Again this simplifies the search for new voicings. With hundreds of F major triads to choose from, and a whole selection of D notes to place beneath these chords, there is an enormous choice of shapes for this one chord.

With a little effort you will find that there are close to 100 playable shapes for any seventh chord (including many inversions). If you take a simple four-chord progression, each chord will have at least 100 possible shapes. So the possible permutations for that simple progression would be 100 x 100 x 100 x 100 – that is, 100 million!

Even if we take 0.1% of those permutations to be practical and playable, that is still 100,000 ways to play the progression! So with only 1% of *those* possibilities you would still have 1000 ways to choose from. Of course you do not need to learn all the permutations. You only need to know the simple rules of chord construction and the name of each note on the fingerboard!

The extension of chords into the 9th, 11th and 13th degree add more and more layers of harmony to a seventh chord. Let's take a chord such as Em9. The notes in Em9 are:

E G B D F♯

The triads available to us within this chord are E minor, G major and B minor. There is even a G maj 7 in there and an Em7! How about G maj 13 – can you see that chord in there? And G5, B5, E5? There is a B sus 4 and an E sus 2. From every angle new chords emerge. This method of chord analysis is useful when you want to find new ways to voice chords. For example, if you play a B minor chord over an open E bass the result is effectively Em9. While there is no G in the chord to create the minor third sound, there is by the same token no G♯ to create a major third sound. The chord is open to both major and minor melodies and harmonies. These ambiguous voicings are very common in guitar chords.

By extending our harmony to the 13th degree we find even more angles! Let's take A13. This chord has seven notes, only six of which, if desired, are playable at any one time on the guitar. You can always play across time. Where a bar of music calls for four beats of A13, why not include some chord tones on beat 1, and some others of beat 2? In this way the chord can shift and change colour over four beats or longer. Back to our A13. The notes are (drum roll please...):

A C♯ E G B D F♯

This chord is a whole scale – the D major scale – or any one of its modes! (more on modes shortly!). Any of the chords of the key of D can be found here – including all the extensions, inversions, additions, suspensions, augmentations, diminutions, you name it!

Start to look at chords in this way and many of the mysteries of harmony and music theory will begin to unfold!

Modes

Acoustic guitarists don't play modes – do they?

Perhaps, more than any other topic, modes create the greatest reverence, confusion, fear, and discussion among guitarists. Modes are often held up as the holy grail of guitarmanship and musicality. The modes have been in use for thousands of years (many modes have fallen out of use over time) and the Greeks in all their mathematical and musical genius discovered them within the order of music over 2500 years ago. The word 'mode' comes from the Greek word 'mood' and this gives a good insight into the true nature of modes. Modes are essentially scales – a fixed series of notes. Each mode has a unique sound and creates a unique musical effect. In an era where we are desensitised by music – music in elevators, our cars, computers, homes, even outdoors – it has hard to appreciate the deep and profound effect music had on people up until only 100 years ago. Before the gramophone and radio music, in particular, high quality music was a luxury. Go back to the time of Aristotle and Plato in ancient Greece and you might begin to imagine the reverence and respect in which music was held. Even today, music still has the power to change our moods – music can make us cry, laugh, dance, sleep and angry. It can sweep us up on an emotional wave and change how we think and feel about the world. Back in ancient Greece the effect was even more dramatic. Each mode had a corresponding mood associated with it. While the names and their moods have been lost and changed over the millennia, the following excerpt from Aristotle's *Politics* will give you a sense of the ancient Greeks' respect for the power that music had over the psyche. Remember that the names of the modes have been lost and changed over the years so don't associate the names in the extract below with any modes which you may already be familiar with:

'The musical modes differ essentially from one another, and those that hear them are differently affected by each. Some of them make men sad and grave, like the so called Mixolydian; others enfeeble the mind, like the relaxed modes; another, again, produces a moderate or settled temper, which appears to be the particular effect of the Dorian; and the Phrygian inspires enthusiasm.'

– from *Politics*, Aristotle

The same thinking is prevalent in today's community leaders who insist that certain music inspires violence and hatred. I would suggest that it is not necessarily the music, but the *behaviour* of certain performers that is to blame! In essence however, it is certainly true that each scale and mode has a unique construction and tonality (modality). The slightly darker colours of the modern day Phrygian mode is in direct contrast to the brighter sounds of the Lydian mode.

So what are modes? Their evolution and development is a little too complicated for this book, but in summary, after thousands of years of use and gradual decline, the western system of major and minor scales was consolidated in the 17th century. Many old church modes disappeared, and what remains is a system based primarily on the major scale. A mode can be thought of as an *inversion* of a scale, much like the inversion of triads. However, each major scale (and each of the modern minor scales) has seven different notes. There are therefore seven modes for each scale. Any one note can be chosen as the starting point – the tonal centre – or more correctly the *modal* centre.

By selecting any note of, for example, the major scale we can give that note an importance over the remaining notes. As we have learned in this chapter and the previous, not all notes are equal in tonal music (music with keys). The tonic note is the most important note in any key. Each of the other notes in the key has a relationship with the tonic. Each of these relationships is unique in correlation with their distance from the tonic. We learned in our discussion of intervals that the fifth note of the major scale has a strong yet relaxed relationship with the tonic, while the seventh note has a particularly tense and restless relationship – it usually wants to move back to the tonic or its octave partner. And so it goes with all the other notes in the scale and the notes outside the scale. We can move to any note of the major scale and grant it the title of 'tonic'. Each of the seven notes can be used as the starting point for each of the seven major scale modes. For example, starting on the D note of the C major scale and playing all the notes from D, through the C major scale for an octave to the next D note an octave above will create a Dorian Mode. Starting on the G note of the C major scale and following the notes for an octave will give you a Mixolydian mode. Each note of the major scale will produce a unique mode.

Each note in music will have some degree of tension with the prevailing tonic note. When the key changes, so do all the relationships, shifting around on an invisible sonic wheel of hierarchy. Only when music becomes *atonal* – as in the work of composers such as Schoenberg, Webern and Berg – does this hierarchy break down into a world of total equality. In atonal music all notes are equal. There are no keys or key centres, no tonic or dominant chords, in fact, there is nothing to tie down any one note as being more important than any other. Listen to recordings of atonal music to understand better this feeling of 'centrelessness'.

A Simple Modal Analogy

An analogy I often use is that of the Rubix Cube ®. The cube has (as all cubes do) six faces. Each face has a different colour – the correspondence between colour and sound is well documented – F♯ is red after all! No matter which face (tonic note) you look at, you are still looking at the same cube (scale). Each face gives you a different and unique perception of the cube – in one case the cube looks blue, in another it is green and so on. Similarly with the major scale you can choose to play or hear the scale from one of seven different 'angles'. Each angle has a unique sound and mood, although it is still connected to the parent scale – they do share the same notes after all! Only their relationships with each other change. In fact, the analogy of a six-sided cube is more relevant than you might think. The seventh mode – the Locrian – was created much later to complete the system and to fill the gap!

Modes Of The Major Scale

The modes of the major scale are considered the reference point for all other modes. To help with the learning process, we will work with the modes of C major, therefore minimising the need for sharps and flats.

Mode 1: Ionian

Example 4.47

The Ionian mode is the major scale by its modal name. The interval pattern as we have discussed is:

T – T – S – T – T – T – S

The scale degrees are:

R   2   3   4   5   6   7

Where R is the modal root note (the tonic) and 2–7 are the major and perfect intervals from this note. This mode is one of the three major modes of the major scale. There are effectively an infinite number of combinations of chords and notes possible with this mode. It would be impossible to try to list even a small percentage of them. However, typical chord progressions in C Ionian will centre on the C major chord:

C • F • G • C

Listen to the CD for reference. Another typical progression would be the II V I:

Dm7 • G7 • Cmaj7

You could say that any series of chords from the C major scale is exclusively a C Ionian progression but this isn't necessarily true. You could play the chords Am and Em, and while they both belong to C major, neither explicitly gives a sense of the C major scale. C major is not only a series of seven notes but a series of seven notes where C is the key note.

Mode 2: Dorian

Example 4.48

CD2, Track 22

The mode beginning on the second note of the major scale is the Dorian Mode. In the case of the C major scale, it produces the D Dorian mode.

The interval pattern is now:

T – S – T – T – T – S – T

The scale degrees are:

R   2   ♭3   4   5   6   ♭7

Where R is the modal root note (the tonic). The Dorian mode differs from the major scale in two places – the flattened (minor) third and seventh notes. The Dorian mode is one of the three minor modes of the major scale. These alterations are the modal *flavours*. One other typical Dorian modal note is the major sixth. This major sixth note distinguishes this mode from the closely related natural minor scale (also known as the Aeolian mode). By making these alterations to a major scale, you can quickly create a Dorian mode. With this simple method in mind, you can create the C Dorian mode by chromatically (keep the letter name) flattening the third and seventh notes of the C major scale:

C major: C D E F G A B C
C Dorian: C D E♭ F G A B♭ C

As with the Ionian mode, there are effectively an infinite number of combinations of chords and notes possible. Typical chord progressions in D Dorian will centre on the D minor chord:

Dm • G • Dm • G

or:

Dm7 • G7 • Dm7 • G7

Listen to the CD for reference. Another typical progression would be:

Dm7 • Em7

Again, a typical D Dorian progression is one where the Dm chord is the tonic chord, and the other chords are built from the notes of D Dorian, in particular, the modal flavours of the minor third, major sixth and minor seventh.

CD2, Track 23

Mode 3: Phrygian

Example 4.49

The mode beginning on the third note of the major scale is the Phrygian mode (pronounced *fridge*-ee-an). In the case of the C major scale it produces the E Phrygian mode.

The interval pattern is now:

$$S - T - T - T - S - T - T$$

The scale degrees are:

$$R \quad \flat 2 \quad \flat 3 \quad 4 \quad 5 \quad \flat 6 \quad \flat 7$$

Where R is the modal root note (the tonic). The Phrygian mode differs from the major scale in four places – the flattened (minor) second, third, sixth and seventh notes. The Phrygian mode is one of the three minor modes of the major scale. These alterations are the modal *flavours*. By making these alterations to a major scale, you can quickly create a Phrygian mode. With this simple method in mind, you can create the C Phrygian mode by chromatically flattening the second, third, sixth and seventh notes of the C major scale:

C major: C D E F G A B C
C Phrygian: C D♭ E♭ F G A♭ B♭ C

The minor second note is a distinguishing sound in the Phrygian mode. The darker tension is typical of Middle Eastern and flamenco music. As with each mode, there are effectively an infinite number of combinations of chords and notes possible. Typical chord progressions in E Phrygian will centre on the E minor chord:

Em • F • Em • F

or:

Em7 • F/E • Em7 F/E

Listen to the CD for reference. Another typical progression would be:

Em7 • Dm7

A typical E Phrygian progression is one where the Em chord is the tonic chord, and the other chords are built from the notes of E Phrygian, in particular. the modal flavours of the minor second, minor third, minor sixth and minor seventh.

Mode 4: Lydian

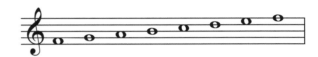

Example 4.50

The mode beginning on the fourth note of the major scale is the Lydian mode. In the case of the C major scale, it produces the F Lydian mode.

The interval pattern is now:
$$T - T - T - S - T - T - S$$

The scale degrees are:

$$R \quad 2 \quad 3 \quad \sharp 4 \quad 5 \quad 6 \quad 7$$

Where R is the modal root note (the tonic). The Lydian mode differs from the major scale in one place – the sharpened (augmented) fourth note. The Lydian mode is one of the three major modes of the major scale. This alteration is the typical Lydian modal flavour. However, it is important to include the major third and seventh in any discussion of the Lydian mode. This is because the augmented fourth appears very commonly in a very different type of scale – the blues scale. You can create the C Lydian mode by chromatically sharpening the fourth note of the C major scale:

C major: C D E F G A B C
C Lydian: C D E F♯ G A B C

Typical chord progressions in F Lydian will centre on the F major chord:

F • G • F • Em

Listen to the CD for reference. Another typical progression would be:

F maj7 • G/F

A typical F Lydian progression is one where the F major chord is the tonic chord, and the other chords are built from the notes of F Lydian, in particular, the modal flavours of the augmented fourth.

Mode 5: Mixolydian

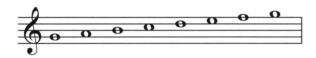

Example 4.51

The mode beginning on the fifth note of the major scale is the Mixolydian mode. In the case of the C major scale, it produces the G Mixolydian mode.

The interval pattern is now:

T – T – S – T – T – S – T

The scale degrees are:

R   2   3   4   5   6   ♭7

Where R is the modal root note. The Mixolydian differs from the major scale in one place – the flattened (minor) seventh note. The Mixolydian is one of the three major modes of the major scale. This alteration is the typical Mixolydian modal flavour. Major third and perfect fourth are the other main modal flavours. The combination of the major third degree and the flattened seventh produce the main elements of the dominant seventh chord, most commonly associated with the Mixolydian. The perfect fourth note also sets this mode apart from a very closely related scale called the 'overtone scale', which is a Mixolydian mode with a *sharpened* fourth note. You can create the G Mixolydian mode by chromatically flattening the seventh note of the C major scale:

C major: C D E F G A B C
C Mixolydian: C D E F G A B♭ C

Typical chord progressions in G Mixolydian will centre on the G major chord, and more specifically the G7:

G • F • C • F

Listen to the CD. Other typical progressions would be:

G7 • F/G

and:

G7sus4 • Dm7

CD2, Track 26

A typical G Mixolydian progression is one where the G7 chord is the tonic chord, and the other chords are built from the notes of G Mixolydian, in particular, the modal flavours of the major third, perfect fourth and minor seventh.

Another typical Mixolydian example is:

A • G • D • F♯ • A

Mode 6: Aeolian

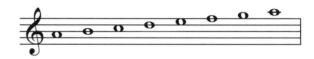

Example 4.52

The mode beginning on the sixth note of the major scale is the Aeolian mode. In the case of the C major scale it produces the A Aeolian mode.

The interval pattern is now:

T – S – T – T – S – T – T

The scale degrees are:

R   2   ♭3   4   5   ♭6   ♭7

Where R is the modal root note (the 'tonic'). The Aeolian differs from the major scale in three places – the flattened (ie minor) third, sixth and seventh notes. The Aeolian mode is one of the three minor modes of the major scale. These alterations are the typical Aeolian modal flavours. You should also consider major second as the other main modal flavour as it helps to distinguish the Aeolian from the Phrygian mode. You can create the A Aeolian mode by chromatically flattening the third, sixth and seventh notes of the C major scale:

C major: C D E F G A B C
C Aeolian: C D E♭ F G A♭ B♭ C

Typical chord progressions in A Aeolian will centre on the A minor chord:

Am • G • F • G

Listen to the audio CD for reference. Other typical progressions would be:

CD2, Track 27

CD2, Track 28

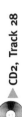

Am7 • Dm7 • Em7 • Am7

and:

Am7 • Em7 • F • Em7

A typical A Aeolian progression is one where the Am chord is the tonic chord, and the other chords are built from the notes of A Aeolian.

Mode 7: Locrian

Example 4.53

The mode beginning on the seventh note of the major scale is the Locrian mode. In the case of the C major scale, it produces the B Locrian mode.

The interval pattern is now:

S – T – T – S – T – T – T

The scale degrees are:

R ♭2 ♭3 4 ♭5 ♭6 ♭7

Where R is the modal root note (the tonic).The Locrian mode differs from the major scale in three places – the flattened (minor) second, third, fifth, sixth and seventh notes. The Locrian mode is the least common mode of the major scale. The numerous alterations, in particular the flattened fifth, restrict its use to diminished chords and their diatonic extensions. You can create the B Locrian mode by chromatically flattening the second, third, fifth, sixth and seventh notes of the C major scale:

C major: C D E F G A B C
C Locrian: C D♭ E♭ F G♭ A♭ B♭ C

Typically the B Locrian mode is used over half diminished chords (the m7♭5 chord):

Bm7♭5

The diminished nature of this chord means that it is rarely used as a tonic chord, but more typically moves from its point of instability to more stable chords, for example, an

A minor or C major. Have a listen to the CD (track 28) for a reference.

CD2, Track 29

Other Scales

There are numerous other scales and modes in common use in music: minor scales, gapped scales, diminished scales and artificial scales. Each of these can have modes. Some only have one mode (the *chromatic* scale and the *whole tone* scale) while others have only two modes (the diminished scales). Other diatonic scales, such as the harmonic minor scale and the jazz minor scale, each have seven unique modes, while the melodic minor scale has one set of notes as it ascends and another set as it descends! So you can see that there is more to music than the major scale! Let's look at some of the most popular scales in use today.

The Pentatonic Scales

These scales are very fashionable in rock and blues guitar. The scales are very widespread across many countries, cultures and centuries. They have been used in the music of the Far East, Celtic music, church music, African music and more. They are easily acquired by musicians and non-musicians alike due to the absence of semitone intervals – the smallest interval in these scales is a tone. The name pentatonic comes from the Greek word *penta* for 'five', and they are five-note scales. There are two modes of the pentatonic scale – major and minor.

The C major pentatonic scale is:

C D E G A

The semitone intervals of the major scale (formed by the B and F notes) are removed. The larger intervals make the scale a little more user friendly and fall quiet easily under the fingers on the guitar fretboard. Here are five shapes for the C major pentatonic scale. Each can be moved into any key. Simply identify the root (circled) and shift the shape into position.

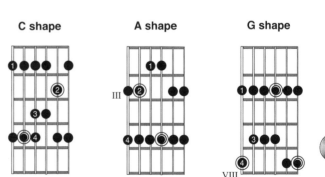

CD2, Track 30

Example 4.54 (continues...)

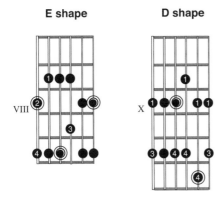

E shape   D shape

Example 4.54 continued

The scale degrees of the major pentatonic scale are:

R 2 3 5 6

There is no fourth or seventh in the major pentatonic scale.

Because of the 'gaps' in the major pentatonic scale, there are in fact three major pentatonic scales contained in the major scale. They are the major pentatonic scales built on the tonic (I), sub-dominant(IV) and dominant (V) notes, as shown in Example 4.55:

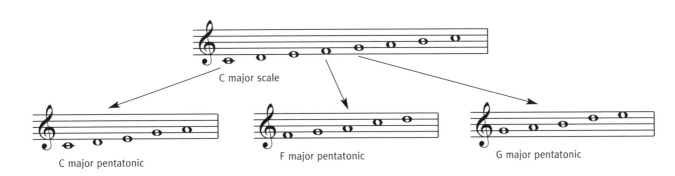

C major scale

C major pentatonic   F major pentatonic   G major pentatonic

Example 4.55

Although theoretically there are five modes of the major pentatonic scale, in practice the only mode used is the fifth mode – built from the major sixth of the scale. In the case of the C major pentatonic scale, it is built on the A note. This scale is the minor pentatonic scale and the notes in A minor pentatonic scale are, on the right:

A   C   D   E   G

As it is so closely related to the major pentatonic scale, the scale patterns on the neck are identical. All that changes is the name of the tonic note. Compare these patterns below with the patterns of the major pentatonic above:

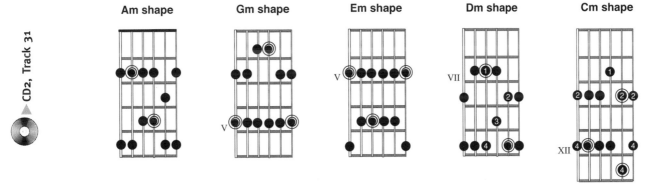

Am shape   Gm shape   Em shape   Dm shape   Cm shape

Example 4.56

The minor pentatonic has evolved as the one of the most popular scales in rock and blues music. Its accessible sound and fingerboard pattern make it one of the most (over-) used scales. The interval gaps give the scale enormous flexibility – it can be used over a huge variety of chord progressions and chord types. It is also the basis of the blues scale (see below).

The scale degrees of the minor pentatonic scale are, on the right:

R ♭3 4 5 ♭7

There is no second or sixth in the minor pentatonic scale.

Again, as with the major scale, these minor pentatonic scales can be connected through 7-note diatonic scales. The A Aeolian mode (also known as the A natural minor scale) which was discussed earlier, has the same notes as the C major scale. The A natural minor scale has three minor pentatonic scales within its notes:

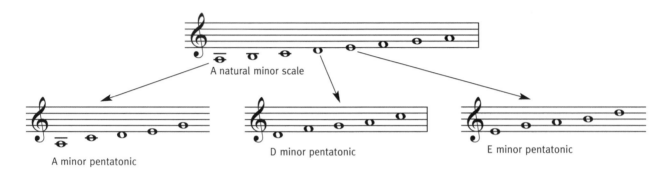

Example 4.57

Again, the pentatonic scales are built on the primary notes – I, IV and V.

The Blues Scale

There are two blues scales in common use which are derived from the major and minor pentatonic scales.

The more common blues scale uses the notes of the minor pentatonic scale and adds one more – the *blue* note. The blue note is the note that falls in between the perfect fourth and perfect fifth notes.

Let's take an A minor pentatonic scale and add in the blue note E♭:

▲ CD2, Track 32

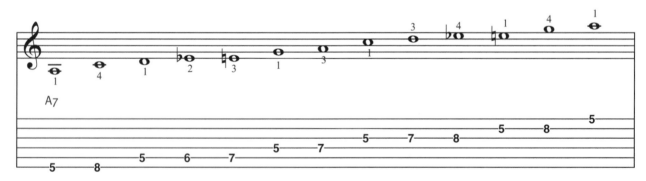

Example 4.58

▲ CD2, Track 33

The blue note adds some extra colour and bite to the scale. The scale is typically played over a dominant seventh chord built on the tonic note. For example, A blues would be played over a A7 chord to produce the following scale steps:

R ♭3(♯9) 4 ♭5/♯4 5 ♭7

As the A7 has a major third, it is theoretically more correct to rename the minor third of the blues scale as an augmented second (or ♯9). The blue note can be seen as an augmented fourth or as a diminished fifth. Either way it produces a tritone interval.

The major blues scale takes its harmony from the major

pentatonic scale. You just add the blue note, in this case the minor third (or more precisely the augmented second or sharpened ninth), in between the major second and major third. This scale can be played over a C7 chord.

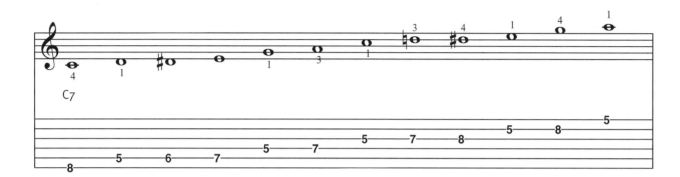

Example 4.59

CD2, Track 34

The strong chord tones of major third and perfect fifth are powerful anchor points over the C7 chord. This scale emphasises different colours to the minor blues scale. Listen to the effect on the CD.

To create a blues sound over major chords you can choose the notes of a minor blues or major blues. For example, over an A major or A7 chord, you can play either A minor or A major Blues scales:

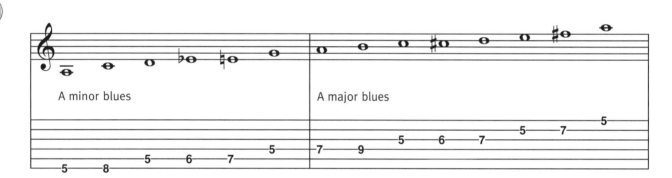

Example 4.60

A very typical approach among more advanced blues players is to combine these scales into a type of 'super scale':

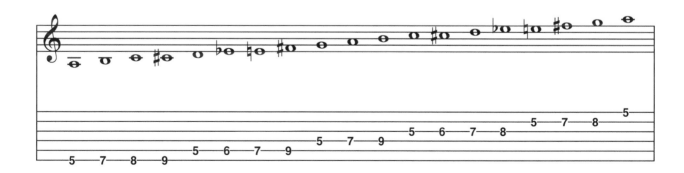

Example 4.61

143

▲ CD2, Track 35

The blue notes – the minor third and diminished fifth – create many semitone steps in this scale. In fact, when you compare this scale with the chromatic scale, the super blues scale has only three notes less. It is an example of 'what you leave out is more important than what you put in'! Listen to the very colourful effect that this scale creates over an A7 chord.

The Natural Minor Scale

We have already met this scale in our discussion of major scale modes. The Aeolian mode shares the same construction and sound as the natural minor scale. The old church modes that were in use during the Dark Ages, through the Renaissance and beyond, were gradually replaced by the major and minor scale system in the 16th and 17th centuries at the beginning of the Baroque period.

The chords of the A natural minor scale are on the right:

Am7   Bm7♭5   Cmaj7   Dm7   Em7   Fmaj7   G7

The scale shares its notes and chords with the key of C major. The key of A minor is the *relative minor* of C major. Conversely, C major is the *relative major* of A minor. These scales are closely related and it is effortless to move between them.

The Harmonic Minor Scale

This scale was developed out of necessity. Chord V of the natural minor is classed as a *weak dominant*. Being a minor seventh chord it doesn't have the same strong harmonic pull of the dominant in the major scale. Composers gradually started to include a strong dominant seventh harmony on the fifth degree of the minor scale. This eventually evolved as a *harmonic* minor scale. The notes of the A harmonic minor scale are below:

▲ CD2, Track 36

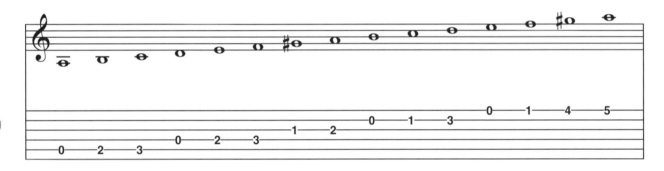

Example 4.62: The harmonic minor scale

The scale degrees are:

R   2   ♭3   4   5   ♭6   7   R

The defining characteristic of this scale is the interval of an augmented second between the 6th and 7th notes. While it is still a diatonic scale, it is unique because of this interval. The Moorish/Middle Eastern sound of this scale is due in large part to this interval. The change from a minor seventh

note to a minor seventh note creates changes in four seventh chords, and ultimately, in all the chords. Here are the diatonic seventh chords of the A harmonic minor scale:

Am maj7   Bm7♭5   Cmaj7♯5   Dm7   E7   Fmaj7   G♯dim7

The G♯ note changes the I, III, V and VII chords to give us some chords we haven't met yet. Here are some standard shapes for the chords of the A harmonic minor scale:

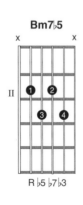

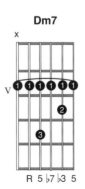
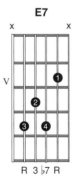

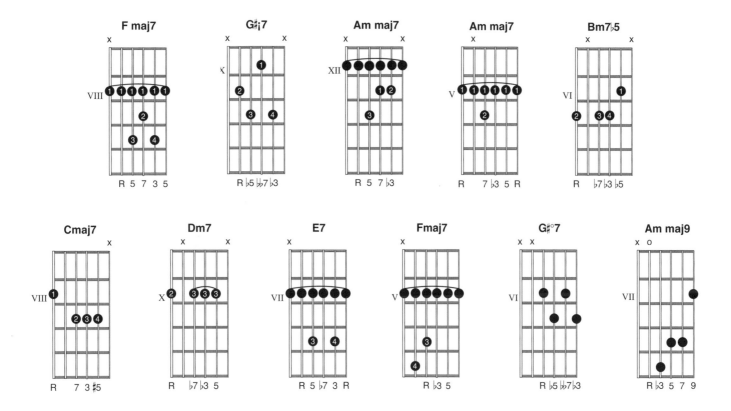

Example 4.63

Nice James Bond moment in that last chord! However, the dominant harmony of chords V and VII is the main focus of this scale. If we extend the E7 chord to its diatonic 9th degree we get the following chord:

Example 4.64: E7♭9

This chord is the most characteristic chord of the harmonic minor scale. The chord tones are:

R   3   5   ♭7   ♭9

Why not use your knowledge of the fretboard to find other voicings? Remember that you don't necessarily need the fifth in your voicing.

The other dominant family chord is chord VII. This chord

is a fully diminished seventh chord. It has some very unique properties. Firstly, while not exclusively a harmonic minor chord (it is the basis of the diminished scales), it is very often associated with it. More importantly. however, is its construction. The chord is perfectly symmetrical. All the notes are the same distance apart – a minor third. This means that each of the inversions remains the same shape as the root position chord. Let's look at this in more detail:

Exercise 4.65

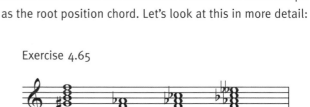

G#°7   B°7   D°7   F°7

Example 4.65: G#°7 and inversions

At first glance these chords may seem completely unrelated. But if you look at the enharmonic equivalents – G# and A♭ are the same note – then you will see that these four chords share exactly the same notes and sound. So while they can viewed as four independent diminished chords, they are also the same chord inverted!

The symmetrical harmony gives us the following formula for the chord:

R ♭3 ♭5 ♭♭7

The 'double flattened' seventh is enharmonically the same as a major sixth. By flattening the major seventh note twice, you move down a whole tone to the major sixth. However, in the interests of consistency and triad harmony, the note is named the double-flattened seventh.

 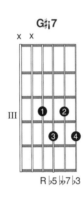 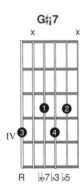 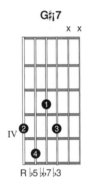

Example 4.66

These shapes are all *closed* and perfectly movable.

Because each diminished seventh chord is actually four diminished seventh chords, there are in fact, only three distinct diminished seventh chords in music. For the sake of simplicity, these could be named as:

G♯°7 • A°7 • A♯°7

Although they could just as easily be given any one of their four names. You'll notice that I have chosen three names that are a semitone apart.

Here are those three chords shown in standard notation:

Example 4.67

Use Of The Diminished Seventh Chord

The primary use of the diminished chord is as a substitute for dominant seventh chords. Let's go back to the dominant chord of the harmonic minor scale.

Look at the fourth voicing in the shapes above. The F dim 7 requires a doubly-flattened E note.

From a guitarist's perspective the symmetry makes things very easy. By taking a diminished seventh chord anywhere on the neck, the shape can be transposed up or down in intervals of a minor third while remaining the same chord!

Try moving these shapes up and down the neck in minor third (three-fret) intervals:

The fifth degree, when harmonised in diatonic thirds, produces a dominant seventh chord with a flattened ninth. The added tension created by the flattened ninth gives the chord an extra push back to the tonic minor chord.

Let's look at the E7♭9 chord in even greater depth:

Example 4.68

The top four notes form a G♯°7 chord. This diminished seventh chord can be used as a substitute for the dominant chord. Just take a diminished seventh chord built on the major third of the dominant. In fact, in most situations a diminished chord can be substituted for a dominant chord. As we have seen any diminished seventh chord can be seen from four angles – in each of its inversions. Let's take a simple progression:

E7 • Am

If the theory is correct, we should be able to substitute any one of G♯°7, B°7, D°7 and F°7 for the E7. Let's hear what it sounds like:

CD2, Track 37

G♯°7   Am   B°7   Am   D°7   Am   F°7   Am

Example 4.69: Diminished chords substituting for dominant chords

Modes Of The Harmonic Minor

The most commonly played mode of the harmonic minor is the fifth mode. Taking the A harmonic minor as our reference point, its fifth mode would be the same notes starting on the dominant – E:

CD2, Track 38

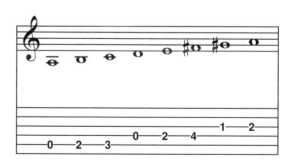

Example 4.70

This mode is commonly known as Phrygian dominant as the intervals are very similar to the Phrygian mode but with one important difference – the third note is major and the tonic chord is a dominant seventh.

The scale degrees of the Phrygian dominant are:

$$R \quad ♭2 \quad 3 \quad 4 \quad 5 \quad ♭6 \quad ♭7$$

The Melodic Minor Scale

The melodic minor scale is the last of the common minor scales. In the past, composers used two different forms of the scale – the ascending and descending forms. The descending form was similar to the natural minor scale, while the ascending form has the following scale degrees:

$$R \quad 2 \quad ♭3 \quad 4 \quad 5 \quad 6 \quad 7$$

It is effectively a major scale with a flattened third. The ascending form is often known as the jazz minor due to its popularity among jazz musicians. There are two particular modes which are commonly used. These will be discussed below.

Here are the notes of the A melodic minor scale:

Example 4.71

The chords of the harmonised melodic minor scale are:

Am/maj7   Bm7   Cmaj7♯5   D7   E7   F♯m7♭5   G♯m7♭5

147

The two most commonly used modes are the IV and VII modes.

Mode IV Of The Melodic Minor Scale

Starting on the fourth note of the melodic minor scale produces an interesting set of notes. Take the fourth mode of A melodic minor, starting on the D note:

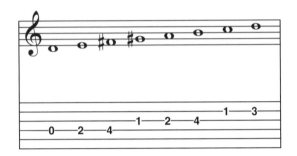

Example 4.72

The mode is often called the Lydian flat 7 scale because of its raised fourth and flattened seventh notes. The scale degrees are:

R 2 3 #4 5 6 b7

The tonic chord is a dominant seventh chord which gives the mode its other name – the Lydian dominant scale. It is also referred to as the *overtone scale* because it contains the same notes as the natural overtone series (which was discussed in chapter 1).

The Lydian dominant is used over dominant seventh or dominant ninth chords with or without an augmented eleventh. It shouldn't be used over dominant seventh sus 4 chords or over any chord with a perfect eleventh.

The other popular mode of the melodic minor scale is the seventh mode. For ease of understanding, let's look at the seventh mode of C melodic minor:

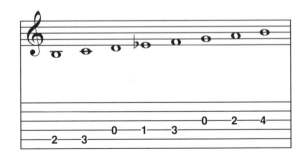

Example 4.73

The mode produces the very rare *diminished fourth* interval on the fourth degree. If we rename some of the scale degrees, we can produce the following series of notes:

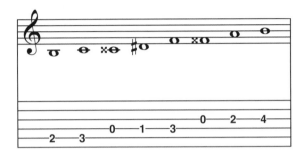

Example 4.74

This scale is commonly known as the *Superlocrian Scale*. Other names include the *Altered Dominant Scale*. The scale degrees are:

R b9 #9 3 b5 #5 b7

I have renamed the second degrees as ninths due to its dominant construction. You can see that by simply using the alternative names for the notes (the scales are identical in sound and pattern) we can uncover the true nature of the scale. The scale has a major third and flattened seventh which gives it its dominant flavour, while the sharpened and flattened fifths and ninths are the altered aspects of the scale.

This scale is used over dominant seventh chords whose fifth and ninth are:

- absent
- sharpened
- flattened

The scale has no fourth or sixth degree. Here is an audio example of this scale being used over an altered dominant:

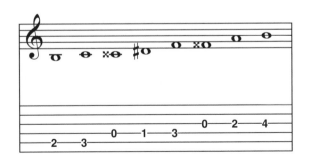

Example 4.75: B7 alt

There are numerous other scales used in a wide variety of cultures and styles. Here is short list of just some of them:

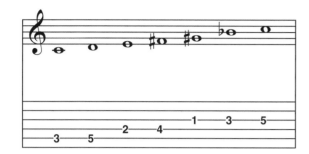

Example 4.76: Whole-tone scale

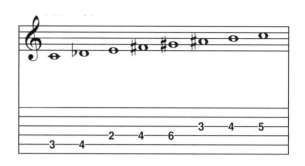

Example 4.80: Enigmatic scale

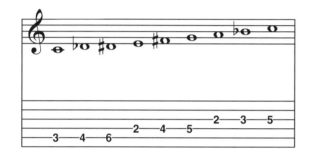

Example 4.77: Whole-tone half-tone scale

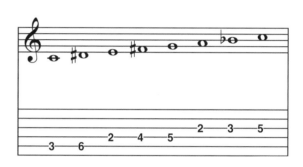

Example 4.81: Hungarian major scale

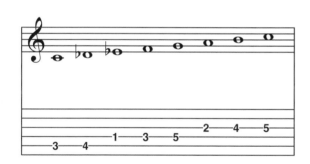

Example 4.78: Half-tone whole-tone scale (diminished)

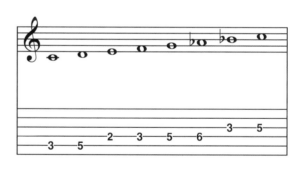

Example 4.82: Hindu (aka melodic major) scale

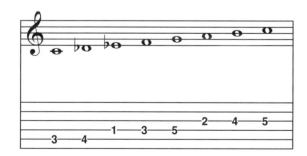

Example 4.79: Neapolitan major scale

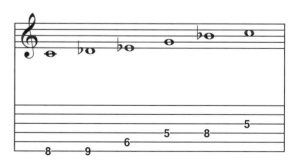

Example 4.83: Pelog scale

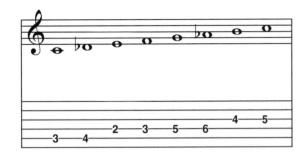

Example 4.84: Gypsy scale

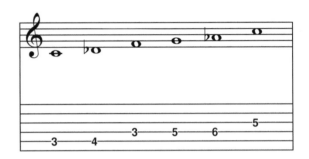

Example 4.86: Jewish scale

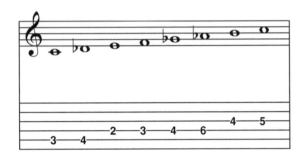

Example 4.85: Persian scale

Example 4.87: Japanese scale

Now that you have been around the world in almost 80 scales, we will move onto more useful guitar techniques!

5 THINKING OUTSIDE THE BOX

Alternate Tunings And Unorthodox Techniques

'The Earth forms the body of an instrument, across which strings are stretched and are tuned by a divine hand. We must try once again to find the secret of that tuning...'

– R Murray Schafer

What is an 'alternate' tuning? For that matter what is 'standard' tuning? Apart from percussionists, the guitarist is probably the only musician who employs such a wide variety of tuning systems for his or her instrument. Often denounced by more 'educated' guitarists as 'cheating' and 'laziness', the enormous variety of guitar tunings is not a recent phenomenon. The history of the instrument, as outlined in the chapter 1, has been marked by radical changes of design and construction. These changes necessitated the development of suitable tunings at successive stages, as the instrument moved from being strung with courses (pairs of strings in unison or octaves) to single strings, and from five strings (often tuned ADGBE) to six (becoming EADGBE) and beyond (7-string guitar is often tuned BEADGBE)

The geographical spread of the instrument's development in Western Europe, Southern Europe and later North America meant that many players and luthiers developed new approaches to tuning and construction to suit the demands of the music for which it was used. Spanish luthiers developed very different strutting and body shapes for flamenco guitar compared with the dreadnought-style body created by the Martin Guitar Company (itself built on 19th-century German guitar traditions).

In its early days the guitar was generally played by uneducated musicians and entertainers. Tunings such as the 'Vestapol tuning' (open D tuning) and 'Spanish' tuning (from an 18th century guitar piece called 'Spanish Fandango' in 'open G' tuning) evolved from a need to keep the instrument as simple as possible to play. These tunings were very common in the 19th century and continue to be used today.

The revival of the acoustic guitar, and in particular, fingerstyle guitar, received a world wide boost in the folk boom of the late 1950s and the 1960s. The trans-Atlantic trade in guitar music and tunings helped to accelerate the development of fingerstyle playing and altered tunings in both the UK and the US. UK players who were exploring the tunings and techniques of the pre-war American bluesmen had an influence on other UK guitarists in the blossoming folk circuit.

Guitarists such as Davey Graham and Martin Carthy, and Pentangle members John Renbourn and Bert Jansch developed complex styles in instrumental fingerstyle and song accompaniment. These four players in particular are mostly responsible for the spread of a variety of altered tunings in the US during the 1960s. While the American guitarists had a history of open tunings in the blues and the musical osmosis of some tunings from the banjo repertoire, the UK guitarists had a history of dance-band music, European jazz music and classical guitar repertoire as reference. As a result, the UK experience of altered tunings was much more eclectic. The influence of Irish and Scottish traditional music, as well as the influence of the blues and American country music, added to the wide variety of styles that UK players drew on.

Over in the US, musicians such as John Fahey and Leo Kottke started to define the contemporary acoustic fingerstyle genre as an artform in its own right. Their music was initially blues-based and both players were distinguished slide players. Kottke emerged early on as a player with a formidable right hand technique and took 12-string guitar playing onto a higher level. The mid-sixties folk-rock scene in the US saw guitarists such David Crosby, Stephen Stills and Neil Young exploring altered tunings and their influence on the young Joni Mitchell is well documented. Using dozens of radical tunings, these players were responsible for some of the most sophisticated folk-pop music ever produced. Players like Paul Simon and Graham Nash had roots in both countries and acted as messengers for the altered tuning world by introducing players on each side of the Atlantic to new developments on the other.

Meanwhile back in the UK, the scene had moved on and now featured the dark and heavy sounds of Deep Purple and Led Zeppelin. Jimmy Page, founder of the latter, was influenced by the music and tunings of players from both sides of the pond and incorporated American open tunings with the more Celtic tunings of the British isles. He was also responsible for the creation of some unique tunings for the electric and acoustic faces of his band. British songwriters such as John Martyn and Nick Drake in the early '70s experimented with dozens of altered tunings.

In the background the maestro player, producer and A&R executive, Chet Atkins was taking it all in and in 1973 released an album *Chet Atkins Alone* in which he recorded arrangements in a variety of tunings. He had been using altered tunings from as early as 1952 in his recording of 'Blue Gypsy' in Open G.

The next wave of altered tunings development came in the 1980s with the revival of Celtic music in the US. Folk festivals all over the country enjoyed a renewed interest and many musicians from the British Isles found a new and large audience there. In tandem with this development was the massive growth of the Windham Hill label. Three guitarists in particular – label founder Will Ackerman, Alex DeGrassi and most notably Michael Hedges – added a whole raft of new tunings and techniques to the acoustic fingerstyle arsenal. That generation of guitarists paved the way for another renaissance in the acoustic guitar idiom and were a defining influence on the current crop of acoustic fingerstyle guitarists.

Pitch Notation

Before we discuss tunings, altered, unaltered or otherwise, we need to standardise the notation of the wide range of pitches involved. There have been numerous systems, particularly those developed by organ builders to cope with the wide range of pitch that the organ uses. The system I suggest is a variation on that developed by Hermann Von Helmholtz (1821–94), a German physicist, in his book *Sensations of Tone*.

'Middle C' below is notated as c'. Even though the guitar in standard tuning is in fact an octave *lower* than that, we still use a lower-case c:

Example 5.1: Middle C on the guitar is written as c'

The 'Middle C' note is written as c for guitarists. The note an octave above that is c' and the note an octave above that written as c''. The note an octave below middle C is written as C.

Below are those four C notes in four different registers together with the tablature:

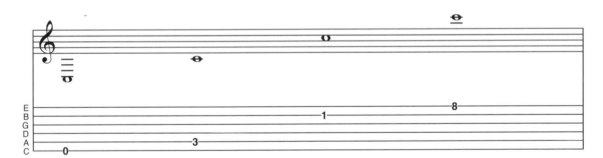

Example 5.2: Detuned low E string

These 'C' notes are the only possible ones on an unmodified guitar (although a harmonic c''' is possible). The very low C is only possible by detuning the low E string by two whole tones.

The notes of a standard tuned guitar are written as:

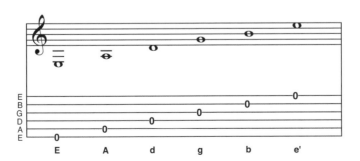

Example 5.3

Categories Of Tunings

The term 'altered tunings' is used to explain a whole variety of tunings. More specifically tunings can be categorised into *open tunings, modal tunings, cross-note tunings, drop tunings* and more. Each tuning that follows will be cross-referenced to one of these categories.

Drop D Tuning (D A d g b e')

The 'drop tunings' are a particular type of tuning. They are simple alterations of standard tuning and are normally used to extend the range of a particular key or song. In *drop D*, as the name implies, you simply drop the E string one whole tone to D. The tuning is popular in all styles from classical guitar pieces, folk and ragtime to rock.

Drop D obviously enhances the key of D major and any related keys such as D minor, G major and minor and the key of A. It obviously affects every single key on the guitar fingerboard. Keys which were previously more remote, such as the key of E♭ receive a new lease of life in the *drop D* tuning.

Neil Young is one of numerous songwriters particularly fond of this tuning. Try the following progression:

CD2, Track 40

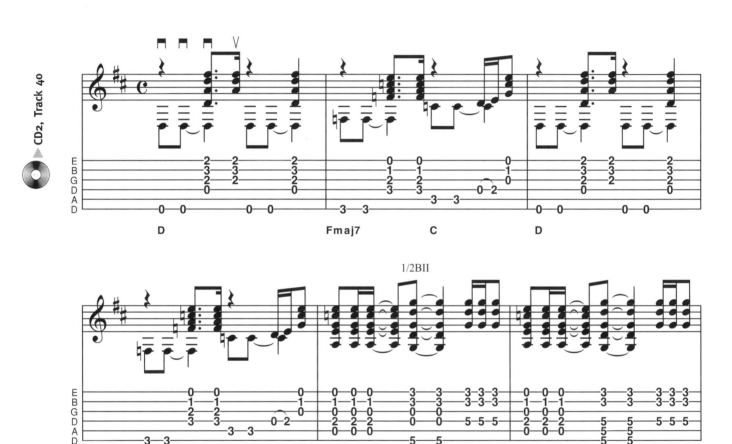

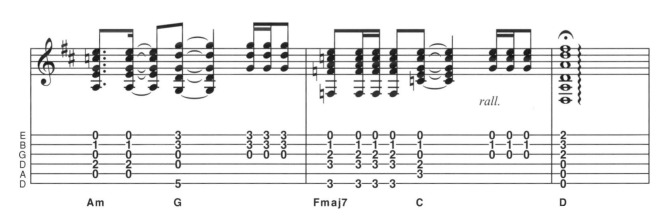

Example 5.4

Here is a small selection of common chords in drop D tuning:

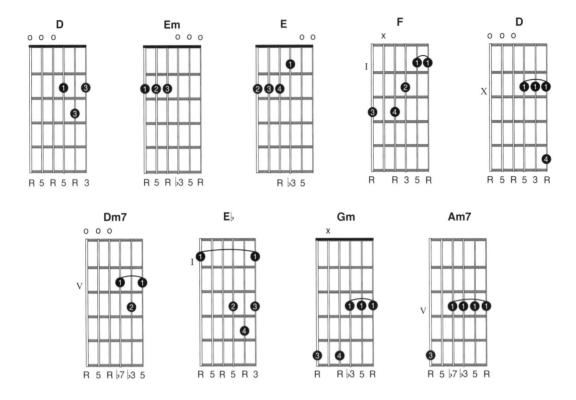

Example 5.5

Double Drop D Tuning (D A d g b d')

The 'Double Drop D' tuning is a simple variation on the drop D tuning with both E strings dropped a whole step to D. This tuning is useful for creating drone-like voicings and is another favourite of Neil Young.

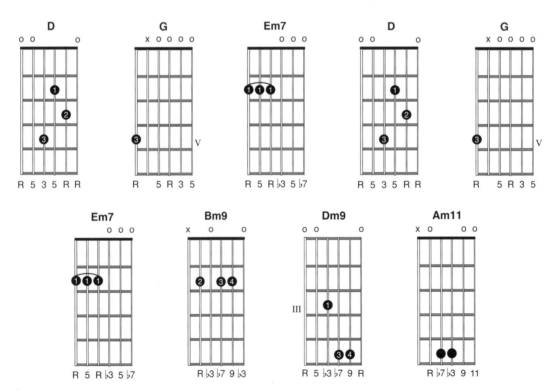

Example 5.6

Drop D, Drop G (D G d g b e')

This tuning is also known as G6 tuning and was used, by among others, the late great Chet Atkins.

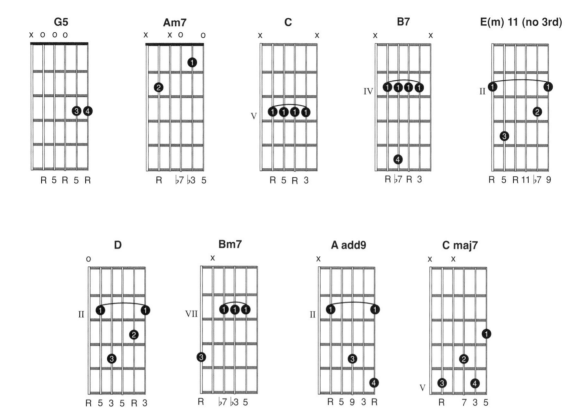

Example 5.7

Other Drop Tunings

Other drop tunings include *drop* C (**C A d g b e'**) and *drop A*. Although not technically a drop tuning (could we call it a 'lift tuning'?) **F A d g b e'** was used by altered tuning wizard Michael Hedges on his track 'Lenono' and was simply standard tuning with the low E string raised a semitone to F (even though the composition was in the not-so-related key of G major!).

Drop A is a tuning I came across from guitarist and producer Martin Taylor on his tune 'Song for Alex'. The tuning **A' A d g b 'e** was used by Martin to provide a deep bass line and grounded root notes for the chords in the key of A major:

CD2, Track 40

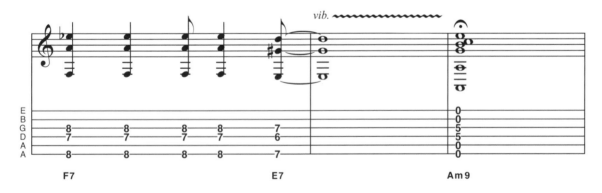

Open Tunings

Open Tunings are so named because the notes of the open strings form a major triad. The most popular are as follows:

Open G (D G d g b d')

The tuning is called 'slack key' (through it's association with Hawaiian musicians) and also 'Spanish tuning' (from its association with the 19th century guitar tune *Spanish Fandango*). The tuning was popular in early blues music and mountain music in the US. In fact, the similarity between this tuning and the tuning of the 5-string banjo led many to suggest that the tuning was the only true North American tuning (in my first encounters with the tuning in Britain, it was called American Standard Tuning).

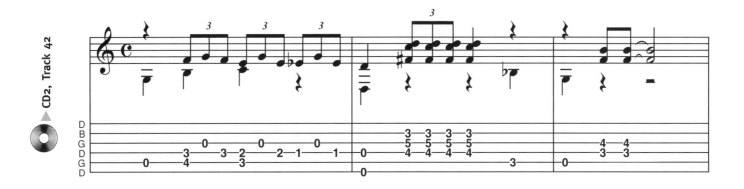

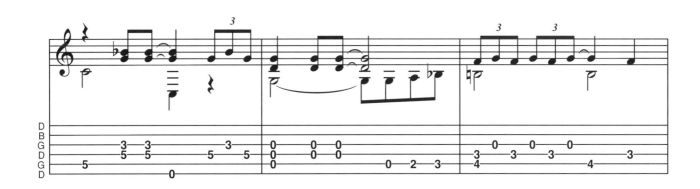

Example 5.9

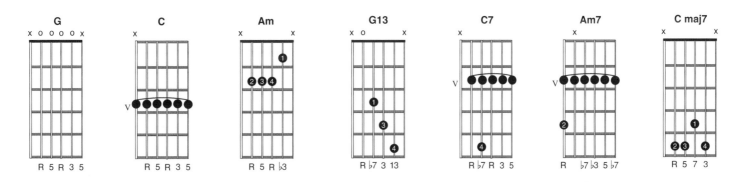

Example 5.10: Open G chord shapes

Open D (D A d f♯ a d')

This tuning has the alternative names of *Vestapol* and *Sebastopol* following its use in famous 19th-century tunes of those names. Like open G tuning, it was initially popular among bluesmen who found the tuning perfect for slide playing and strong six-note voicings of the major chords. The position of the root note at the top and bottom of these voicings gave the open D tuning a particularly grounded nature.

CD2, Track 43

p i p m p i p a p i p m p i p a etc

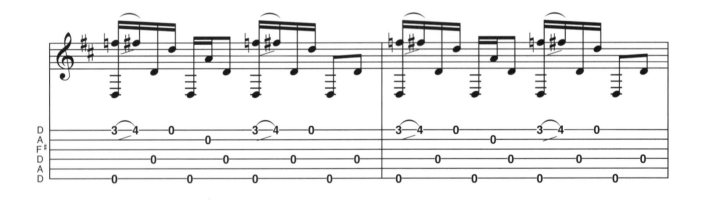

Example 5.11

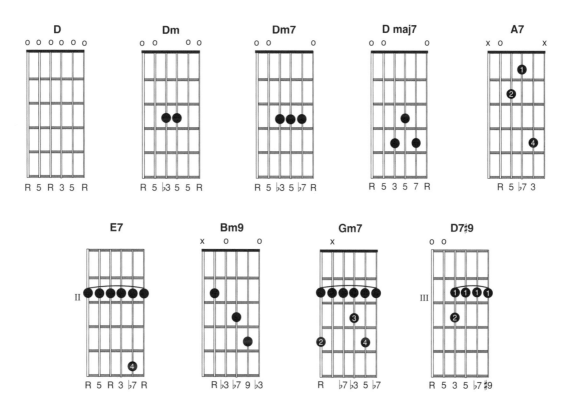

Example 5.12: Open D chord shapes

Other Open Tunings

The other most common open tunings are open C (C G c g c' e') and open E (E B e g♯ b e'). Generally the tunings are employed to facilitate the major key of the open 6th string.

One way to explore any tuning is to investigate other keys within the tuning. Generally in these open tunings the key based on the open fifth string is a close relative so why not start there?

Modal Tunings

This family of altered tunings are more flexible than the open tunings. They allow easier access to a wider variety of keys. They are identifiable by their lack of a major or minor third in the interval pattern of the open strings, although they would also exclude inversions of these intervals (that is, major and minor sixths) and the tritone interval. They are predominantly constructed with major second, perfect fourth, perfect fifth and octave intervals and are often referred to as sus 2 and sus 4 tunings.

DADGAD Tuning (D A d g a d')

One of the most commonly used modal tunings, the tuning's origin is popularly credited to British fingerstyle innovator Davey Graham whose encounters with local musicians in North Africa led him to devise the tuning in the early 1960s. The strong intervals of a perfect fifths and octaves give the tuning a rich resonance of parallel overtones and sympathetic vibrations, while the interval of a major second between the second and third strings allows for easy fingering of melodies. The suspended fourth quality that the open strings create (D sus 4) give the tuning an in-built tension that, once resolved, allow for very satisfying chord changes. It is popular among Celtic fingerstyle guitarists although it has become recognised as an inspiring tuning for contemporary songwriters. As with other tunings, you should explore keys other than those offered by the open sixth string. The following examples in D major and C major indicate two approaches to the tuning:

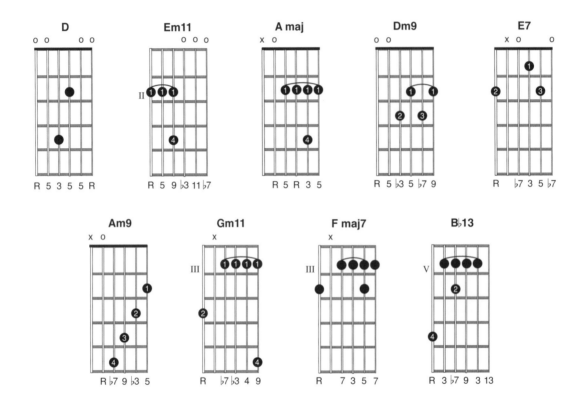

Example 5.13

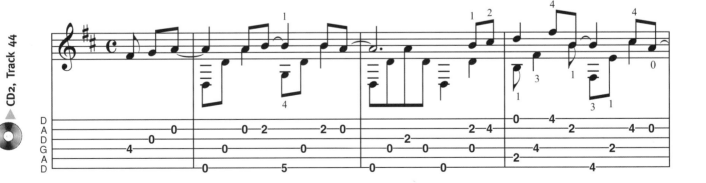

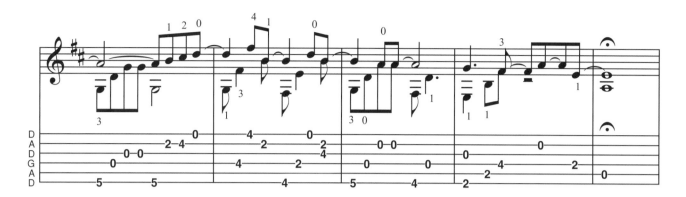

Example 5.14

The Water Is Wide

CD2, Track 45

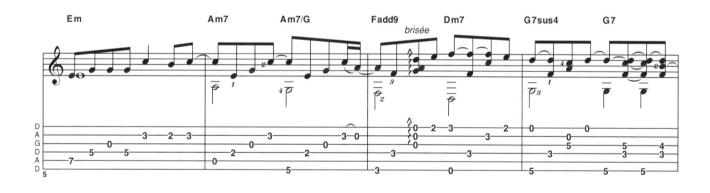

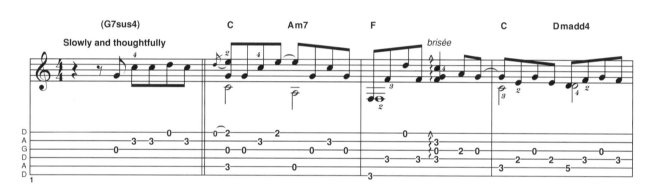

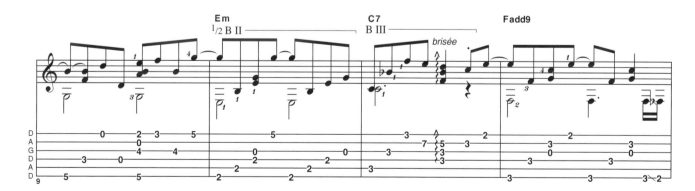

Example 5.15 (continues...)

Example 5.15 (continues...)

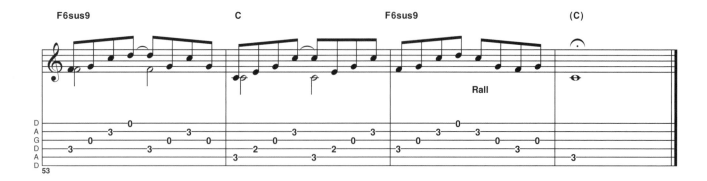

Example 5.15 continued

DADEAD Tuning (D A d e a d')

The tuning is another modal tuning and is of the sus 2 variety. The major second interval between the third and fourth strings allow for some interesting effects. The audio example below will give you an introduction to the tuning's possibilities:

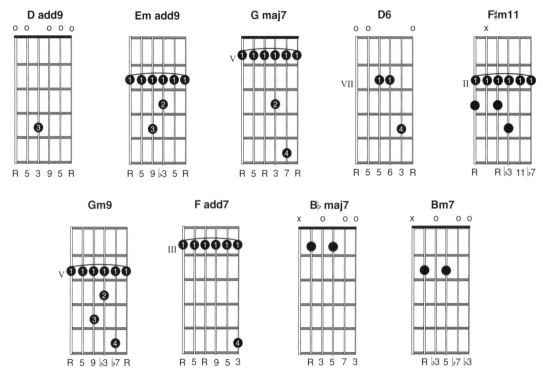

Example 5.16

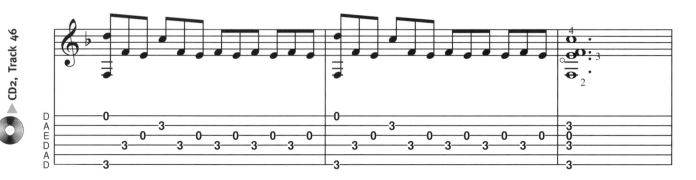

Example 5.17

G Modal Tuning (D G d g c' d')

Also known as G sus 4 tuning, this tuning is a guitar adaptation of the popular 'sawmill' tuning employed by 5-string banjo players. Another name, though now out of use, is 'mountain minor' tuning (the tuning *isn't* minor in nature). It is most useful as a variation of open G tuning allowing the player to make major and minor chords quite easily.

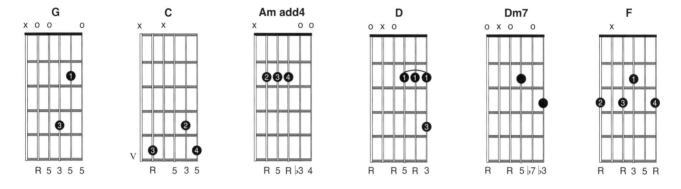

Example 5.18

Example 5.19

C Modal Tuning (C G d g a d')

A simple variation of the DADGAD tuning, this C modal tuning gives access to very resonant chord voicings in both the keys of C and G among many others.

165

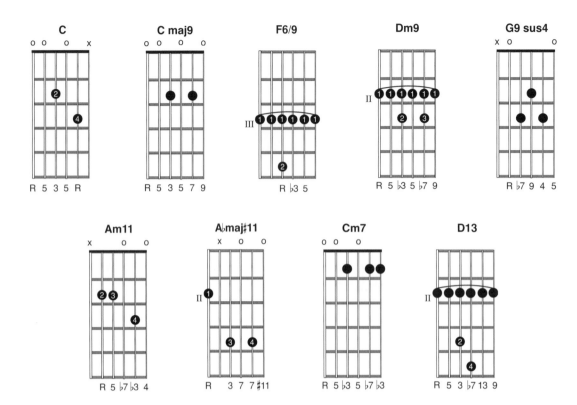

Example 5.20

Cross-Note Tunings

These tunings are in fact open tunings based on minor triads. Some of the most common are:

- D minor tuning: D A d f a d'
- G minor tuning: D G d g bb d'
- E minor tuning: E B e g b e'
- C minor tuning: C G c g c' eb'

More Radical Tunings

There are almost as many tunings as there are players. Many players have devised tunings to accommodate just one of their compositions. Guitarists such as Michael Hedges, Nick Drake and Joni Mitchell have rarely used the same tuning twice in their recording career, while others such as Pierre Bensusan have spent a lifetime exploring one altered tuning.

Here is a short list of some of the more radical altered tunings:

- C G d g b d' – 'C wahine' tuning from Hawaii
- C G c d g a – Synonymous with Martin Carthy
- E E e e b e' – '4+20' by Stephen Stills
- B'b F Bb f bb c – Martin Simpson's *Raglan Road*
- E A d f# b e' – John Renbourn, *Lute Tuning* for 'The Bicycle'
- B F# c# e f# b – Joni Mitchell 'Hejira' tuning
- E B B g b d' – Ani di Franco, 'Not a Pretty Girl'

Nashville Tuning

This tuning is a simple adaptation of the standard tuning of 12-string guitars. It is also commonly known as high string (hi-string) tuning.

From low to high:

e a d g' b e

The bottom four strings are an octave higher than standard tuning while the top two treble strings are tuned at their normal pitch. This of course requires different gauge strings to cope with the radically higher pitches. From low to high I would recommend the following gauges:

.030w | .020 | .014 | .009 | .016 | .012

The 'low' E string is the only wound one. I don't know of any specific 'Nashville tuning' string sets. You should either get these strings from a standard 12-string set or piece one together from other sets of strings.

The Nashville tuning is useful for 'doubling' parts on a recording. I have recorded a simple rhythm part and 'doubled' it with the exact same shapes on the high string. I have panned the hi-string guitar slightly right and the normal guitar slightly left so that you more clearly hear it. I finish on a simple back-stroke on the hi-string guitar. A hi-string guitar is a standard tool in the session guitarist's 'bag'. It can add a subtle sparkle to a guitar track without getting in the way. On many recording sessions I have pulled out the hi-string and helped to add a bright texture to the guitar rhythm track. Interlocking rhythms, and panning a normal and high-string guitar hard left and hard right in the stereo field can be very effective too.

CD2, Track 48

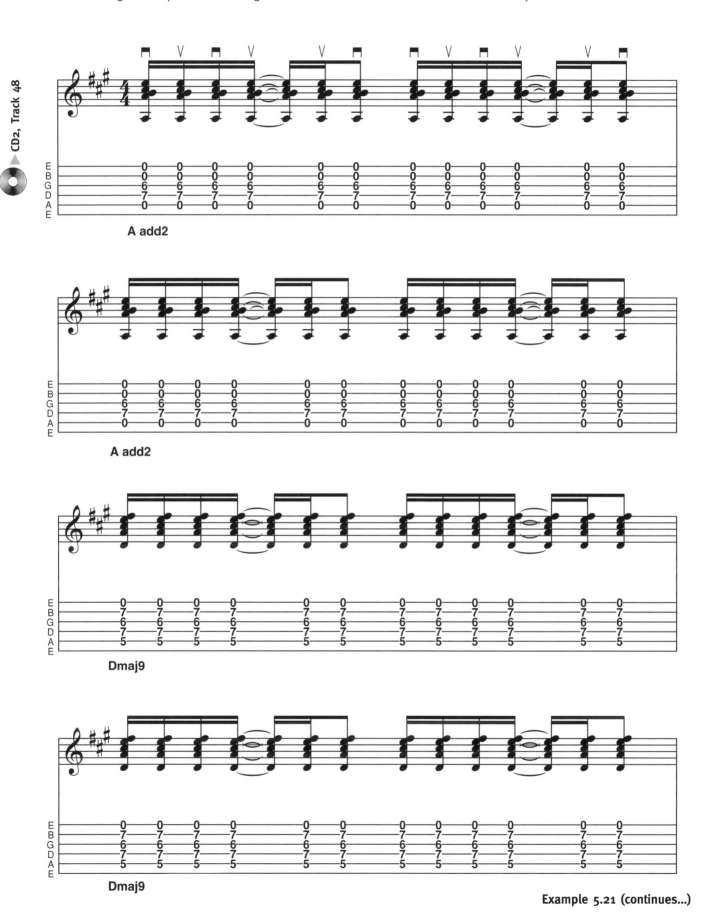

Example 5.21 (continues...)

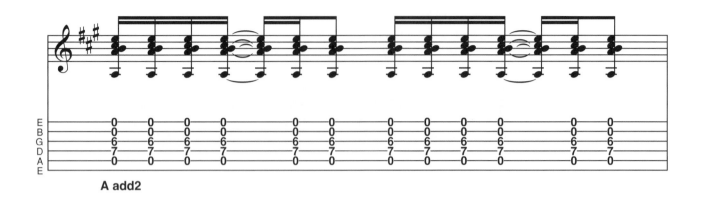

A add2

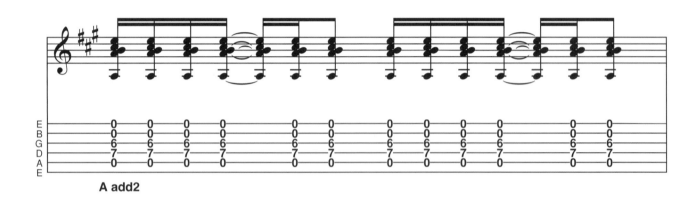

A add2

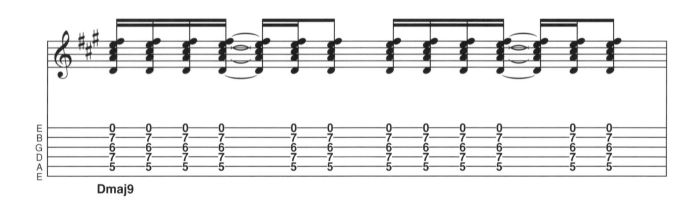

Dmaj9

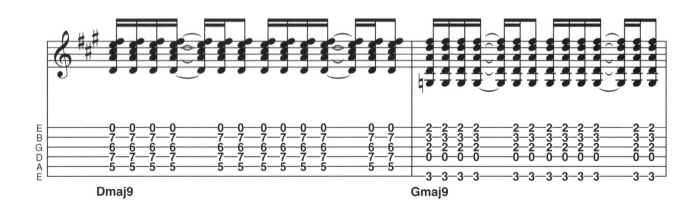

Dmaj9   Gmaj9

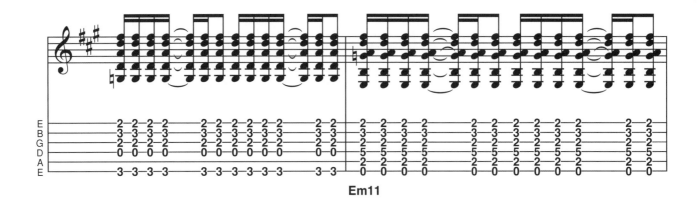

Em11

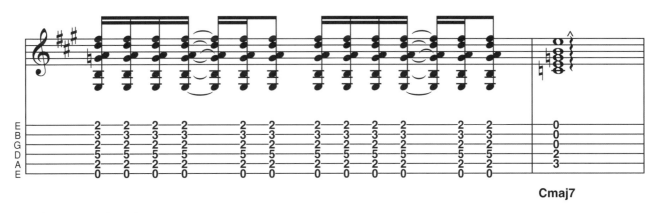

Cmaj7

Example 5.21 continued

String Gauges And Altered Tunings

While it is nearly impossible to put a guitar in Nashville tuning without altering the string gauges, you can in theory apply many of the other tunings in this chapter without changing the strings.

The majority of altered tunings are de-tunings – the strings are lowered in tension rather than raised. While there is no rule that says that you must lower the tension and not raise it, in practical terms, the lowering of a string's tension makes new notes available in an accessible part of the fingerboard. Raising the pitch of a string will obviously give you extra notes at the very top frets, but these are not so commonly required.

The majority of tunings are used as a way of creating greater resonance and easier fingerings in particular keys. As noble as it is to work in the key of E flat with drop D tuning, most guitarists will use this altered tuning as a way of enhancing and broadening the possibilities of keys more closely related to the D note.

By lowering the tension of a string, you change the way it behaves. The tone quality of the string also changes. More importantly though, its ability to play in tune diminishes as you lower the tension. In short, the lower you tune a string, the less able it is to play in tune

accurately. One way to compensate partially for this is to increase the gauge of the string.

Personally I suggest that the minimum gauge strings on a standard jumbo/dreadnought-style acoustic guitar should be:

.012 | .016 | .024w | .032w | .042w | .053w

With this as a starting point, I would suggest that you move up a gauge for each whole tone that you drop in pitch, so for example, **D A d g a d'** tuning would call for the following string gauges:

.013 | .017 | .024w | .032w | .042w | .054w

The Martin Carthy tuning **C G c d g a** could use the following gauges:

.016 | .018p | .026w | .034w | .044w | .056w

The p here means 'plain' (unwound) and the w means 'wound'. In this set I have increased some of the gauges by .001 to compensate for the radical lowering in tension that this tuning creates.

If you intend to leave an instrument in an altered tuning virtually permanently, then I would recommend that you bring the instrument to an experienced repair man who can reset the truss rod and neck tension to compensate for the permanent change in string tension.

Radical changes in string gauges should be done with caution, particularly on lighter guitars. There are certain guitars on the market that come with a string gauge warning. Pay attention to these warnings from the manufacturer – otherwise you could end up with a damaged soundboard, or in extreme cases a damaged guitar neck.

Capos And 'Altered' Tunings

There are a number of 'partial capos' on the market. These capos are designed to cover anything from 1 to 5 strings. There are models that will cover three strings but not the outer ones (see the photograph in the accessories section, pg 210). The very innovative 'Third Hand Capo' is used extensively by players such as Harvey Reid, Chris Proctor and singer songwriter David Wilcox. This capo has the capacity to capo any combination of strings, from one to six. While leaving the guitar in standard tuning you can

create the impression of altered tunings while working with familiar shapes and patterns. With some practice you can also play on both side of the capo, as some strings are left open.

Harmonics: Notes From Heaven

As we saw in the section about intonation and overtones, it is possible to access a wide range of notes in the overtone series of any note. To quickly summarise, any note that you play on the guitar will have a whole series of related notes that sound at the same time. Any one note in fact is composed of an infinite series of notes extending upwards in a fixed sequence. These overtones can also be played as *harmonics*.

Natural Harmonics

There are a number of techniques used to create harmonics on the guitar. The easiest harmonics to play are those that are found on an open string. They only require the standard technique of a fretting left hand and a plucking right hand.

These *natural harmonics* can be found, among other places, at the following frets:

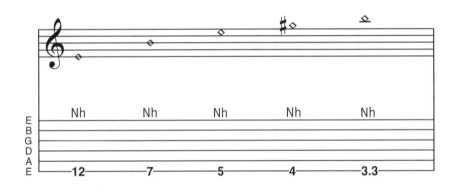

Example 5.22: First five harmonics on the low E string

The series produced here is:

- Octave
- Perfect fifth
- Octave
- Major third
- Perfect fifth

The last two harmonics in this sequence are technically impossible to tab. As the harmonic series doesn't correlate precisely with the frets of the guitar: the further up the series you go, the further the harmonics stray from the fret markings. The major third, for example, is just on the 'nut' side of the fourth fret, while the following perfect fifth is on the 'bridge'

side of the third fret. See the diagrams in the Intonation section earlier to find the next harmonics in the series.

Playing Natural Harmonics

The crucial part of this technique is finding the harmonic – the *node* point – on the string with the left hand. The sounding of the harmonic with the right hand is no different to the technique in sounding a 'normal' note.

Let's start with the first harmonic that appears at the 12th fret on an open string. Bring the left hand middle finger (any finger will do, but for the moment use the longer and more controllable middle finger) to the low E string at the 12th fret. Touch the string gently but without applying pressure just above the 12th fret, not in the space where you place your fingers for chords and scales, but rather directly above the fret wire at the 'bridge' end of this fret space. Do not depress the string, but remain in contact with it. Pluck the string with the right hand. Here are the 12th-fret harmonics on each of the open strings, from low to high. They form an Em11 chord:

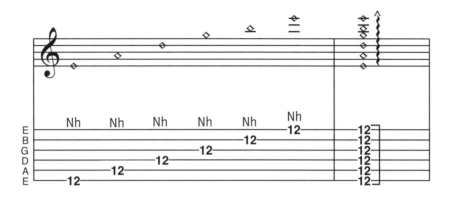

Example 5.23: 12th-fret harmonics

The same technique can be applied at the 7th fret. These notes form a Bm11 chord:

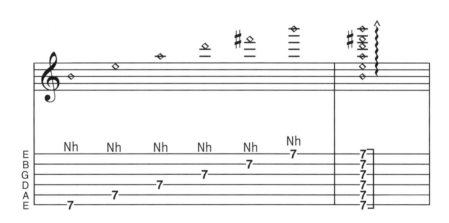

Example 5.24: 7th-fret harmonics

And also at the 5th fret where you can form another Em11 chord:

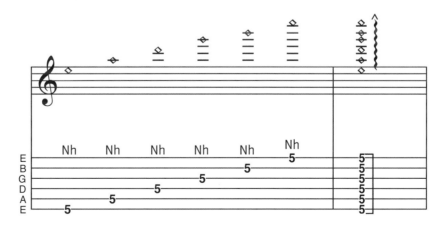

Example 5.25: 5th-fret harmonics

You can produce some interesting chords by replacing the bottom note with a fretted note. For example these chords:

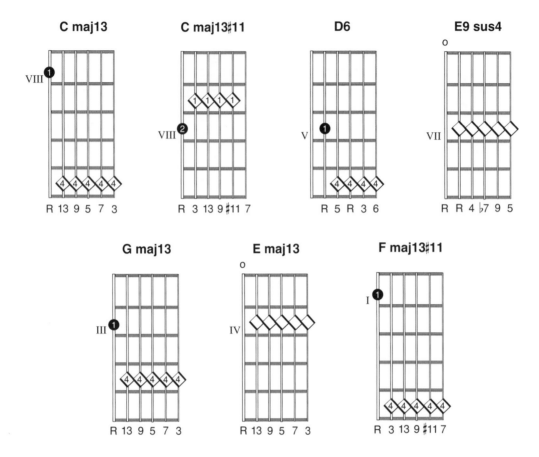

Example 5.26

You can also play scales. Here is a D major scale played with natural harmonics:

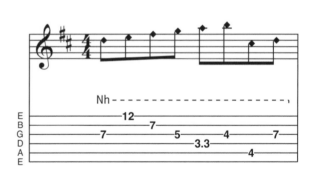

▲ CD2, Track 53

Example 5.27

And here is the A major scale played with natural harmonics:

▲ CD2, Track 54

Example 5.28

Here is a melody in A major played exclusively with natural harmonics:

CD2, Track 55

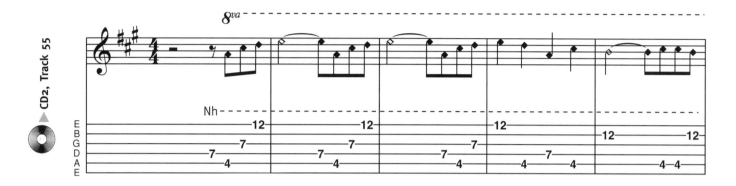

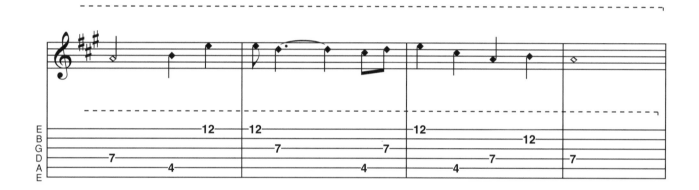

Example 5.29

Here's a simple but effective phrase using only the harmonics on the 7th and 12th frets. Starting on the B string 7th fret, it simply alternates 7,12, 7, 12, etc.

CD2, Track 56

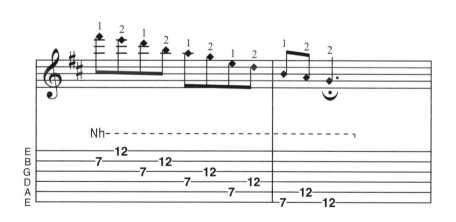

Example 5.30

Artificial (Harp) Harmonics

These harmonics are created by altering the length of the string (by fretting it). The harmonic series remains unchanged, it just shifts over on the string in relation to the new string length. For example, if you fret a note at the 5th fret, its first overtone or harmonic can be located just above the 17th fret. This technique is also known as the Koto technique.

To play this harmonic requires a particular technique for the right (plucking) hand. The picture on the right shows you. In this case the index finger is touching a node point at the 12th fret of an open E string. The right hand thumb then plucks the E string to sound the harmonic. You should practise plucking the same note with the thumb, middle and ring fingers in rotation as an exercise. Although particular players favour one finger over another, ultimately it would be beneficial to have the choice of which finger plucks.

In artificial harmonics, you are playing harmonics on fretted strings. Try this simple passage in Example 5.31 with a barré across the 5th fret:

▲ CD2, Track 57

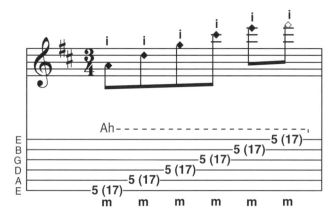

Example 5.31

As with the natural harmonics you can create different chords by substituting various bass notes:

▲ CD2, Track 57

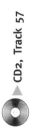

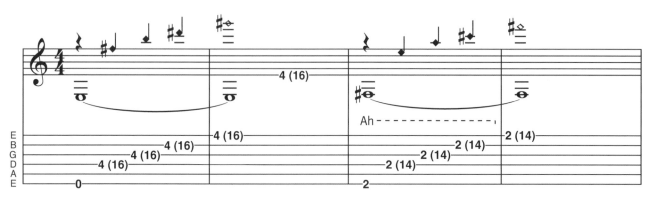

CD2, Track 58

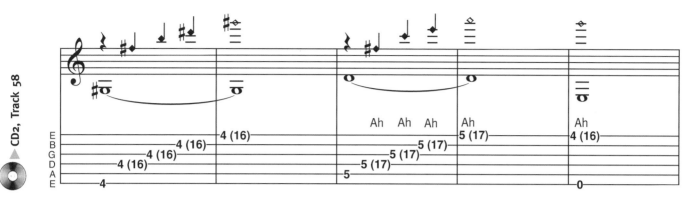

Example 5.32

Combining Harp Harmonics And Fretted Notes

One of the most exciting uses of harmonics is their combination with fretted notes. This combination of sounds can produce a harp-like effect. In the example below you need to simply barré across the 5th fret. With the right hand you select alternately fretted notes and harmonics. Let's look at the opening notes of example 5.33 below. The right hand ring finger plucks the fretted D string. This note is followed by a harp harmonic on the low E string at the 17th fret. The harmonic is touched by

the right hand index and plucked by the thumb. This pattern of fretted note–harmonic is repeated on the next pair of strings until you get to the high e' string at which point the process reverses. Here it is in detailed tablature. Refer to the CD to hear the effect. It is important to carefully balance the volume of fretted notes and harmonics. Your first attempts will probably be a little unbalanced. You should aim for louder and clearer harmonics while subduing the stronger nature of the fretted notes. As usual, practise slowly and listen carefully to each sound as you play it.

CD2, Track 59

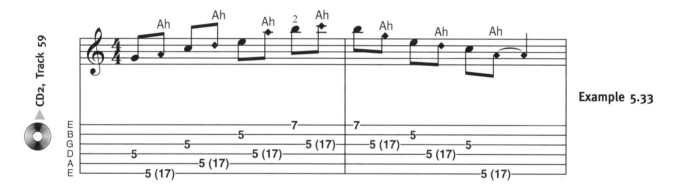

Example 5.33

You can also combine legato – pull-offs – with artificial harmonics. Look at example 5.34 below. Play a barré at the 5th fret and play an artificial harmonic on the 3rd string. Pull off on the high E string with the third finger.

CD2, Track 60

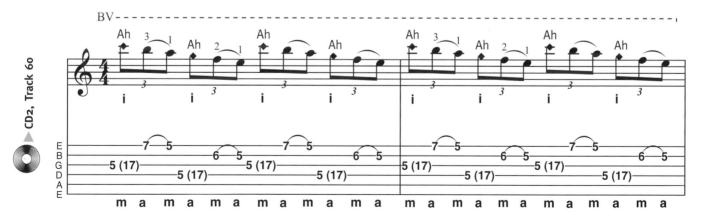

Example 5.34

You can also apply the technique to more colourful chord shapes such as these dominant ninth #11 chords:

CD2, Track 61

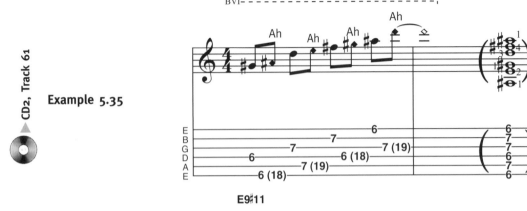

Example 5.35

Raked Harmonics

In this technique the approach is very similar to harp harmonics. Take a simple chord such as E minor. Holding down the chord with the left hand, touch the first string, as if you were about to play a harp-harmonic with the index finger of the right hand at the 12th fret. Your right hand ring finger needs to be in 'pluck' position. At this point make a mental note of your right hand shape and position. Tense the muscles in your right hand and forearm slightly to lock the hand position and then draw upwards across the strings.

Your ring finger sounds the notes while the index selects the harmonics.

When the index crosses the fretted D and A strings the technique is ineffective unless you move right along the string to the 14th fret to mirror the fretted notes. Often I will slightly raise the index out of 'touch' position and let the ring finger sound the fretted strings and the open low E string. Other times you can rake the hand back at an angle to produce raked harmonics for chords such as Fmaj7 (see Example 5.37). Listen to the sound of raked harmonics on the CD:

CD2, Track 62

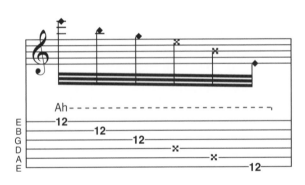

Example 5.36

The technique can be applied to chord sequences also. Play through the following example to hear the results and apply the technique to your own repertoire and compositions.

CD2, Track 63

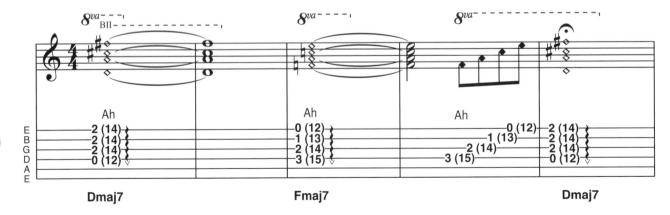

Example 5.37

Strummed Harmonics

This can be thought of as the reverse of raked harmonics. Whereas in raked harmonics the right hand is drawn back across the strings to produce a series of harmonics, in strummed harmonics the right hand is moving *downwards* against the strings to produce them. The approach however, is significantly different and in some ways, more challenging.

Take a simple chord again, such as E minor. The right hand wrist needs to be angled quite dramatically – up to 60 degrees – so that the sledge of the hand is parallel to the frets. Place the sledge of the hand gently on the strings at the 12th fret to produce the usual degree of gentle but consistent pressure needed for harmonics. The right hand index, and if possible the middle finger, should then strum downwards to produce the harmonics at the 12th fret.

CD2, Track 64

Example 5.38

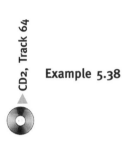

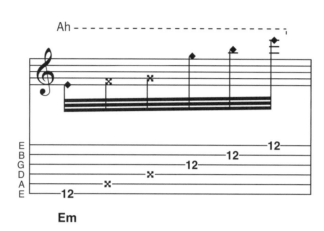

Here is a short piece for you to practise with. It combines some of the harmonic producing techniques that we have explored in this chapter. In a later chapter we will look at some other techniques to produce harmonics.

CD2, Track 65

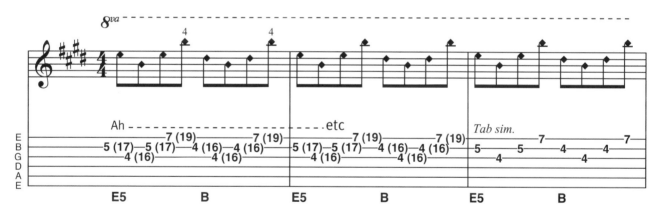

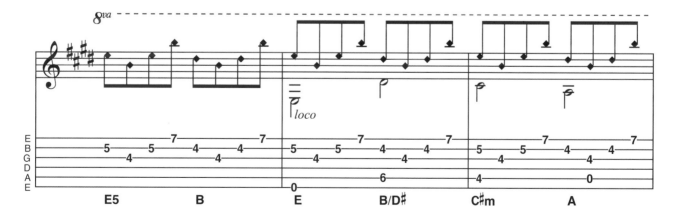

Example 5.39 (continues...)

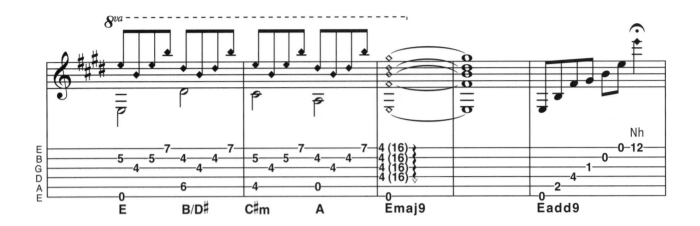

Example 5.39 continued

6 'WHAT BOX?'

The Guitar Is A Drum, And The Drum Is The Ear Of God

'Find out what the drum does to the body. Find out about Rhythm.'
– *Professor John Blacking*

The body of an acoustic guitar has much in common with a drum. Although it doesn't have a skin, the thin, carefully braced soundboard is tuned much in the way that a drum-skin is. The soundboard has to be flexible enough to respond to the loudest and deepest frequencies and sensitive enough to amplify the slightest string noise and overtone.

Although many guitarists may not appreciate it, the body of the acoustic guitar has been used as a source of percussive sounds for over a hundred years. Flamenco guitarists and blues guitarists have been tapping and slapping the soundboard from the earliest days. However, the acoustic guitar until the 1930s, wasn't as strong or as large as today's instruments. The dreadnought guitar was built to live up to its name. Large and strongly built, the guitar was able to withstand far greater knocks and bangs than its predecessors.

There have always been superfluous string and guitar body noises that have become part of accepted guitar vocabulary. The simplest form of percussive sound on the guitar is achieved by bringing the right hand back onto the strings firmly. The strings should strike the frets and produce a simple 'chink' sound. The technique involves moving the fingers in one plane to produce the notes and the hand moving in another plane to come back down on the strings for that percussive effect. This technique was used very effectively by guitarists such as John Martyn. Try the following example:

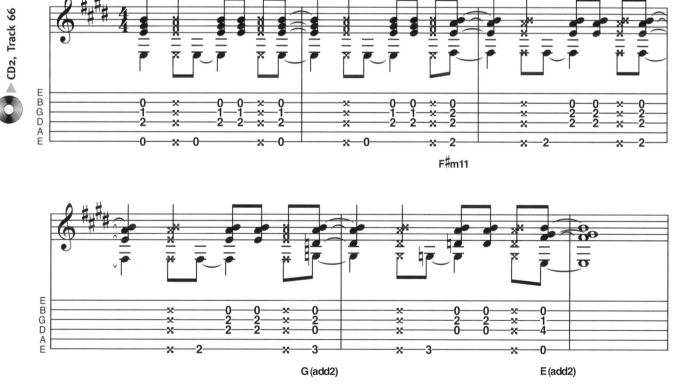

CD2, Track 66

Example 6.1

179

The same technique can be used on the soundboard. The X marking on the stave below denotes a percussive tap with the right hand fingertips just below the soundhole.

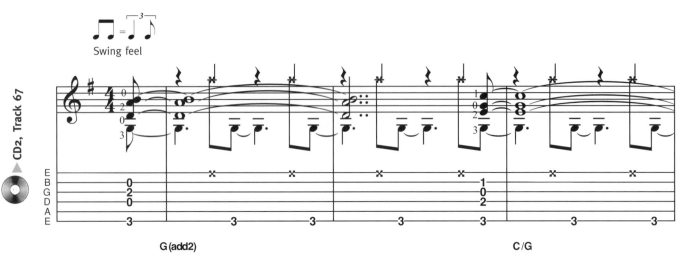

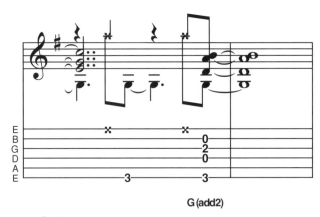

Example 6.2

The heel of the right hand is usually free to play some deeper 'bass drum' type tones. By bringing the heel of the hand down onto the soundboard just above the soundhole, a low bass-like thud can be produced on even the smallest guitars. The combination of these two percussive sounds is not too unlike a pair of congas. Listen to the following example to hear the effect.

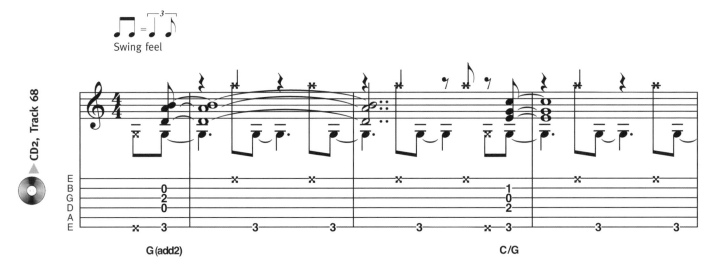

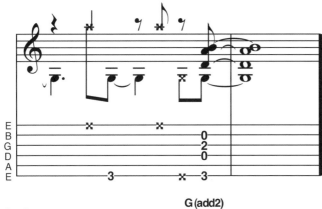

Example 6.3

There are a number of other textures available at various points on the guitar body. Using your right hand fingernails firmly on the underside of the lower bout, you will produce a definite click, not too dissimilar to the sound of a drummer hitting the rim of his snare drum.

Bring the heel of the hand down firmly on the soundboard, just above the lower bout and you should produce a low bass drum tone. In the example below, I have marked the bass drum with the lower X and the cross-stick tone with the upper X.

CD2, Track 69

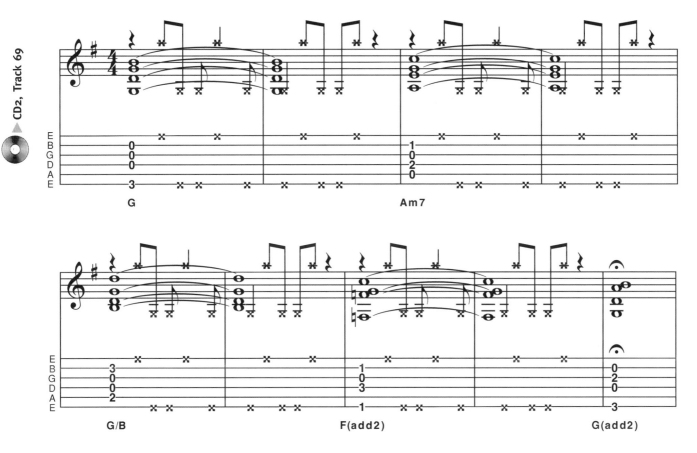

Example 6.4

The left hand can also join in on the fun. It takes careful co-ordination, but the following example involves a left hand slap on the side of the guitar, just underneath the heel of the neck. The heel of the right hand comes down

on the soundboard just above the neck to play a bass drum tone. The tuning is DAdgad'. The final chord is struck by the side of the right hand thumb knuckle.

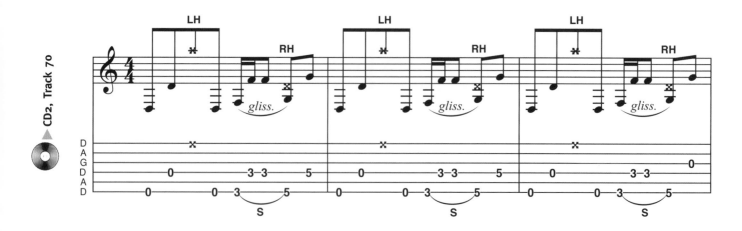

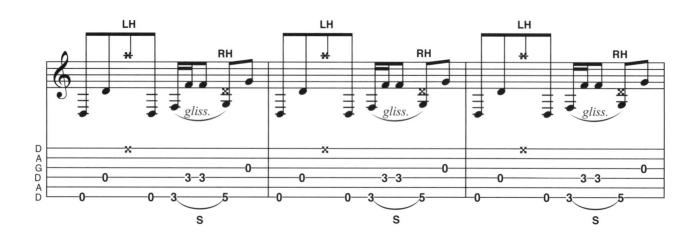

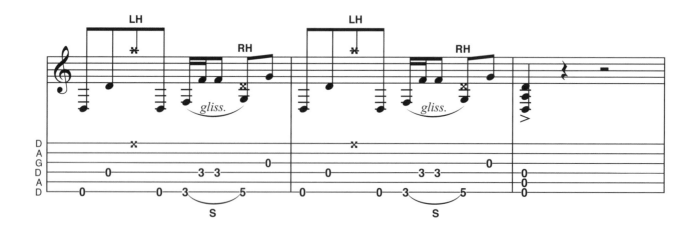

Example 6.5

The following example is a two-handed percussion rhythm. There are four different tones detailed in the legend below. The lowest of these tones is the bass drum sound produced by the heel of the right hand on the soundboard. The next tone is a right hand slap on the muted strings at the soundhole. The next highest tone is the conga style right hand slap on the soundboard just underneath the soundhole. The fourth and highest pitched tone is produced by the left hand tapping on the off beats against the strings on the neck. Have fun!

CD2, Track 71

Right hand · Left hand

Right hand

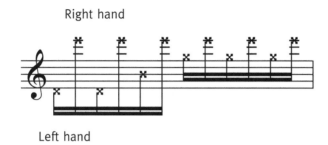

Left hand

Key

Left-hand string tap

Strings
(soundhole)

Bass drum
(soundhole)

Soundboard

Example 6.6

Two-Handed Acoustic Tapping.

This technique, most commonly associated with electric rock guitar, can also be applied to the acoustic guitar. It was adapted and brought into the acoustic guitar vocabulary by the late great Michael Hedges and developed by the following generation of guitarists such as Billy McLaughlin, Preston Reed and Thomas Leeb.

The following example requires the fretting of notes on the fingerboard by both hands. The right hand taps (marked T) need to be firm and as close to the fret wire as possible. The left hand taps (marked L/H) are effectively hammer-ons 'from nowhere'. Some notes are produced by the right hand pulling-off an already tapped note. These notes are marked RPO (Right-hand Pull-Off). Again the fingers on each hand should come down as sharply and as close to the fret wire as possible. In this example the tuning again is Dadgad'.

CD2, Track 72

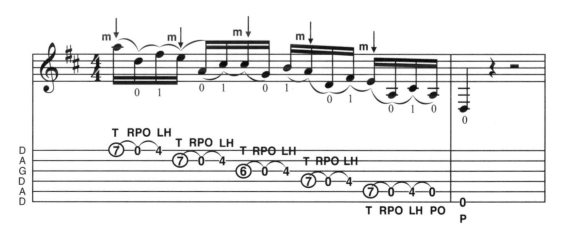

Example 6.7

The next example is a development of the two handed tapping technique. The following bass line from my track 'Roundabout' is harmonised in octaves. The whole piece is presented at the end of the book.

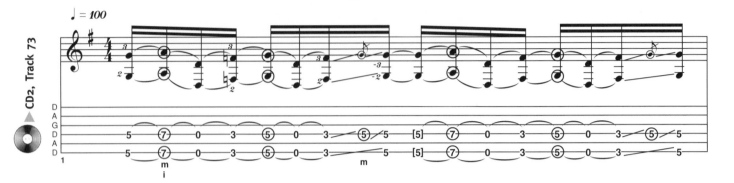

Example 6.8

Slapped Harmonics

Another way of selecting the overtones on a string is to hit the string precisely on one of the node points, such as the 12th fret, 7th fret, or 5th fret. The technique requires some practice but can produce dramatic results. The sound also has a percussive element as the finger hits the fretboard. The right hand index or middle finger should be extended to full length. Slap sharply at the node point with the underside of the finger. The finger, as far as possible, should be kept parallel to the frets. Listen to the following example to hear the effect:

Example 6.9

You can also apply this technique to other chord shapes. Try these major seventh chords. Turn your right hand index until it is generally parallel to the chord shape.

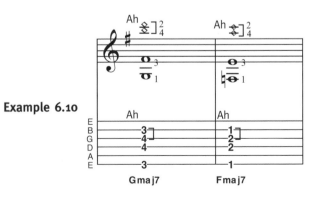

Example 6.10

You can combine the Celtic percussive rhythm from earlier on in the chapter with these slapped harmonics. The tuning again is DAdgad'.

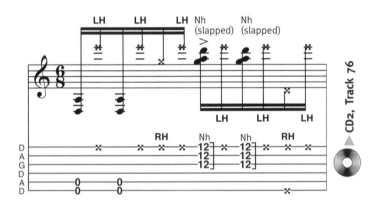

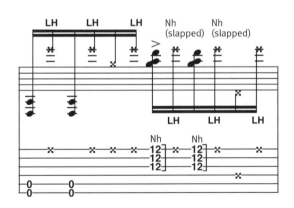

Example 6.11

These techniques are great fun to use and can add a whole range of new textures to the sound of the guitar. Use these techniques as a way of expanding your own compositional and performance repertoire.

7 LET THERE BE SOUND!

Amplification And Performance

'We cannot close our ears; we have no earlids.'

– From 'The Tuning Of The World', Murray Shafer

In the past ten years, the amplification and recording of acoustic guitar has undergone huge change. As the interest in acoustic guitar and acoustic guitar music has ballooned, so too has the technology and investment by guitar companies. In the 1970s the best that you could expect was a microphone placed in front of the soundhole. In both performance and recording situations this is probably the *worst* place for a microphone. A whole barrage of overtones and undertones, rushing air and strumming fingers will ensure that the microphone never reproduces the sound of the instrument. More on that later.

Pickup Systems For Acoustic Guitar

Pickup technology for flat-top acoustic guitars was in its infancy only 20 years ago. Today pickups come as a standard accessory on many models. The term 'acoustic' has become almost synonymous with 'electro-acoustic' in the acoustic guitar community, with certain guitarists such as Pierre Bensusan labelling themselves 'electro-acoustic guitarists'.

The amplification of an acoustic guitar's sound has been the key to the growth in popularity of the instrument. Because the instrument was traditionally difficult to amplify, the acoustic guitar was often perceived as the poor cousin of its arch top and solid body relations. Electric guitarists have many generations of experience in treating the instrument and the amplification as a unified whole – they play the guitar and its amplifier simultaneously. In many ways the guitar *plays* the amplifier. Acoustic guitarists have travelled a different path – the instrument itself is its own amplifier. The soundboard and soundbox are the means by which the guitar amplifies its own sound. A well-trained classical guitarist can use a well-built classical guitar to project sound to the back of a medium-sized hall without any electric sound amplification. In some ways it's surprising that the flat-top acoustic guitar survived at all in the wake of electric guitar pickups. The reasons are manifold although the instrument's ease of portability was probably its saving

grace. It's much easier to sit under a tree by Walden Pond and strum some chords on your acoustic guitar than it is to set up a PA (Public Address) system in the same setting. Not nearly as soul-satisfying either, is it?

However in recent years, the acoustic guitar has moved more to the electric guitar side of the playing field. Acoustic guitarists now use electronic pickups and amplification as much as electric guitarists. The processing that some acoustic guitarists use rivals that of many arena-playing rock guitarists. It is easy to become confused with the huge array of equipment and terminology that has suddenly been sprung on the unsuspecting fingerpicker. Piezo pickups, compressors, pre-amps, valves, condenser microphones, magnetic pickup systems and phantom power are terms that are now common place in any discussion of acoustic guitar amplification. In the world of recording and performance, the acoustic guitarist has to be *au fait* with these terms and more so that he/she can know that they are reproducing the sound of their instrument faithfully.

The equipment that turns an acoustic sound (sound waves) into an electrical signal (which can then be transported via cables to an amplifier) is called a *transducer*. These transducers appear in a wide variety of forms, from large condenser microphones, through to magnetic pickups (commonly used on solid body electric guitars) and to undersaddle piezo-electric pickups. This electrical signal needs to pass through a number of stages to process this electrical signal and create an acceptable reproduction of the original acoustic sound.

Magic Crystals: The Piezo Pickup

This system of amplifying acoustic guitars has been in existence for many years. It has become the most popular way to amplify acoustic guitar – particularly in the production-line sector of the market. They are cheap and easy to install and use.

The piezo (pronounced 'pee – *aytz* – oh') pickup converts each note and sound on the acoustic guitar into a small electrical signal. The piezo crystal has a unique property – when it is crushed, even by tiny amounts, it produces a tiny electrical signal. The vibrations of strings pulled taut across the bridge of a guitar, or the vibrations of the soundboard, produce enough of a 'crushing' effect to produce various electrical signals for each and every sound on the instrument. Clever stuff indeed.

They are used in two very different forms:

The Under-Saddle Piezo Pickup

This pickup, in recent years the most common, is usually a thin, flexible ribbon or wire of piezo material which fits under the saddle. The advantages of the under-saddle piezo system are its simple and inexpensive installation. It is virtually invisible, the only visible clue to its presence being a 1/4 inch output jack doubling as a strap button located instead of the end-pin at the bottom of the guitar! Guitarists who prefer to keep their guitar free of extraneous fittings will find this type of pickup aesthetically pleasing. They are feedback-free due to the rigid placement of them under the bridge. They really require no experimentation with placement. Just pop them in and they are ready to go. The disadvantages of this most popular approach to amplifying acoustic guitars are the sound and their inconsistency in response. Although they have improved a lot in recent years, under-saddle piezo pickups are notorious for their plastic tone. They overemphasise the high and upper-mid range of frequencies, reproducing little or none of the instruments 'bottom end' or extremely high 'sparkling' frequencies. A piezo pick-up will always need modification of their frequency output (*Equalisation* or *EQ*) to help them reproduce an acoustic-like tone. They are normally used in conjunction with some type of pre-amp and on-board EQ adjusters. The EQ adjustments that are fitted to many factory fitted pre-amps have very broad settings such as Low, Mid and High. Ideally you would use 32-band graphic equaliser which gives you much more control over the frequencies that are amplified. The inconsistency in the response of these under-saddle piezo pickups means that certain strings will sound louder than others. Even a new set of strings can sometimes change the performance of the pickup.

The main disadvantage of this style of pickup is its inability to reproduce accurately the tone of an acoustic instrument without careful equalisation of the sound. The attack of the sound is usually short and sharp. The piezo pickup reacts mostly to the string vibration and less to the vibrating soundboard and air in the sound box. The sound is therefore a little less natural than other styles of pickup.

The Contact Piezo Pickup

This pickup works on the same principle as the under-saddle – vibrations caused by the strings produce an electrical signal in the piezo crystal. These vibrations occur very significantly on the soundboard of the guitar. The contact pickup is attached to the soundboard and responds to these vibrations. As we discussed in an earlier chapter, the soundboard vibrates in a highly complex way. The placement of a contact pickup is critical to its performance. Usually the bridge plate on the underside of the soundboard is a good place – it is a very strong and feedback-resistant part of the soundboard and is close to the bridge where the strings make contact with the soundboard. They should be fitted on the outside (towards the bottom of the guitar) edge of the bridge plate somewhere between the G and D strings. They also can be fitted to the exterior (top) of the soundboard, although I find it safer and neater to fit them to the underside. In the past many guitarists fitted these pickups to the top of the soundboard, using a sticky putty to attach them. If placed correctly, these pickups produce a very natural tone, and are more consistent in performance than the piezo pickup.

Magnetic Pickups

These pickups are based on the same technology as electric guitar pickups. They use an electro-magnet which produces a magnetic field. This magnetic field detects vibrations of the strings and produces a corresponding electrical signal. These electro-magnetic pickups are normally placed across the soundhole of an acoustic guitar. They can be mounted on the soundboard although this will have the detrimental effect on the vibration of the soundboard as well as requiring significant string clearance.

The placement of these pickups in the soundhole reproduces very different aspects of the sound than the piezo pickup. They tend to produce a fatter tone and are isolated from the vibrating air and soundboard so they are virtually feedback free. Like piezo pickups they need careful equalisation to reproduce an acoustic-like tone. These pickups respond better to steel strings than to bronze. This can result in an unbalanced output although many of the recent developments in magnetic pickups for acoustic guitar have overcome this problem.

The modern electro-magnetic pickups produce a very smooth and even tone that suits very quiet playing or techniques. Normally, they can be used at very high volumes, with careful equalisation. For some players the main disadvantage is the appearance of a relatively large bar of metal across the soundhole. There is very little that can be done about this, although many of the modern systems are very subtle in appearance, their chrome plated ancestors went out of fashion many years ago! The main advantages are the ease of installation and relatively cheap cost. They are commonly combined with some type of pre-amp stage (see below) that improves their tone.

Internal Microphones

Of the various types of pickups discussed so far, these are the most difficult to install. They usually need to be fitted by a qualified repairman or luthier. They will often require phantom power (the mixer or pre-amp you are using has to send power *back* down the guitar cable to the microphone). Without exception, these internal microphones will be condenser microphones and are quite small and subtle, if not invisible due to their location. Condenser microphones work by applying a small voltage across the small gap between two conductive plates. The air in the gap forms a *capacitor*. When soundwaves hit the plates, the distance between the plates varies, producing a change in the voltage. This change translates as a signal which can then be amplified.

The internal microphone has advantages and disadvantages. On the plus side, the sound reproduced by an internal microphone is particularly realistic. It is quite close in quality to the sound created by an externally placed microphone. However, both internal and external microphones are very sensitive to increases in signal gain. They are more prone to feedback, although careful and precise equalisation can help to reduce this risk significantly. Condenser microphones are very sensitive to impacts and bangs and are more easily damaged than other types of microphone.

These types of pickups are very responsive to the natural highs – overtones – in the sound of a guitar string. As a result these internal mics are best used in combination with other types of pickup (see below).

External Microphones

These are by far the most effective at recreating the true sound of an acoustic guitar. In a recording situation they are by far the best option. However, there are inherent problems with this type of 'pickup'.

The main disadvantage is the difficulty in correct microphone placement. If you are the type of player who stands and moves while you perform, this solution to your amplification needs will be the least satisfactory. Even a small deviation from the original placement will produce highly significant changes in the performance of the microphone and the quality of the sound.

Even relatively medium quality microphones are more expensive than some of the higher quality under-saddle pickups.

External microphones are notoriously difficult to equalise and will almost always produce feedback at higher volumes. While some guitarists may want to suffer these disadvantages in the pursuit of high quality sound reproduction, the impracticalities usually outweigh the benefits.

Pickup Combinations
A 3D Approach To Acoustic Guitar Amplification

As you will have realised from the above descriptions, each type of pickup has strengths in different parts of the sound spectrum. Some combination of the above transducers will have a synergistic effect – the combination will produce an effect greater than the sum of the parts. An obvious combination is the internal microphone and under-saddle piezo pickup. Various manufacturers produce this combination. The internal microphone captures many of the natural features of the air and wood of the guitar while the under-saddle pickup deals with the direct string vibration. The internal microphone will pick up many of the aspects of a guitar tone that the piezo ignores. The internal microphone adds a very 'real' dimension to the sound.

Another common combination is the magnetic soundhole pickup and internal microphone. The magnetic has a warmer and smoother sound than the under-saddle piezo-electric pickup and is complimented by the ability of the internal microphone to capture many of the upper overtones and the sparkle of the acoustic guitar.

The issue of acoustic guitar amplification always centres on *equalisation*. Each signal from an acoustic guitar has a particular set of characteristics that require individual equalisation. However, for most practical situations, you cannot have a lead coming from each and every different pickup in the guitar and process each individually. Most factory-fitted pickup combinations will allow you to set a balance between the two signals. You can choose, for example, to have more internal microphone than piezo, although the pre-amp will combine the signals and only allow you to equalise the combined signal. This is not ideal but obviously better than having only one signal. Ideally the signals could be separated and treated individually.

Pre-amplifiers

Pre-amps boost the relatively weak and high-impedance signal of a guitar pickup so that it can survive the journey through a long cable to the power amplifier. Without the assistance of a pre-amp, the signal is too fragile to reach the mixer or power amplifier effectively. Many factory built guitars these days are produced with a piezo and pre-amp already installed. All pre-amps will 'colour' the tone of the signal to some degree. This colouration is usually preset by the electronic circuitry of the pre-amp. The colouration of the tone is achieved by filtering certain frequencies and enhancing or damping them. Some pre-amps offer the guitarist a certain amount of tone control in the form of a control panel mounted on the top side of the guitar. Many guitar pickups will have an internally mounted pre-amp which is usually no bigger than a matchbox and powered by a 9v battery. The output of most pre-amps is 'line-level' which means that it can be handled by most mixers and amplifiers. Pre-amps vary in size from the small internally mounted pre-amps to large complex, rack mounted units with sophisticated signal-modifying ability and equalisation. These larger units can often take a number of inputs from separate pickups – offering an opportunity to blend signals optimally before sending the signal to the amplifier. There are numerous 'stomp box' style units or microphone-stand mounted units that are reasonably priced and make an enormous difference to the quality of the signal being sent to the power amplifier.

DI Boxes

These simple devices are used to convert the high impedance output of a pickup and its pre-amp to a low impedance signal which can be sent long distances to a house PA system or mixing desk. The cable from the DI (Direct Injection) box to the mixer–amplifier is normally a *balanced* (with three pins) one which will help to eliminate any hum or radio interference normally experienced with cheaper unbalanced cables. These days the DI box has evolved into a unit that is similar to the floor mounted pre-

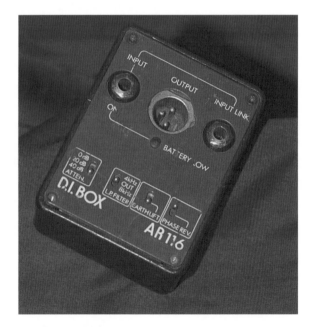

Example 7.1: DI box

amp. They now offer more features and degrees of tone control than older DI boxes.

Equalisers

An equaliser is a unit which takes the signal from an instrument and allows the user to control the behaviour of some or many of the numerous frequencies the signal contains. Some equalisers are very simple, such as those found on the front panel of many home-stereo systems. These simple equalisers will normally have a Bass and Treble (and occasionally a Middle) control. The frequency being controlled is preset and the knobs allow you to increase or decrease the volume of that frequency. Slightly more advanced are the Five-band EQ systems found on home-stereos which allow you to control the amount of five pre-set frequencies covering a wide spectrum of the audible range. These types of units don't give the user any accurate control to select 'problem frequencies'.

In a live performance situation every room is different. The shape and volume of the room affects how the sound in that room is perceived. Certain frequencies will be exaggerated by the room while others will be soaked up and disappear. The materials used in the construction and decoration of any room can radically affect the listeners perception of sound. Hard flat surfaces tend to reflect and bounce back the higher frequencies, while other surfaces and shapes may absorb the low-mid range of the sound. Fill that room with an audience and the sound is once again affected!

There are two types of equaliser. The *graphic equaliser* is a set of slider-control buttons, each corresponding to a particular frequency. The more sliders, the more control you have. The picture below shows a 31-band equaliser (as stereo model with controls for the left and right images in a stereo field).

The graphic equaliser shown in Example 7.2 has slider controls for frequencies as low as 20Hz (or 20 vibrations per second – very deep!) to 20,000Hz (20kHz) – close to the extremes of human hearing. The slider works in a volume range of +12 decibels down to -12 decibels (Db). There are also controls to the left which allow certain frequencies to be cut. These 'cut' controls appear in the form of the *parametric equaliser*. With a parametric equaliser you can select a precise frequency and boost or cut it as far as necessary. Parametric equalisers are useful for selecting a particular frequency, particularly ones that are causing feedback and controlling them. The parametric equaliser is very useful for this type of precision control while graphic equalisers offer a more general style of control and are often easier to use in performance situations.

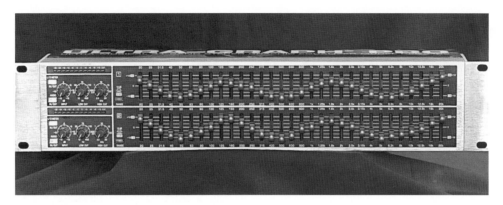

Example 7.2: Graphic equaliser

Feedback

Although used to great effect by certain electric guitarists, feedback is normally not welcome in the context of acoustic guitar. Every guitar with its unique combination of shape, size and construction material will have certain resonant frequencies that are prone to feedback. Feedback is where the 'input' (the guitar signal) and the output (the sound from the speaker) forms a closed loop. In simple terms, the sound from the speakers is strong enough to cause the guitar top to vibrate at certain sensitive frequencies. This vibration is amplified again and again forming a continuous loop which sounds like a screeching hum. Imagine a cat chasing its tail!

As it is only one particular frequency or two that are the source of the feedback, an equaliser in the loop will help to select and control that frequency. These frequencies are typically between 100Hz and 200Hz for a flat top acoustic guitar.

'Gain' in the amplification part of the loop is a critical factor when controlling feedback. The relative positions of the input and output signals are also a factor. What follows is a description of a typical setup for a solo guitar and vocal performance.

Stage Setups

It is important for the speakers to be positioned far enough forward of the source signal so that the sound emanating from them will not reach the acoustic guitar (and any other input signal such as a vocal microphone). This arrangement will have its own drawbacks. The musician will most likely need to hear the sound of their instrument and voice. With the speakers facing away from them, it is necessary to re-

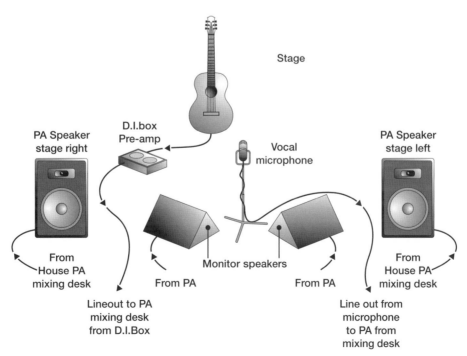

Stage

PA Speaker stage right

D.I.box Pre-amp

Vocal microphone

PA Speaker stage left

From House PA mixing desk

From PA

Monitor speakers

From PA

From House PA mixing desk

Lineout to PA mixing desk from D.I.Box

Line out from microphone to PA from mixing desk

Example 7.3: Typical stage setup

route some of the output *back* towards the musician. Some type of monitoring system is needed. This can be in the form of speakers set up on the stage area or a more personal monitoring system such as in-ear monitoring systems. Of course the floor mounted monitor speakers themselves can produce enough sound to create a feedback loop. It is unlikely however, that the monitor volume level needs to be set at the same volume as the PA speakers facing the audience. In an ideal situation the monitor signal will also have an equaliser somewhere in the 'chain'.

These mixers tend to combine in one handy unit many features already discussed. They vary from 4 to 12 channels and can handle that number of independent signal sources simultaneously. Each channel typically has its own EQ controls and its own gain and volume controls. There can be additional features such as auxiliary channels through which effects like reverb and chorus can be added. There may be overall EQ controls to finely tune the output of all the combined signals, pan buttons to move any one signal across the stereo field, as well as frequency-cut buttons and more. Many will also have some phantom power which can be used to power internal microphones.

Where a guitarist is using multiple signals (such as those from a combination of pickups), a small onstage mixing desk gives the musician a lot of control over the mix and tone of those sounds. The output signal from many of these small mixers is a balanced and low impedance signal which doesn't require a DI box.

Example 7.4: Typical live mixer

Soundcheck Fundamentals And Etiquette

The soundcheck I am going to discuss is the very typical style of soundcheck that you will encounter in acoustic clubs and venues, singer-songwriter events, small theatres and arts centres. These venues vary in seating capacity from 30 to 300 and this is where the majority of artists operate from in their early careers and beyond.

Most of these venues will offer some type of PA system. You should be warned that the quality of both the equipment and the operator (often called a *sound engineer,*

although that term is sometimes applied very loosely!) will vary enormously from venue to venue. In all cases the PA will comprise three main components:

- Speakers (usually a pair set up in stereo)

- A power amp from as low as 100 watts of power to 1000w and beyond in some venues (this amplifies the sound)

- A mixing desk which processes and manages the signals from the performer and their instrument. The signal from the desk goes to the amplifier and from there to the speakers.

In smaller venues the power amp and mixer may be a small combined unit with very basic equalisation controls.

Any venue providing a sound system will also provide a minimum number of basic microphones and stands. You can also expect them to provide DI boxes (if required) and all the required cabling for the sound system. Don't expect them to provide guitar cables, although many will have a supply of relatively inexpensive ones.

There are various 'extras' that will form part of the sound system as you move to bigger venues. These may include:

- 'Outboard' gear like reverb units, compressor units, equalisation, and multi-effects units

- Stage monitors

- Recording facilities for recording performances

One of the first rules is to establish a good working relationship with the sound engineer. He will be responsible for your sound and ultimately has a great effect on the audiences perception and enjoyment of your music. Get on 'first name' terms with him or her (and in my experience *female* sound engineers are among the best in the business – they *have* to be in order to compete in the male-dominated music industry!). Addressing the engineer more personally when making requests during the soundcheck will make the whole process go more smoothly.

No matter how many performances you have done, it is more likely that the engineer is more familiar with the process than you. The venue is *their* territory. They are more familiar with the various quirks of the performance area and the sound equipment, so bow to their experience. This, however, is not to demean your own experience. You are the other half of the equation. There is no soundcheck without *you* the artist. And nobody knows your musical material better than you. Learn to trust your ears and instinct.

Sound behaves peculiarly in confined spaces. Any two rooms are likely to be radically different in terms of their sound. Parallel surfaces will set up standing waves, whereas balconies will reflect the sound. Hard floor surfaces will affect the sound one way, while a 'red seat' theatre with plush carpet will affect it another way. The length, breadth, height, shape and construction of the performance area, the position of the speakers and the position of the engineer as they process the sound all affect the sound dramatically. A member of the audience in the front row is going to have

a different aural experience of your music than someone in the balcony or in the back row of the stalls. A good engineer will maximise the quality of each of these people's experience.

Your *own* experience of the sound will differ from that of any member of the audience. As a performer you will have a different agenda than the audience. Your position in the room – normally on some raised platform – gives your ears a different perspective on the sound. Trust that the engineer will be able to deliver the sound equally well to all parts of the room. In my own experience, once the sound on stage is good, I let go and give the engineer the trust to do his job well. If the engineer enjoys your music, it makes their job easier, although any engineer worth discussing will have had many years of experience in engineering music that isn't necessarily to their taste.

Have an effective mode of operation during soundcheck. The sound engineer is primarily interested in *tone* and *dynamics*. In that light you should run through your quietest number and your loudest. If you are going to change instruments during your performance, don't forget to soundcheck that too. You know your material and performance style better than anyone, so think carefully about what the sound engineer needs to hear. There may be moments where the guitar is very quiet but the vocal needs to be very loud or vice versa. Put yourself in the engineer's shoes – he doesn't know your material so he needs to know the extremes to which it will travel. Most engineers will be very experienced, so unless you are truly unlike anything he has ever heard before, he will be using his intuition to anticipate your needs, particularly during the performance itself.

Your Equipment

We will discuss equipment maintenance in another chapter but for the moment it should be mentioned that your guitar and any accessories need to be in good working order. No matter how good an engineer is, there is nothing they can do to improve the tone of a low quality instrument, old strings, buzzing capos or faulty pickups. Equally they can not do much to improve the sound of a player with poor tone and technique. I remember fondly a situation some years ago where an act who were opening for me were on stage going through their soundcheck. (It is normal practice in many venues for the opening support act to soundcheck last so that their equipment stay in place for their performance.) The bassist was having a particularly difficult time communicating his requests clearly to the sound engineer. He was obviously not pleased with the sound that the engineer was creating for him and asked the engineer to 'make it sound more funky!' – to which the engineer muttered under his breath 'Well, why don't you go and get some funk bass lessons then!' Some musicians put too much faith in equipment to produce the sound that they want. The sound starts with you and your instrument. Once that is sounding as you want, the engineer's job is a lot easier.

What To Bring To A Performance

It is difficult to say which equipment you should bring to a performance – venues vary from one to another. Here is a general list for you to pick and choose from.

- Guitar (and a spare if you intend using different tunings)
- Guitar amplifier and stand (if you use one)
- Guitar stand
- Pre-amp
- Power supply and batteries for any electronic equipment
- Spare strings
- Tuner
- Capo
- Plectrums/thumb picks if you use them
- Strap
- Guitar cables and spares
- Foot stool (if you use one)

For extra comfort and security you could also bring one or all of these items:

- A direct box
- A small personal mixer
- A quality vocal microphone with cable and boom (adjustable) stand
- A multi effects processor for the guitar

If you are performing regularly, you may want to consider bringing along promotional material and merchandise. Promotional material might include:

- Details of other upcoming performances
- Short biographies with contact details for you or your agent
- Mailing list forms for audience members to complete
- Souvenir postcards/pictures with details of your website

Merchandise is a way for artists to supplement their performance fee and it also acts as a promotional tool. In the early stages it could be sales of your home recordings on CD or cassette tape. As you develop your act you may feel that a full album is more appropriate. Defining your image with a catchy logo or trademark can be a way to focus your self promotion. Using a logo in a fashionable way on clothing can broaden the range of merchandise and will increase the possible funds that your merchandise stall will generate.

The Art Of Stage Performance

'Without a good listener, even the best performer is useless. And if a performer is not a good listener, the performance is useless.'

– *Mickey Hart, The Grateful Dead*

A performance on any public platform is an opportunity for communication. The communication is in the form of music transmitted through the musician to the audience. The communication cannot happen if one or both parties are not committed to communicating. Communication requires skilled transmission and reception.

Of course very often the transmission goes in one ear and out the other, even that of the performer himself! People listen to music for many reasons – for purely aesthetic reasons, to feel good, to worship, to reminisce, to dance, to find hope, to be inspired, to be woken up, to be put to sleep and for ceremony.

For these many reasons and more, people listen to music to receive but also to give. In my own experience, any performance which is not sincere is not valid. Somebody on a stage holding a musical instrument and playing the 'right' notes in the 'right' order with the 'right' equipment and wearing the 'right' shirt cannot automatically move an audience to laugh, cry, dance or to dream. However, a musician playing the 'wrong' notes in the 'wrong' order with the 'wrong' equipment and 'wrong' shirt, but with the right intention and right spirit, can change the world.

Let's Get Real

Now that the sermon has ended, let's look at some more practical guidelines to performing:

- Always turn up well in advance of your performance time.

- Familiarise yourself with the stage area and venue.

- If there is a sound engineer, learn their name – you'll be using it a lot.

- Make sure that all your equipment is in working order and that you have all the spare accessories you need – strings, strap, capo, tuner, stand and leads.

- Think about which kind of audience and venue you will be performing to and answer the following questions:

- Is it a sit down 'listening' audience, or more like a 'bar' audience who may talk and drink as you perform?

- Is there a cover charge? If people are paying to see you, they will have a different attitude to an audience who are just passing through.

- Are you the main act or an opening act? If you are an opening act you should tailor your set so that the audience can appreciate you rather than alienating them and the main act.

- Is this your first time at this venue or is it a regular 'gig'? If this is a weekly or other regular gig, you should consider varying your set from night to night. Why not present at least one new song each time you play? If it is your first performance for that audience, do a set which will attract the widest range of people and possibly encourage them to see you again.

Performance Tips

- **Look directly at the audience.** Even if they haven't paid to see you, they are still listening. Remember it's about *communication*. You know what it feels like when someone is talking to you and they don't look at you as they speak. Give the audience that small amount of respect. They will give it back to you. Likewise they will hand back any disrespect that you show them. Dress appropriately for the venue and the material. You are a complete package of audio and visual stimuli! How you look and move on stage should connect with the material you are playing. Singing a song about 'why she left me' when you are dressed like a sack of potatoes and looking at the ground as you sing, might bring you a few sympathy votes but will probably lose most of the audience. They may well decide to let you know before you've got to the chorus! The simple solution is to be yourself and be comfortable but remember that people are looking up to you on stage, and while you don't need to dress like you are on the Milan catwalk, make sure that you are pleasing to the eye!

- **Project your sound to the back of the audience.** Don't just play to the person in the front row. When I perform for an audience I make myself aware of every part of the room and where the audience are within that space. I then play beyond those edges to encompass the whole audience in sound. The better your equipment and the better the sound engineer, the easier that will be.

- **Arrange the order of your musical set with the audience and venue in mind.** If the audience is 'yours' you may not feel obliged to grab them with a strong up tempo number – it's interesting how a more subdued piece can draw the audience in towards you. Hit them hard with the second number! If the set is short (where you are the opening act for example) then present a representative but contrasting set. Think of the variety of keys, textures, tempos, lyrical subject matter and energy levels that your material has. Use these categories to choose an interesting set for that performance. Choose interesting cover versions to break up the impact of all your own original material. Remember that you can make a cover song your own in the way you treat it. Take it in under your skin and then give it back to the audience. If you succeed, they will remember you. But be warned, if you fail they may also remember you!

- **Speak to the audience in between numbers.** Use your taste and instinct to gauge how much is appropriate. Keep it lightly humorous. The audience are at your gig to get away from their everyday routine. You and your music provide an escape for them. You have a responsibility to them. The audience often enjoy extra context to the music they are hearing. However, segueing songs or pieces together can be very effective. Look at your material carefully and try to spot the opportunities that it presents. Key changes from one song to the next can be very effective. Speaking between those songs can break the flow of energy created in those songs. Cover versions can be most effective when not introduced. However, it is usually good policy to at least name them once you have finished your rendition. Unless it's 'Happy Birthday' then don't expect every one to know your choice of cover tunes.

- **Thank the audience for coming.** Gently remind them about merchandise (but don't overdo it!) and your mailing list. If you are pleased with the efforts of the sound engineer, thank him publicly too. Then close with your final number. If you are the main act, then be gracious and accept the call for an encore if it comes. However, (and this is important!) if you are the opening act, do not let a call for an encore distract you from your role. Your job in that situation is to open for the main act, not take away from the amount of time that they can play (sometimes a curfew will mean the main act has to finish promptly) and you may come across as arrogantly 'stealing the show'. If the main act is gracious enough then they may invite you on at the very end for a duet. Otherwise, be pleased in the knowledge that you have won over another artists audience and put it down to experience.

After The Show

I have always found it useful and enjoyable to interact with the audience after every show. I will generally need a few minutes alone to gather myself, catch my breath and settle down before I do that, but wherever possible I will make my way to the audience area and greet them informally. There will always be people who want to give back to you in the form of praise and thanks. Be gracious and accept their gift for what it is. Many times a member of the audience has approached me and begun: *'I know that you've heard this many time before but I really enjoyed.....'* I always accept their thanks graciously and take it inside and hold onto it. To turn a ancient proverb on its head, 'It is better to give *and* receive.'

The universal law of dynamic exchange tells us that giving and receiving are different aspects of the flow of energy in the universe. Some people may also want to ask about particular songs, techniques, tunings and your equipment. Very often they have to pluck up some courage to ask you, so be aware of them.

On bigger shows it is not so easy to 'meet and greet' the audience, although I will make the dressing room available for a short while once the bulk of the audience have left the venue. Genuine well-wishers will make the effort to see you.

Criticism, Compliments And Fragile Egos

When you put yourself in a performance area and share your music, talent and energy with people, you are at the same time offering up your music for interpretation, appreciation and analysis by the audience. Each person will hear your music through their own 'filter' of experience, taste, knowledge, intelligence and self awareness. As we know, this can vary enormously from person to person. That does not mean that your music will have a completely different effect on each audience member. They may well all hear your music in broadly the same way with subtle variations. Each will have some sort of opinion of their feelings about your music and lyrics. These feelings are totally valid given that each person is recognising those feeling through their own 'filter'. However, when that person then decides to tell you about those feelings, they go through another 'filter' – yours. Here is where things start to get complicated. As the subject of their analysis, you can become very vulnerable. One of the traps that we performers can fall into, is believing that the analysis of our music is

an analysis of us. So, when someone compliments or criticises our music, we tend to take it *personally*. Some people are so tactless and ignorant that they make their compliments and criticisms *sound* personal. I want to give you a few tips about dealing with complements and criticisms.

Our ego is our false sense of ourselves. The ego is built up with all the things that we feel constitute the royal 'I' – our name, personality, our job, our status, our music, our equipment, our credit cards, house and friends. Of course these things are a part of us, so when someone insults our car, they are insulting us, when the compliment our home, they are naturally complimenting us. When the criticise our choice of friends or partner, they are criticising us, and when they compliment our songs, they are complimenting us. Do you see where this is leading? Pretty soon your sense of yourself is a series of compliments and criticisms of 'you'. The truth, of course, is that all of these things that make up 'you' can be changed or gone in a moment. Everything.

In my experience it is best to accept a compliment or criticism graciously but also try to recognise the true nature of that compliment or criticism. What is behind it? Here are a few thoughts for you:

There are three types of criticism:

- Criticism from someone who is ill-informed and inexperienced to properly judge and comment on your music – the 'armchair' critic.

- Criticism from someone who wants to get something from you. They may want to put you down to feel better about themselves or to create a situation where they can gain something from criticising you. These people are self-serving.

- Criticism from someone who wants to help you to grow and become better at what you do. These people are teaching you.

You will appreciate that there are also three types of compliment:

- Compliment from someone who is ill-informed and inexperienced to properly judge and comment on your music – the 'armchair complimenter'.

- Compliment from someone who wants to get something from you. They may want to build you up to make you feel better about them and so create a situation where they can gain something from complimenting you. These people are self-serving.

- Compliment from someone who wants to help you to grow and become better at what you do. These people are teaching you.

The trick, every time, is to recognise what lies behind the criticism or compliment. In my experience it will be clearly be coming from one of these three places. I have come across all of these varieties in my years as a performer. It can be difficult though. Bob Dylan was criticised heavily in the '60s when he switched from acoustic guitar to electric. The loudest and most vociferous criticism came from those who didn't want to open their ears and hearts to what Dylan wanted to explore. They wanted the 'old' Dylan for themselves. In their selfishness they criticised him. Through his strength, self-awareness and knowing his truth, Bob Dylan did what he had to do – grow.

Learn to accept all compliments and criticisms with grace but also learn how to 'file' them. Keep your ears and heart open for the teachers who will help you to grow and deepen into your art. Those teachers don't necessarily know that they are teaching – they are doing the only thing that comes naturally and that is *giving*.

Recording Your Music

Recording acoustic guitar is not easy. Capturing the sound of an acoustic guitar requires a good pair of ears, some reasonably decent (although not necessarily very expensive) microphones and lots of experimenting. It will also require a good recording space, as well as a decent instrument. If an instrument sounds bad acoustically, it may well record very badly too. I will give you the golden rules of acoustic guitar recording a little later on.

One of the main problems in the recording of acoustic guitar is the excessiveness of particular frequencies at different points on the soundboard. The placement of the microphone or microphones is critical. In fact, an inch in either direction can make a radical difference to the sound that the microphone picks up. With different types of construction, tone woods and size, every guitar will require a unique approach. Ask four different sound engineers how they would approach an acoustic guitar recording session and, if you are lucky to get an answer, you will probably get four (or more!) different ones. However, it's most likely that their answers will centre on the tried and tested stereo miking approach.

Up Close And Personal

The miking of acoustic guitar is generally best achieved using 'close miking'. This is where the microphone is placed between 6 and 12 inches from the guitar. You should ideally use directional condenser mics, preferably cardioid (uni-directional). These microphones are best able to deal with the excessive bass frequencies that emanate from the guitar.

The following methods are based on the use of two microphones set up in stereo.

Spaced Microphone Placement

Place the microphones at the same height spaced apart. One is pointing at the 12th fret and the other pointing just behind the bridge. There is a simple rule in miking techniques. The '3 to 1' rule says that the distance between the two microphones should be at least three times the distance that each microphone is from the sound source. This helps in the elimination of phase cancellations (which occurs when the same sound reaches two different points at different times – like when it reaches two different microphones at different times). The microphones will then pick up the sound at different points in the phase of the wave cycle. The placement of the microphones is critical in the elimination of this effect. Using the '3 to 1' rule, if the microphones are placed 6 inches from the guitar, they should be at least 18 inches away from each other.

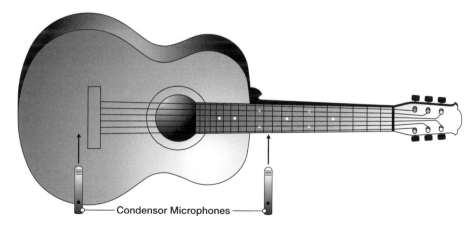

— Condensor Microphones —

Example 7.5: Spaced microphone placement

Coincident Microphone Placement

This method involves placing the microphones with their tips almost touching. The connector (rear) end of the microphones are angled at approximately a right angle (90 degrees). They can be positioned around the 12th fret. Because they are so close, you will eliminate any 'phasing' that could occur if they were further apart. As they are pointing in different directions each microphone will emphasise a different range of frequencies. The microphone pointing up towards the nut will capture the higher frequencies and overtones, while the microphone pointing in the direction of the bridge will emphasise the bass end frequencies. By placing the microphones about 6–8 inches from the 12th fret, they will both act to in a way that reduces the overemphatic recording of the mid-range frequencies.

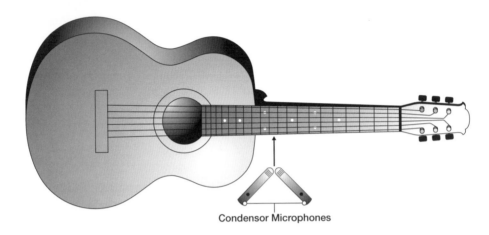

Condensor Microphones

Example 7.6: Coincident microphone placement

This style of miking will produce a far narrower stereo image of the acoustic guitar, but it can add a warmer, more natural sound to the acoustic guitar. Of course, with so many variables such as the room size and resonance, the microphone type and placement, the instrument, the player and the music, the key word here is *experimentation*.

Microphones And Recording Acoustic Guitar

Assuming that you will want to record in stereo, you will need two microphones. Over the years it has been discovered that condenser microphones offer the best choice for acoustic guitar recordings. There are numerous styles of condenser microphones, many requiring phantom power. Smaller condenser microphones (those with a diaphragm diameter less than 2.5cm) will capture a very detailed sound. Where possible, select a microphone that will have a 'cardioid' setting – many good condenser microphones will have a selector switch to adjust the microphones field of response. A cardioid setting will cause the microphone to only record what is directly in front of it, while ignoring much of the sound around it and behind it. By using these cardioid (that is, uni-directional) settings on a pair of microphones you can more effectively create a stereo image of the guitar.

Larger condenser microphones (those with a diaphragm diameter less than 2.5cm) will produce a warmer and rounder sound due to the slower reaction of the diaphragm. They are in fact, more commonly used as vocal microphones, as they can warmly colour the sound on its path to the recording.

Ambient Microphones

If the room or space in which you are recording adds some quality to the sound of your instrument, it may be worthwhile placing a mic further back from the instrument, between 8 and 12 feet. This microphone will capture the sound of the guitar as it is reflected around the room. If possible, send this signal to a separate channel on your recorder. This will give you more choice at the mixing stage. It will give you some natural reverb to bring into the mix.

Golden Rules For Recording Acoustic Guitar

• Invest in the best condenser microphone (or preferably *pair* of condenser microphones) that you can afford.

• Find the sweet spots on your guitar. Simply ask a friend to play your instrument, get down on your knees and move your ear around the soundhole, bridge and neck area to locate the best sounding spots on your instrument. Make a note of them, as these are the best places for a microphone.

- Use some type of compressor to control the peaks in the guitar output.

- Use new, or nearly new strings. For a brighter sound try a lower gauge.

- Many acoustic guitars suffer from a 'boominess' which can ruin a recording. This low-end boom usually resides in the 100–300Hz area. Try pulling out frequencies in this low-mid part of the spectrum.

Once you are satisfied that the recorded sound is as good as possible, concentrate on giving a good performance. It is far better to have an average recording of a great performance than a great recording of an average performance.

Leave as much time as is practical between the *recording* process and the *mixing* process. Ideally you should get a night's sleep before attempting to mix a recording. However, time and cost constraints may have to be considered. They are two different stages that require two different hats.

Mixing

This stage is very important. You may have a great performance on tape (or hard disc), and be pleased with the quality of the recording. That recording needs to be polished and shaped so that it can be used.

The main considerations at the mixing stage are:

- **Equalisation** – Balancing the relative levels of the many frequencies. The more sophisticated your equalisation controls, the greater control you have. At this stage you are concerned with reproducing the sound of an acoustic guitar in the monitors. You have an opportunity at this stage to be very experimental and creative.

- **Effects** – You may want to process the sound of the guitar to create a certain mood or atmosphere. Effects such as *chorus* can help to gently thicken the sound of the guitar. *Reverb* can be used to recreate the sense of different size recording spaces from a small bathroom size reverb to a huge cathedral.

- **Levels** – If there are different instruments, or even different signal sources for a solo instrument, you will need to find the correct balance between their volumes. Careful

choice of EQ and reverb settings can also help to subtly adjust the levels. You will also want to consider the overall volume level of the music. If it is set too high, the sound may start to distort. If it is set too low, there will be a poor ratio between the system noise and the music.

At this stage you may be ready to commit this recording to a CD or master tape. One final stage – *mastering* – can be the final polish and adjustment of the track. Depending on the nature and quality of your project, you may choose to skip this stage. Unless the recording has been made on very high quality recording equipment, the mastering stage could be wasted.

Some Final Thoughts On Recording

As we move on through the 21st century, with technology developing at an exponential rate, it can be hard to reconcile the simple activity of music-making with banks of processors and hard disc recording machines. However, at the very heart of the relationship between art and technology, is our human need to express ourselves. We continue to build tools to help us to be more efficient and more productive. Recording technology is no different. In the early days of recording there was a closer link between the act of music performance and the art of sound recording. For many years, although the technology improved, a musician went into a room with a microphone and gave the best performance that they could. Groups of musicians would give multiple performances of the same song until the producer was satisfied that they had a good recording, or a good 'take'. However with the invention of multi-track recording (of which *Sergeant Pepper's* by The Beatles is an early example), musicians could record at different times, and indeed different locations. Tape editing became even more sophisticated and the complexity of recording production increased a hundred fold. Producers began to realise enormous soundscapes and productions, and musicians had the opportunity to make endless attempts to get the perfect take. Most famous of all in studio lore perhaps are Steely Dan who would spend endless months on a single song. They were notorious for putting their studio musicians under great pressure to provide as close to perfect a performance as possible.

As digital technology and the compact disc replaced the older analog and vinyl media, the standards of recording rose even higher. Musicians were put under even greater pressure to give flawless performances. In the popular music sector of the recording industry, this led to a degree of blandness in recordings. The synchronisation of rhythms to time-codes and over-processing of the sounds left many recordings sounding lifeless.

At the time of writing, the industry is swinging back to more 'organic' methods of recording and business. The internet is changing the way people buy and distribute music. Singer-songwriters, who a few years ago were effectively locked out of the industry, have found a channel to make themselves heard.

The recording process and the art of performance, while related, are and always will be very different. A performance happens and disappears where a recording (audio or visual) is more like a photograph. You can return to it again and again. All its character – warts and all – can be experienced over and over. It is important to give your best at the recording stage. Once the track is mastered, the picture is set. In the words of Philip Sudo in his book *Zen Guitar*, 'What do you want [the recordings] to say about yourself? Will they inspire those yet unborn? Consider this deeply before you commit yourself to record. Then, when the red recording light goes on, be in it with your whole self.'

8 DO UNTO OTHERS...

Instrument Selection, Maintenance And Care

'Take care of the little things and the big things will take care of themselves.'

– Anonymous

Choosing A Life Partner

For most of you, your relationship with your instrument is very personal. You probably spent a reasonable amount of time, effort and money in the purchase of it. You may even have consulted friends, guitar teachers and even professional players in the selection process. However, just picking up a guitar 'off the peg' in your local store, or for that matter a handbuilt instrument from a renowned luthier is no guarantee that the instrument will be a perfect match for your style and technique. Every guitar, in a respectable guitar store, will have been given a very general 'set up'. The set up will normally consist of setting the intonation, string height, truss rod tension, fitting and tuning in new strings and other smaller touches. The guitar is then ready to be picked up and played by numerous different players throughout each day of business. This style of set up is designed to allow the guitar to appeal to as wide a variety of players and styles as possible. However when you select a guitar from a guitar store, you need to keep this in mind. It's rather like shopping for a new apartment – you need to be able to visualise the property beyond the horrible wallpaper, carpet and furnishing that were the taste of the previous owner. Now that might seem a little harsh on our friendly guitar store repair man, but there is such a wide range of styles and techniques that any one guitar is not necessarily going to appeal to two different players. Some guitarists, for example, those coming from a rock guitar background, will probably not enjoy playing heavy gauge strings, while a guitarist who normally plays a nylon string guitar may not find extra light strings easy to play. Similarly, the height of the string above the fretboard action will vary according to a player's taste and experience.

I am often asked by guitarists which criteria I use when selecting a guitar. There are some general criteria I will have in mind even before I select an instrument:

- **Guitar shape and size** – There is a world of difference between a 'dreadnought' style instrument and a smaller 'parlour' type guitar. They each have a different relationship to your body and your style of posture. They generally have very different tones and dynamics, although with the explorations in bracing these days, it is more difficult to generalise. Do you want a cutaway? If your style involves (or may one day involve) single notes played high up on the fingerboard, then you should consider an instrument with a cutaway. Cutaways can be put in later on, but are very expensive, and are uneconomical on cheaper instruments.

- **Tone wood and construction material** – As the supply of traditional tone woods diminishes, guitar builders and luthiers are turning to less traditional tone woods to create their instruments. Woods such as spruce, cedar, mahogany, rosewood and walnut have been used for decades and are becoming rarer and more expensive for guitar use. Woods such as cypress (for flamenco), maple, redwood, koa (from Hawaii), paduk (an African hardwood) and cherry are more and more common. The soundboard can be a solid piece of wood (a 'solid top') or a laminated top (similar to plywood – where three or sometimes more thin layers of wood are bound together to form a guitar soundboard). The laminate top will always have a inferior sound to the solid top (assuming of course that the soundboards are intelligently braced!). Each tone wood and all the various combinations will have characteristic tones. In general a spruce top, with its tighter grain, has a brighter sound than cedar. In general rosewood, used for back and sides has a deeper bass and a crisper high end than mahogany which is not as 'brilliant' due to its lighter weight. (Remember that tone is highly subjective, as variables like guitar shape, tone woods, string gauge, tension and a musician's technique all affect it.)

- **Brand reputation** – Again this can be highly subjective. All of the world's greatest guitarists play every recognisable guitar brand. The search is for an instrument that suits *you*. A Martin guitar will *never* sound like a Lowden guitar and vice versa. Therefore it is good to have a general idea of how the main brands differ. You will find that many of the lesser known brands tend to be derivatives of these older established brands. It is important to remember though that just because a particular brand is played by a world class player and has a history dating back over a century, does not necessarily mean that you will like it or that it will suit your style of playing. There is a particular series of guitars made in the 1970s by the largest Japanese guitar company, that are comparable to many 'vintage' flat top guitars. These 'freaks' had a particular combination of tone wood, shape and bracing to produce a classic sound. Once every few years I come across one, and normally the owner is unaware of the high quality of their instrument. These guitars were, and still are, produced and sold relatively cheaply, although they have never since reproduced this 'freak' range of guitars! While generally you will see a correlation between price and quality, buyer beware! I have been less than impressed with the output of one of the world's leading brands in the past ten years and have seen numerous luthiers spring up all over the place with incredible instruments.

Once I have generally fixed on a guitar shape, tone wood combination and brand, I go shopping! All the time, remaining flexible – you never know what surprises await you.

Once I have an instrument in my hands, all logic and planning go out the window! It is down to simple touch and emotion. At this point I am interested in only two things in this order:

- **The shape and feel of the neck** – The neck is one of the main points of contact with the instrument. Here you select your notes and chords. Here your left hand (or fretting hand) will be permanently fixed. It has to feel right. If your left hand is uncomfortable then the whole experience is uncomfortable.

- **The tone of the instrument when *I* play it** – Almost immediately my attention turns to the tone of the instrument as I play it. The important point here is what the tone sounds like when I play the guitar *myself*. It is not much use hearing what the store salesman sounds like when he plays it. It is a good guide, but ultimately the tone is a result of *your* technique and approach on the guitar. Having passed the neck and tone test I can turn my attention to other features such as pickups, saddle buttons, oh yes … and price! I am a firm believer that if you shop around you can find a great guitar that suits you and your style for reasonable money ($700-$1200). Of course once you get into more expensive tone woods and quality of workmanship, the price rises accordingly. Any guitar less than $700 may start to show signs of poor workmanship, cheaper tone woods and less than adequate construction. Again these are generalisations to which I have seen every exception!

And don't forget that you most certainly will want the guitar set up specifically for you. You can make suggestions to the store repairman regarding you string preference and tension, string action and tone. It will take some time, months probably, for you to discover how the instrument should best be set. It is extremely useful to build a working relationship with a reputable repairman who is familiar with your style of playing and preferences. I found one almost ten years ago and will only use him exclusively. In this way he can work more effectively without having to continually find out what I require. You can think of it as something like the relationship you might have with an osteopath or chiropractor. In the first visit you will spend the first 30 minutes covering your medical history and details. Only then can the body worker move on and begin to treat your ailments. If you continually change from one chiropractor to another, you will spend a lot of time and money as you go over your medical history. In my case I only have to leave my instrument with my guitar repairman who knows what work needs to be done!

Changing Your Strings

Some of the questions I am asked most frequently are about strings – which brand, which type, coated or uncoated, how often do I change them, and what is the best way to change strings. Changing and maintaining strings is one of the most direct and simplest ways that a guitarist can improve the performance of their instrument.

Which Brand?

Like guitars, there are numerous brands of guitar strings on the market. Although I have been playing the same brand all my life (in the beginning I had no choice – it was the only brand that the local store carried) I do recognise that many of the other brands are equally good. Many of them use identical processes in their production. They are generally geometrically shaped steel wire cores which are wound, like a spring, with an alloy winding that can be adjusted to change the mass of the string. I would suggest choosing a brand that has a wide variety of string types and gauges so that you can customise your own sets without swapping across brands too much.

Which Type?

I have tended to favour phosphor-bronze strings over other types of strings. This alloy, to my ears, produces the best tone for my playing, although I have experimented with a 'coated' string by the same company and used those exclusively for over two years. I recently returned to using the phosphor-bronze strings and realised that the coated strings were restricting many of the upper overtones from sounding. This made them sound slightly duller (often interpreted as warmer). Yes indeed, they lasted a whole lot longer, but with the blessing of a string endorsement from that string company, I am not restricted from experimenting with different string types and gauges.

Coated strings were introduced in the 1990s (although experiments date back many years). The technology involves coating the string with a thin film in a specific way so as to minimise the inherent damping effects. Although certain players and guitar companies highly recommend them, I feel that any coating, while obviously lending longevity to your strings life, will also adversely affect the tone. Once again this is highly subjective.

How Often Should You Change Strings?

There are a number of variables here that need to be considered before you answer this question for yourself. In short, the strings should be changed as soon as they stop playing in tune and with the quality of tone you expect from strings. This depends on the accuracy and experience of your ears and the tolerance of your audience! I have met guitarists who haven't changed their strings in over a year and the strings still sound great (that may be that the guitarist never practises and plays one gig a year!). Other guitarists have to change the strings after every gig and at most every week. Personally, playing uncoated strings and playing about 120 shows a year, I like to change my strings every couple of weeks. I like the 'played in' tone of strings that have had a bit of use. The 'ping' of brand new strings is not so appealing and I tend to play them in for a couple of hours before recording or performing. What are the signs that indicate you should change your strings?

- **Poor intonation** – The strings don't seems to play in tune any more.

- **Corrosion** – The strings are dirty and worn looking. The dirt and grease that comes from your fingers and the places where you play the guitar has a very corrosive effect on the strings. You can counteract this by always wiping down the strings after playing and using some string cleaner.

- **String Damage** – The winding seems to be coming loose, particularly where the string meets the frets. There may also be kinks or bends in the strings at these points.

- **Poor tone** – The strings don't sound good anymore. They have lost their life and sound dull. The notes decay more quickly.

- **Breaking strings** – When a string breaks after a number of weeks playing, it can be a sign that the whole set needs changing. It is not good practice to only replace the broken strings. The net result of this is that after a while you will have six strings of different ages, each breaking at the end of its life. It is much better practice to replace the whole set with a brand new set.

For an amateur guitarist who plays purely for pleasure, I would expect that a string change every 6–8 weeks or longer is adequate. For a guitarist who is doing 2–5 shows a month I would suggest every 4–6 weeks. However, once again these are very general guidelines. Use them as an approximation of when you should consider string changes. One thing is for sure – the most expensive guitar in the world will sound no good when the strings are past their prime.

What's The Best Way To Change Strings?

This method is the one I employ on all my guitars. I learned this method from experienced guitar repairmen and it is also the one used by many reputable guitar stores and factories.

Removing The Strings

Slacken the strings and free them from the bridge pins or through the string holes in the saddle. You can safely remove the strings all together. There is an old man's tale that you should only remove the strings one by one as to do otherwise would damage the truss rod. Any truss rod that can't take this change in load isn't doing its job properly, so fear not! In any case removing all the strings gives you an opportunity to thoroughly clean the frets and fingerboard. These will remove dirt and grease that may corrode the new set of strings. Remember to clean the grooves of the nut through which the strings must run.

Attaching A String In Six Easy Steps

In this description I will describe the attaching of a low E string (the 6th) to a typical right handed acoustic steel string guitar. All directions and orientation are described from the perspective of looking straight at an upright guitar from the front.

1   Attach the ball end of the string to the bridge pin as normal and then run the string directly up the neck to the tuning peg.

2   Turn the tuning peg so that the string hole is aligned 180 degrees with the neck. Pull the string directly through the hole and pull the string taut by hand.

3   Pull the string back through the nut by about an inch, with the right hand maintaining a little tension to hold the string in place.

4   Pull and loop the free end of the string in the clockwise direction around the tuning post, down through the centre of the headstock. Bring the free end underneath the string (between the nut and the tuning post).

5   Now bring the free end of the string back over the string and form a sharp kink over the string. The free end is now parallel to the nut.

6   Tune the string with the tuning peg, ensuring that the string is winding in an anti-clockwise manner. The kink ensures that the string stays in place. You should maintain some tension in the string with the right hand half way down the neck by pulling gently against the tension of the tuning peg.

Some Tips For Winding The Strings

This method will give you about 2–3 complete winds on the tuning post. This is adequate. If you have any more, you risk having the string rewinding onto itself and becoming messy. Many tuning problems result from the string not sitting neatly on the tuning post. The string criss-crosses itself several times and spends its short working life trying to settle down into the grooves and ruts that it has created for itself. Intonation becomes a nightmare!

•   Always wind the string on the inside of the tuning post, away from the edge of the headstock. All the strings should meet the tuning post on the side closest to the centre of the headstock.

•   Always clip any excess string away as close to the tuning post as possible. This will eliminate string rattle and confusion about which string runs to which peg.

•   There will always be some excess play in the string at

first. Tune the string to pitch. Gently grab the string at about the 12th fret and pull the string away from the fingerboard about an inch. Run your hand along the length of the string (slowly if you want to avoid string burn!!). Let the string back down gently and re-tune. You may need to do this a small number of times to stretch out the string. This will minimise the chances of the strings going out of tune so early on in their life!

General String Care Tips

•   Keep the strings clean by wiping them down after every use. You should use a lint free cloth for this. There are special micro-fibre cloths available for string care which don't leave hairs or fibres on the string – it's surprising how even one tiny fibre can affect the tone of a string. There are also numerous products on the market that can be used to clean the strings.

•   Clean your hands before you play the guitar. This minimises the amount of grease and dirt that will be transferred to the strings.

•   Avoid any damage to the strings. This can be caused banging the strings against the frets too harshly, using a metallic or similarly hard object to sound the strings, or letting the strings come in hard contact with a sharp edge (for example, a table edge).

•   If your strings break frequently, check to see if there are any sharp edges or burrs on the tuning post, nut or bridge. Remove the string(s) and file down these sharp edges carefully.

•   Avoid over-tightening a capo against the strings. This can permanently kink the strings.

Storing Your Guitar

Almost without exception, I store all my instruments in their hard cases. This protects them from dust and damp. It also protects them from accidental damage. Unfortunately it also inhibits spontaneous indulgence! I have always recommended that my students keep their guitars on stands so that the instrument is always in view and calling for practice time! I do defend my apparent hypocrisy by suggesting that I have a busy office/studio with 15 instruments. If I didn't keep them in cases, they would be in the way and a danger to themselves and me. For the average guitar student/enthusiast it is probably more practical to keep the instrument closer to hand. For a more valuable instrument, I would still recommend that they are kept in a case. If you do choose to keep the guitar on a stand then try to place as far into a corner as possible, where it will be out of harm's way. Keep any objects which could conceivably fall or move against the instrument as far away as possible.

Another popular storage solution is to hang the guitar, guitar-store style, on a wooden guitar hanger attached to the wall. This keeps them out of harm's way but keeps them in view.

Guitars And Direct Sunlight

You should always store guitars, in or out of cases, out of direct sunlight. The heat that can build up on an instrument can cause irreparable damage: Necks and soundboards can warp and even crack; finishes can become tarnished. Similarly, too much damp and moisture can have an adverse effect on the instrument. In itself, damp can be dried out. The serious problems occur when a crack has developed through the instrument being overheated and dried out. The crack is then in danger of soaking up moisture which will swell the wood and cause all sorts of damage. A crack on the soundboard (often the most susceptible to heat and moisture damage) can cause braces to loosen, or in worst cases, to completely fall off.

Heat that damages instruments commonly occurs in the trunks of motor cars. Leaving a guitar, in its case, in your trunk at, for example, a summer folk festival can cause severe damage. On a typical summer day with temperatures approaching 30 degrees Celsius (86 degrees Fahrenheit) the temperature in a trunk can quickly start to climb to 60 degrees Celsius (140 degrees Fahrenheit) which is the temperature than many modern guitar glues start to liquefy.

Guitars And Humidity

Low humidity can cause more damage than high humidity. Low humidity can dry out an instrument so much that the wood cracks. This is most common in the case of the soundboard, which is already under a lot of tension from strings and braces.

The ideal conditions for a guitar are a temperature of around 21 degrees Celsius (70 degrees Fahrenheit) and a humidity level around 45%. You can buy a relatively inexpensive humidifier for guitars these days and they are well worth the investment. As the global climate pattern changes, this is not a problem that is restricted to certain parts of the US. I have suffered from various humidity problems with my guitar in Sweden and the UK.

It is also obvious that you should never store your guitar, with or without a case, near a heater, fireplace, damp wall or outside over night. These instruments may forgive you the first time, but regular abuse of a guitar by storing it in extremes of temperature or humidity, will guarantee the instrument's demise.

Travelling With Your Guitar

At some stage you will want to transport your instrument in a car or plane. You may even want to ship it across the world. I have had experience of each of these types of transport, and experience with the types of damage that can occur.

Travelling By Road

This is probably the most common type of transport for musicians and their instruments, particularly amateur and semi-professionals. If your instrument is of any value to you, you MUST have a hard shell case. These are typically supplied as a standard accessory with most high end ($1500+) guitars. They protect the instrument from the typical knocks and shocks that you can expect from loading a guitar in and out of car trunks, in and out of venues and on and off stage. They tend to fit the guitar quite snuggly and will normally have a small accessory compartment for spare strings, capos and electronic tuner. Some, in addition to a standard carrying handle, will have fittings for the attachment of a carrying strap. You can also purchase case covers – typically made of a hard wearing fabric that will protect the case itself. These usually have some strap system so that the case can be carried on the owner's back.

These cases are not, as we have seen above, particularly effective at protecting the instrument from extremes of temperature or climate. If you leave these instruments in a car trunk overnight, or during a hot day, both the case and the instrument are at risk of damage.

Travell-ing By Air

With the advent of budget airlines, more and more musicians are choosing to fly to gigs. Venues that were once a four or five-hour drive can now be reached by a short one hour internal flight. The costs can often be less than the cost of car fuel. However, not all musicians take the necessary precautions to protect their instruments from the irresponsible and unthinking actions of underpaid baggage handlers! I have seen, from my window seat, my guitar being thrown from the baggage cart onto the floor of the baggage-hold area! And why, when I have specifically taken my instrument to the 'fragile-baggage' loading belt, does my guitar still end up on the normal baggage belt at my destination? I am not convinced that the larger, more expensive airlines are much better. I have had every type of guitar-damage imaginable – cracked cases, broken guitar necks, humidity damage and broken pickup systems. I have yet to personally suffer from 'lost baggage' syndrome, but with the amount of flying that I and my guitar do, typically 25–30 flights a year, I am certainly due for a case of it!

Budget airlines, with their smaller aircraft, will rarely let you take a guitar in a hard shell case on board the aircraft. A jumbo or dreadnought size instrument will be too big for most overhead lockers. In a few cases, I have been able to carry a concert-sized classical instrument, which may just squeeze into the overhead baggage compartment. Some aircraft will have a storage area for the cabin crew's personal baggage and overcoats. If you smile the right way, they may allow you to store your instrument in there!

In general you can expect to leave your instrument at the check-in desk, or at best at the departure gate where, if you are lucky, a member of staff will carry it to the baggage hold. Or of course you could buy an extra ticket for the instrument!

(I always smile at the story that Bill Puplett, a legendary guitar repairman and luthier in the UK, told me about British fingerstyle guitarist Adrian Legg. Bill and Adrian designed a very quirky solid body instrument nicknamed 'the Breadboard'! Adrian has gone on to perform and record with the instrument and travel the world with it. Such was Adrian's determination to carry the instrument on board every flight, that he took measurements of every overhead baggage locker on every flight he took. He would send Bill the measurements who would then shave a little more off the instrument so that it would fit! Now I don't recommend that you go to such extremes with your vintage Martin D28, but the story does show some ingenuity!)

Tips For Transporting Your Guitar By Air

Over the years, with the benefit of having made all the mistakes in the book, I have come to the airline-proof method of preparing your instrument for flight. Imagine that you are going to war and that your instrument must be protected at all costs – this will put you in the right frame of mind. Baggage handlers are not to be underestimated in their determination to wreak the most damage on cargo.

- **Do NOT use a hardshell case to transport your guitar.** They will NOT protect it. Baggage holders can puncture these easily when they throw them against the corner of a metal flightcase or reinforced suitcase. I highly recommend that you use a fibreglass flight case such as a Calton (www.caltoncases.co.uk). These custom built cases are well worth the investment and protect the instrument from even the most severe knocks. I have seen these cases run over by cars, caught in an airport cross wind, even struck by a fork-lift and still protect the instrument inside!

- **Always slacken the strings.** One of the most common cases of instrument damage caused by airlines is a broken guitar neck. When a case falls flat on the ground, it creates a whiplash like reaction to the instrument inside. With the combination of this shock and the hundreds of pounds of pressure that the strings exert, the neck will break just behind the nut. The added weight of the machine heads can also increase the risk, although I don't recommend removing them! Loosening the strings adds greater protection. However, don't slacken them to the degree where they have no tension. A little tension will help to protect the neck in a backward fall.

- **Pack some bubble wrap/old newspaper/padding around the headstock.** Ensure that the padding is rigid enough to keep the headstock in position. It should be packed to the degree where the padding offers a little resistance as you try to close the case.

- **Pack everything tightly.** If there are any areas within the case where you feel the guitar may be able to move, pack these tightly also. Any movement can translate into a highly damaging inertia caused by a sudden sharp blow.

- **Remove any loose fittings on the instrument.** This includes capos or batteries (unless they are in sealed battery compartment). A loose 9v battery floating around inside a guitar can wreak havoc on your braces and struts.

- **For long haul flights use a small humidifier.** These are relatively inexpensive (try www.planetwaves.com) and will protect your instrument against the highly damaging effect of low humidity. Many long haul flights travel at 30,000 feet or higher, where the air has a lower humidity. So low in fact, that the soundboard can dry out and crack. Ideally the humidity for a guitar should be around 45%. With the humidifier, the humidity in the case can be maintained at a safe level.

- **Ask your local guitar dealer for a guitar box.** These simple cardboard boxes are used by guitar companies to ship guitars in hard shell cases to guitar stores. You can fit your guitar case in and add packing in and around the case. This provides a virtually damage-proof protection for your guitar.

- **Purchase a 'climate case'.** For even more protection. Made of a material that was designed by NASA, the case is soft-cover designed to fit over your hard, guitar shaped flight case. This cover protects the instrument against the changes in temperature and humidity so common in aeroplane baggage holds. (Check out www.allenguitar.com)

Cleaning Your Guitar

Here are some basic tips to guide you when you need to clean your guitar.

- Use a soft clean cloth to remove any loose dust or dirt. An old cotton T-shirt will often do the trick. There are lint free cloths designed for this job on the market. Slightly tougher spots of dirt can be removed by slightly dampening the cloth with warm water and rubbing firmly over the stain.

- After cleaning, you can bring your guitar up to a nice buffed shine by using one of the numerous guitar polish products on the market. These usually come with a polish cloth. Do NOT use furniture polish. This has compounds and oils that can stay on the guitar finish. If you are at all unsure about the correct products appropriate for the cleaning of your guitar, then consult the guitar manufacturer.

- The fretboard collects dirt and grease in a different way. The strings take the dirt and grease from your fingertips and deposit them on the fingerboard. They tend to build up along the fret wire and work their way into the wood. To clean the fretboard, remove the strings and wipe off the grease and dirt with a dry rag. You can improve the condition of the fretboard by putting a few drops of lemon oil (linseed oil is also good) onto a clean cloth and rubbing it into the wood. This helps to prevent the fretboard from drying out and cracking, and it also brings out the natural colour of the wood. For those tough-to-remove bits of dirt, use a small piece of extra-fine steel wool. This will certainly remove it.

- Very often there will be a tougher stain where your right forearm crosses the lower bout of the guitar. The skin is constantly releasing oils and sweat and these can stain the guitar over time. This area may need a lot more attention.

The Ten Golden Rules of Guitar Care

1 Always store the guitar in its case.

2 Never store a guitar near a heater or a cold draft.

3 Always replace the whole set of strings at once.

4 Never leave your guitar in the trunk of a car in hot weather.

5 Always place a guitar on a stand or back in its case, never against a table or perched on a chair.

6 Avoid dropping or knocking your guitar – sometimes a broken neck can take a few hours to appear.

7 Invest in a hard shell case.

8 Never leave your guitar in direct sunlight or where it can get wet.

9 Change the strings at regular intervals. Old and overused strings have poor tone and intonation.

10 Bring your guitar to a repairman at regular intervals for a set up – you will be amazed at the difference. I promise.

Nail Care

In my list of 'frequently asked questions', it is questions about nails that probably rank highest. The nails of fingerstyle guitarists, in particular those playing steel strings, are vulnerable to the wear and tear of playing. Coming from a classical and nylon string background as I did, the shift over to steel strings was quite a dramatic shock to my nails. I had always achieved my tone with a combination of nail and flesh, but within days I had lost all my nails. I then began to investigate solutions to the problem. I had a choice of:

- Abandoning my 'nail and flesh' approach to tone production and looking for an alternative way to produce it using flesh only

- Trying plastic and metal fingerpicks

- Finding some nail strengthening method that would allow me to continue using the 'nail and flesh' approach I had developed

I was not keen to leave years of practice and tone development behind and begin what seemed to be a challenging search for my tone using only the flesh of my fingertips. I had always used the nail to produce harder and brighter tones on the string. It also gave me a more instant attack. Equally the flesh produces a warmer, rounder and softer tone. The combination, with a customised nail shape, has given me access to a wide spectrum of tone colours, literally at my fingertips.

Plastic and metal fingerpicks, while they suit many of the world's greatest fingerstylists including Chet Atkins, Tommy Emmanuel and Jacques Stotzem to name but a select few, have never appealed to me. Even just using a solitary thumb-pick would require me to re-position my hand and arm dramatically.

I decided to look into the various nail strengthening methods employed by different players. These days there are numerous products available. A simple search on the internet will give you plenty of choices. However, when I was investigating in the late '80s and early '90s there were very few, if any, specific products for guitarists and their nail care. I spoke with Pierre Bensusan, the French guitarist, and he recommended a combination of super glue and baking soda (my poor nails!!!). Gordon Giltrap suggested alternate layers of super glue and tissue paper! I heard of John Renbourn's technique of gluing small crescents of sliced ping-pong balls under his nails! I even came across a flamenco guitarist who used thin shavings of matchsticks glued carefully to the surface of his nail! Juan Martin, the flamenco guitarist, suggested a simple solution of Olive Oil (that's what they use on the horses hooves in southern Spain he told me!!) while Martin Taylor uses a solution of tea tree oil. As my percussive right hand technique developed, none of these methods seemed to suit. I even tried vitamin supplements and lots of calcium enriched milk! Eventually I swallowed my pride and went to a nail salon.

It is a booming industry these days, with the explosion in nail art and fashion, but 12 years ago when I was looking for professional advice on the best way to re-enforce my nails, no nail technician seemed to have any experience in taking care of guitarists' nails. In fact, I found that I had to train them in the particular issues that affect guitarists.

There are a variety of approaches that nail technicians will employ. Here is a simple summary:

- **Nail lengthening – the long and short of it.** The nail technician will apply a plastic nail tip to the end of the nail with a special nail glue. He then cuts it down to the right shape and length. The nail-tip is then filed until it forms a flush surface with the natural nail.

- **Silk wraps and fibreglass.** This method involves small sheets of fibre that fit over the nail. With a glue resin the fibre forms a hard shell that can be filed and smoothed into shape. They are often used in conjunction with false plastic tips.

- **Acrylic coats.** This approach is very common, especially in the DIY world of guitarists. Using a special acrylic powder and resin, and some type of hardening agent, this method requires that you already have the correct length and shape in your natural nail.

If you choose to go to a nail technician then consider investigating each of these methods before you decide which works best for you.

The DIY Kit

A guitarist walks into a nail salon. 'Can you do my right hand nails please?' Pause. 'I'm a guitarist.' Pause. Mimicking of right hand fingerstyle playing…

This story is true. Unfortunately. I sat down. She began work on my nails. We talked about the weather. Then silence. A customer walks in with her four-year old daughter. Calm before the storm…. 'Mommy- Mommy!! Look! That woman has a beard!'. Since that day I have become a DIY nail technician. Here are the some of the drawbacks:

- Whether you're right- or left-handed, you will be applying the nails with your weaker hand to your dominant hand (unless you're one of these left-handed players who choose to play right-handed or vice versa!). You'll be at a distinct disadvantage when trying to do a neat job!

- It can take a lot longer than it takes a professional, mostly due to the awkward orientation that you have to work in.

- Nail glues (and don't let any of the packaging or promotional material fool you – it's quick-drying super-glue!) are runny and get everywhere especially when applied with your weak hand. They do what it says on the packet – 'bonds in seconds'!

- It's surprising how easily horrible things like nail fungus and other nail disorders can develop when the user doesn't have the proper skills. The professionals have the right tools and qualifications.

After many years of experimenting – you name it, I've tried it! – I finally settled on the acrylic coating. There are kits available from most pharmacies or drugstores. I won't recommend any particular brand, as most of them do pretty much the same thing. Look for an 'acrylic nail kit'. These kits will have some basic elements:

- A nail primer to prepare the nail for the application of the coating

- A nail glue or resin (aka a *monomer*)

- An acrylic powder

- An accelerator spray that will speed up the setting process

- A simple selection of nail care tools – a file, buffer, etc.

This forms the core of my nail kit. (See picture below.) My own nail kit, which I bring to concerts and recording studios, has the following list of items:

- A selection of nail files, nail clippers (large and small), nail buffers and emery boards

- An acrylic nail kit as described above

- A microbiological solution which aids in the treatment of nail infections and fungus

- A sterilising spray to keep all the files and buffers infection free

- A selection of large plastic nail tips (see below)

- Nail glue/hardener remover

- Spare pots of nail glue (they often become locked and unusable- it's a good idea to keep some spare!)

- Nail hardening products

- Cuticle oil and nourishment

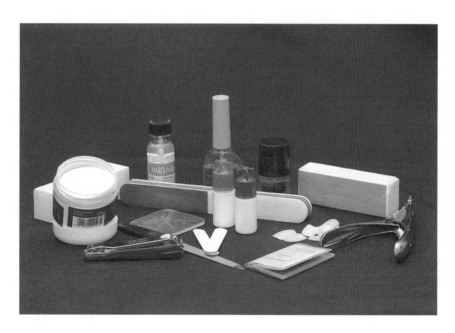

Example 8.1: A selection from my nailkit

All of these products are held together in a small tool box, which goes with me to all shows and recordings. For emergencies I have scaled down the kit in each of my main guitar cases to a mini-acrylic kit and some simple files.

Applying Acrylic Nails

This is a method that I use, although I recommend that you get advice from a qualified nail technician before trying it yourself.

1 **Prepare the area.** Find a suitable flat surface, such as a table, that can be used as a work area. Remember that you will be working with fast-drying adhesives and other chemicals that could permanently damage the finish on some furniture. I use a towel or a few layers of absorbent kitchen paper to form a protective layer for the work surface. Lay out all the necessary tools, files and glues. You should also keep some tissue paper handy in case of accidents or spillages!

2 **Prepare the nail and the nail kit.** Apply a quick spray of the sterilising liquid to the various nail files and clippers. The nails are very vulnerable to infection, especially from bacteria on the tip of invasive items, such as files and clippers. Ensure that your hands are completely clean. Grease and oil can inhibit the effectiveness of nail glues and other adhesives. If necessary apply a coat of microbiological solution to protect the nails against infection.

3 **Apply the nail primer.** The nail primer prepares the nail for the acrylic coating.

4 **Apply the acrylic gel (or monomer).** This is the liquid part of the acrylic solution. To apply it effectively you should squeeze a small drop onto the centre of the nail and spread it out to the sides with the tip or a needle.

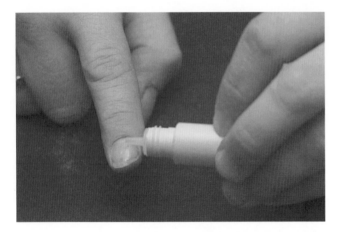

5 **Dip the nail tip in the acrylic powder.** Once the nail is thoroughly coated it can be dipped in the small tub of powder. You should leave a small area at the back of the nail near the cuticle that will allow the nail to breathe.

6 **The setting accelerator.** Some acrylic kits will harden at this point. Others will require a short spray of some setting accelerator. In either case, the acrylic will set very hard within a minute. You can then decide whether to repeat steps 4–6, or to move onto the filing and shaping stage.

7 **Shaping the nail.** You should have a range of files graded from 200–600 grit. These will give you many degrees of accuracy when filing and shaping. When shaping the nail I tend to skew the shape to the right. Place the hand, palm down, flat on the work surface (be careful not to put it on any undried glue or acrylic!). Looking down at the nail, the highest point should be about two-thirds of the nail width to the right. This shape is useful when you are placing your arm and hand at approximately a 45 degree angle to the strings. The smallest twist of the finger gives you a flesh tone, while a small twist to the other side gives you a nail tone. In between is a spectrum of nail/flesh combinations.

I shape all five nails in this way (I rarely use my little finger, but as they say – be prepared!). The length of my nails is relatively short. On the short side of the curve, the nail actually disappears below the curve of the finger. At its greatest height, the nail is approximately 2 millimetres above the finger. The thumb nail will usually be a little longer – as much as four millimetres above at its highest point.

8 **Filing and buffing.** Once the nail is the right shape, you need to smooth it and buff it to get rid of any unwanted edges or protrusions. Choose a high grade nail file or paper (say 400 grade) and gently smooth out any rough edges. You will need to work on two areas: the nail tip and the nail surface. The goal here is to get everything as smooth as possible. With nails as strong as these, you do NOT want them snagging on the strings! Start with the tip. File gently from underneath the tip and work your way over the edge to the upper surface of the nail. Be careful not to file too much of the free edge away. Always work in short gentle movements. One long hard stroke and you might take away the complete edge if you are not careful. Then apply the same file to the surface of the nail. You need to concern yourself primarily with the line where the acrylic ends and the natural nail

begins. This needs to taper smoothly so that there is no tangible difference across the whole surface of the nail. You can finish off with an emery board to bring the nails to a nice, smooth and healthy looking finish.

9   **Oiling the nail.** Using a cuticle oil, massage the whole nail, in particular the back of the nail. This will give a nice, natural looking finish to your nails. It also keeps the cuticles healthy and happy.

10 **The road test.** Run through some standard right-hand techniques including strumming, this will help you to identify any problem areas that should be attended to. Don't wait until the second number in your concert to find out that the thumb nail has a hook in it!

Emergency Nail Repair
Applying A False Nail Tip

Occasionally, even with nail re-enforcement, I will lose the tip or free edge of a fingernail. In these cases I will usually attach a false nail to this finger. The immediate problem for me is that my fingers are slightly wider than average. Most false nails are designed for women, who on average have smaller hands. I often have to pick through the selection and discard 80% of the tips. Even then I am often struggling to find a nail tip large enough to replace my thumb nail. Fortunately, I have found a steady supply of extra-large nail tips through a nail technician trade magazine. The steps are simple:

1   Clean the nail. You can leave any acrylic coat in place – just ensure that it is smooth and clean. Attach a nail to the surface. As this is normally a temporary measure I attach it to the whole surface of the nail, as far back

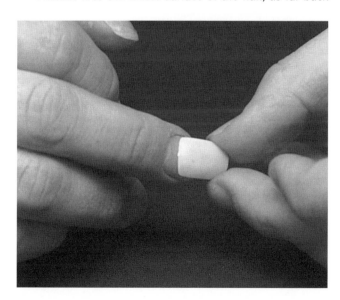

as the cuticle.

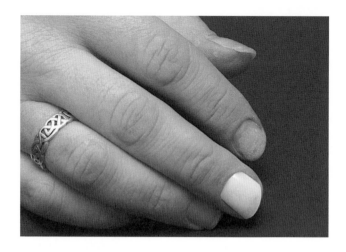

2   Cut the nail tip to size and shape.
3   Smooth out any rough edges on the nail tip.

4   Apply a strengthen coat of clear nail hardener (or any colour you choose!) to the nail tip.

General Nail Care Tips

•   Always dry your nails thoroughly after washing your hands and a bath. Water can make its way down in through the fibres of the nail and cause them to split. Use rubber gloves when you wash the dishes or the car.

•   Keep the nails at a length that is practical for your playing and tone, but no longer. Nails that grow long can become weak and crack. They are also more vulnerable when it comes to catching on everyday objects such as cutlery, door handles, tools and computer keyboards.

•   Use your other hand for simple tasks such as opening drawers or doors. Be aware of the places in your home and workplace which are a threat to your nails!

•   Keep your nails smooth and snag free. The most common way of breaking a nail is catching it in a loose thread or fibre from your clothing or bed clothes. As soon as you see a snag or a split – attend to it. A stitch in time....

•   Stay healthy. The number one cause of weak and broken nails is poor nail health. The nail is the first thing to suffer when you are ill or run down. Eat a healthy balanced diet and remember that nails need calcium.

Accessorise Yourself

There are a huge number of accessories available for the guitar. Here are a few:

The Capo

The capo (short for *capodastra*) dates back to the mid-18th century. It was an obvious accessory for fretted instruments. The first capo was simply a C shaped piece of metal that slid over the neck. Since then there have been hundreds of designs, and even to this day, the capo is being refined and improved upon. The elastic capo was introduced in 1931, and the 1970s and 1980s saw the emergence of various clamp and screw adjustable capos. Designs have included screw, spring, elastic, string and lever mechanisms. There are capos that roll up and down the neck, capos that be used for partial fretting and even a capo which allows you

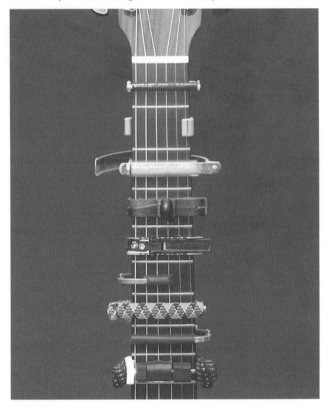

Example 8.2: A few capos!

to select which strings to fret or to leave open (the clever Third Hand capo). The latest development in capo design is the G7th capo (visit www.g7th.com). The picture shows my Nick Benjamin guitar with a variety of capos attached.

Why use a capo in the first place? Well...

- It's useful for transposing guitar parts into other, more difficult keys.

- The capo causes the instrument to behave differently due to its reduced string length. This creates a change of tone – usually tighter and brighter.

- It can be used for children as beginner guitarists to help them work in smaller frets.

The Electronic Tuner

This is an enormously useful accessory. Tuners now come in handy, guitar-case friendly shapes and sizes. Some tuners are small enough to be fitted to the guitar with a simple mechanism. Others are too large for a guitar case and need to be fitted in a rack system. However, I recommend a slightly more sophisticated model like the one shown here. This style of tuner can accept a guitar cable and be used as part of the signal chain as it has an input and output. There is also a built-in mic that allows you to tune without the pickup.

Example 8.3: An electronic tuner

Effects And Processors

Again, these come in all shapes and sizes. They are either floor-mounted with buttons for foot control, or rack-mounted. They are all generally similar with a variety of effects such as reverb, chorus and delay. Many effects and processors come with a built in library of combined effects called patches. Most allow the operator to write their own patches on the unit and save them to an internal memory. The model below features effects that can also imitate the sound of various microphones.

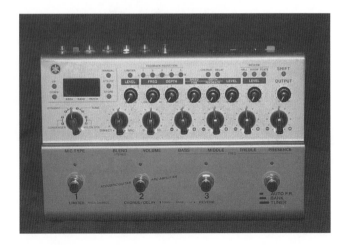

Example 8.6: An effects processor and pre-amp – the AG Stomp Box

Guitar Synthesisers

Although more commonly associated with electric guitarists, it is possible to set up a an acoustic guitar to transmit MIDI signals to a guitar synthesiser like the one in the photograph below. You would need a MIDI pickup or a MIDI signal converter to let your guitar 'talk' to the synth.

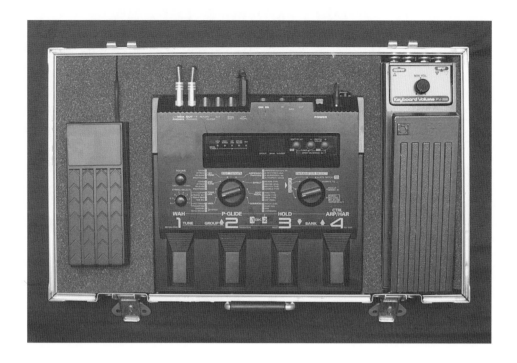

Example 8.5: A guitar synethesiser

This synthesiser allows a guitarist to assign different MIDI sounds to each string, or even to different regions of the fingerboard. For example, you could trigger double-bass sounds with the low E string while triggering a flute sound with the treble strings. The possibilities are endless although potentially annoying to purists!

9 PERFORMANCE PIECES

Building Your Repertoire

'We are the music makers, we are the dreamers of dreams.'

– Arthur O'Shaughnessy

In this chapter I present you with six performance pieces that incorporate all the theory and technique covered in the book. There are altered tunings, all manner of chords and styles, a wide variety of techniques and textures. Good luck with them.

'Si Beag Si Mor'

Pronounced 'shee beg shee more', this tune is supposedly the first ever composed by the blind Irish harpist-composer Turlough O'Carolan (b.1670). It is a staple of many Celtic style fingerstylist's repertoire and there are numerous versions available. The title translates as 'little hill, big hill' and was composed with lyrics to tell the story of a battle between two fairy queens and their armies. They join forces in the end to fight a common enemy. Exciting stuff!

The piece is arranged in drop D tuning and is in a slow 6/4 time signature. It should evoke a very open, atmospheric feeling. Lots of open strings, low D notes and loose time. Listen to the recording to get a sense of the phrasing. The piece is in a standard A B form where each section is played twice. My arrangement starts out with sparse bass notes and simple harmony. By Bar 33 the harmony and bass line are more developed. In Bar 38 I use an A♯ diminished chord to approach the B minor chord. The arrangement continues in this way until Bar 61. A few natural harmonics add a new texture to the melody. An interesting technique here is the combination of these natural harmonics with other notes. In this arrangement you will need to allow room for the other notes on the same beats.

The tune comes to a close with a standard rallentando (gradual slowing down) and sus4 tension and release (a D sus4 chord resolving to D major).

Si Beag Si Mor

Turlough O'Carolan

CD2, Track 77

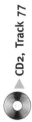

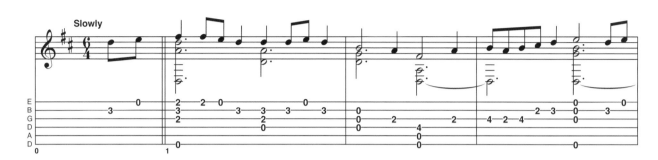

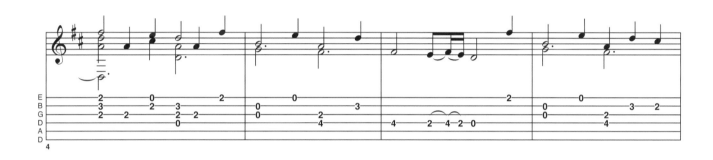

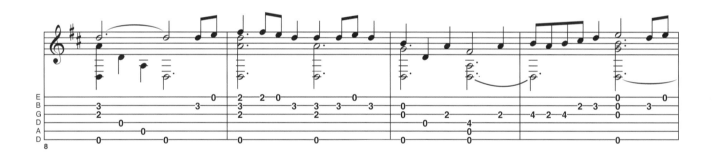

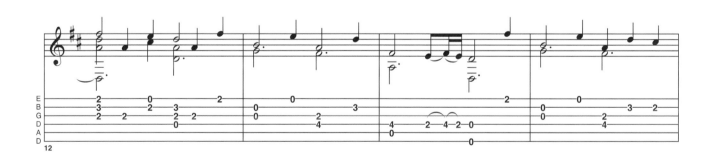

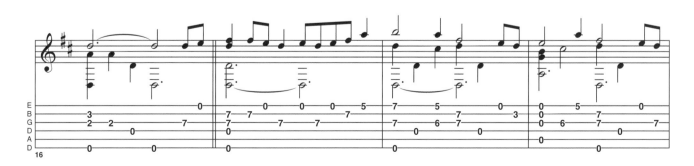

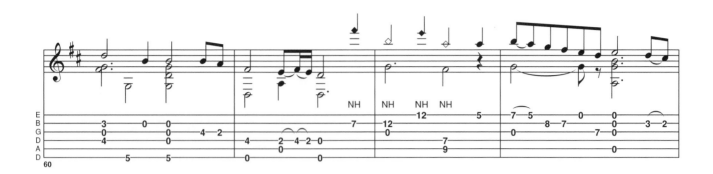

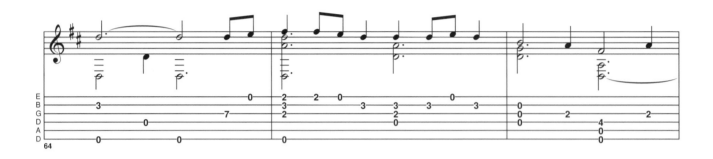

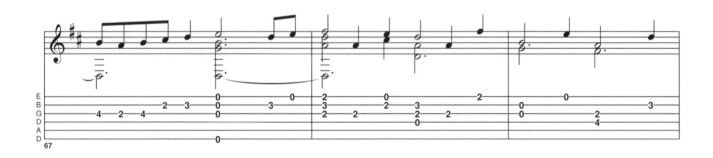

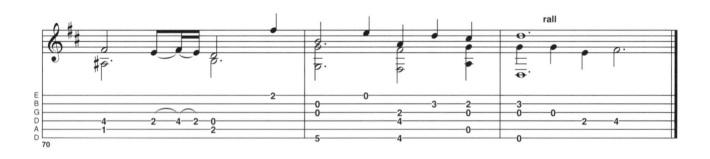

'The Brandenburg Hornpipe'

This is my own arrangement of the main theme of JS Bach's Second Brandenburg Concerto in F major which first appeared on my album *The Perc U Lator*. The second Brandenburg is my favourite of the set of six. The original goes through many key changes, presenting and developing other themes. However, for the purpose of demonstrating how a simple beautiful melody can be rearranged rhythmically and texturally, I have used only the opening theme. Ideally you should refer to a reputable recording of the original to hear the context of my arrangement.

This arrangement (which I have lately been calling *'The Brendan Burke Hornpipe'!*) is a continuation of the Celtic guitar style introduced earlier. To imply the dance rhythms of a hornpipe, you will notice that I have played all the sixteenth notes as swung sixteenth notes. You should refer to the recording to hear the rhythm of swung sixteenths. Rather than complicate the notation with triplet sixteenth notes, I have written out the music in straight sixteenths with an indication that three triplet sixteenth notes are to be played in the time of two standard straight sixteenths. To steady yourself as you work on the feel, you should count eighth notes (**1** + 2 + 3 + 4 + **1** + etc.)

To keep the arrangement in the original key, I have used a capo on the third fret. The notation is straightforward – the tab can be read with or without the capo, the standard pitch and rhythm stave is in the key of F. I also used the modal tuning DADGAD to bring out the overtones and resonances common in this style of music. In choosing appropriate fingerings I have used as many open strings as possible. This allows notes to ring on longer than they might normally.

The Brandenburg Hornpipe

JS Bach

'Bourrée'

This is my own original arrangement of the Bourrée from GF Handel's *Music For The Royal Fireworks*. Handel was commissioned to compose this music for a small orchestra. In my arrangement, I have retained the original melody while embellishing the rhythms and harmony. The tune is a typical *bourrée* in that it is in 4/4 time and starts with a single note on the last beat of the pick-up bar. These pieces were originally written as dances and should be treated as such. Try to imagine people dancing as you play.

As the tune is short with only two themes, I had to employ a number of arrangement tricks to give the piece some substance for the solo guitar. For example, on the first run through, the harmony is more sparse than in the following sections with the melody being played over a single D drone. Rhythmically, I accent certain notes that are not accented in the original. A case in point is the slur at the end of bar 2. I snap the F♯ note by plucking it with my thumb *away* from the sound hole. I then hammer on to a G note on the same string. This produces an accent in an unusual part of the bar and, as you will hear from the recording, is very effective. This technique appears a number of times throughout the piece.

I have chosen, as usual, the altered tuning DADGAD and used a capo at the 3rd fret. This allows me to use some standard voicings while sounding the key of F. I often combine this tune with the previous 'Brandenburg Hornpipe' to create a longer performance piece.

Bourrée

GF Handel

CAPO 3

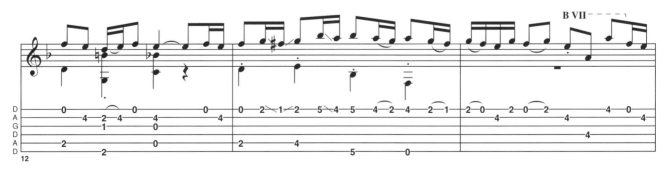

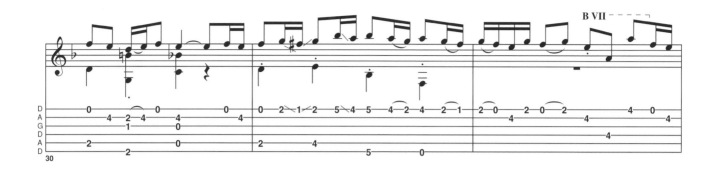

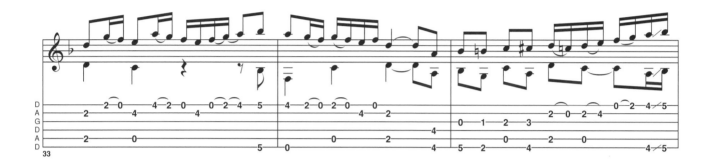

'God Rest Ye, Merry Gentlemen'

For those more seasonal moments I've chosen to put the classic 'God Rest Ye, Merry Gentlemen' through the same Eric Roche arrangement machine. Because of the harmony involved, it was quite easy to come up with some colourful chord voicings and re-harmonisations. The melody of the piece is in E minor, and the harmony I've used is borrowed from the E melodic minor, E harmonic minor and E Dorian mode. It is quite common for tunes in a minor key to have their harmony in the various minor keys and modes of that tonic.

The melody is played down near the nut on the first time (bars 1–25) and then an octave higher the next time. Check out the chromatic chords with their chromatically descending inner voices in bars 27–28. Sweet! The piece ends with some harmonics which ring on to produce an Em add 9 chord.

Try to capture that triplet swing feel which is notated in the transcription. Think swing!! The rests that are indicated are important to give the rhythm its punctuation and feel. Try to observe them as carefully as you can. Refer to the audio recording to get a sense of the feel.

God Rest Ye, Merry Gentlemen

▲ **CD2, Track 80**

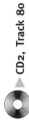

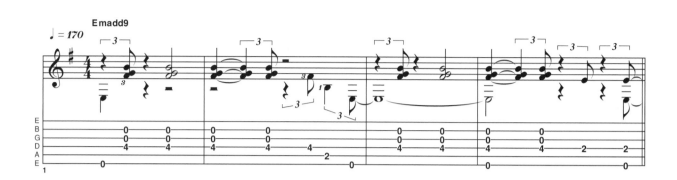

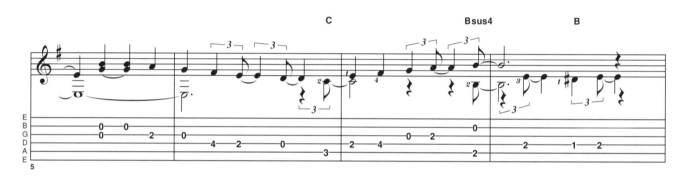

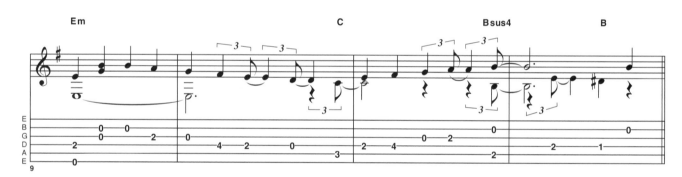

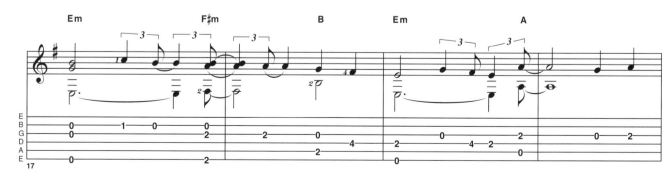

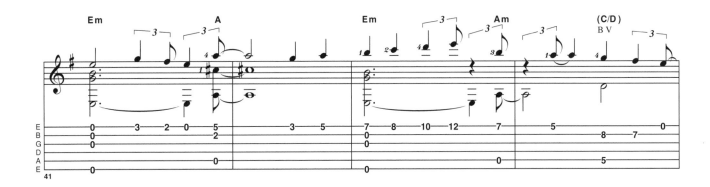

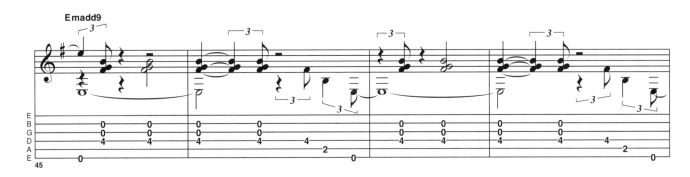

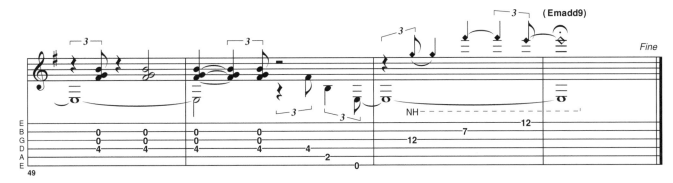

'Eight Years'

'Eight Years' is taken from my second album *Spin*. The tune was composed shortly before the millennium celebrations and lived for a short while under the slightly darker title of 'Seven Year Itch'! The true sentiment of the tune is one of thankfulness, so try to put that feeling into your performance. The tune was written quite quickly (over the course of one afternoon as far as I remember) and follows a fairly standard song structure. There is a wide variety of techniques and sounds in the piece so please follow the transcription and performance notes carefully.

'Eight Years' is one of two tunes on the album which feature the tuning CGDGBD (low to high). This tuning is a Hawaiian slack key tuning used by Joni Mitchell, Martin Simpson and a few others. You may need a heavier gauge string to handle the low C note on your E string.

Bars 1–16

This opening section is based on artificial harmonics. The left hand holds down a simple shape (similar to an open standard Am7 shape) and the right hand reaches over to the 12th fret area and picks harmonics. To achieve this you need to place your right hand index finger directly above the fourth (D) string at the 14th fret and lightly touch the string, using the middle finger or thumb pluck the note. It may require practice. The harmonics produced are called artificial harmonics because they don't occur naturally on the open string. The next harmonic is played in the same way on the open G string and the following harmonic played at the 13th fret. You simply 'trace' the shape of the chord at 12 fret intervals. In the tab, the number in brackets is the position for the right hand to produce these harmonics. Every fourth bar these harmonics contrast with some 'normal' notes played with standard right hand technique.

Bars 17–33

These bars are the main A and B sections of the tune. There are some left hand fingering notated in the standard ('dots') stave. Try to use the fingerings that I have suggested. In particular in bar 23–25 and 27–29 the left hand third finger is creating a half barre on the A, D and G strings.

Bars 34–6

These bars use natural harmonics, mixed with standard notes.

Bars 37–46

These bars are difficult to notate and transcribe. The right hand slaps the treble strings at 12 fret intervals from the left hand position. (If the note/chord is played at the 5th fret then the strings are slapped at the 17th fret.) This slap can produce artificial harmonics an octave above the fretted notes. Listen carefully to the recording and work with the transcription and sound.

This end section is full of unorthodox techniques. The right hand in bar 78 makes percussive sounds on the body of the guitar. These are indicated on the tab stave with an X and on the standard notation stave as *Tam 1* and *Tam 2*. Tam 1 is played by the heel of the right hand on the area just over the soundhole by the bridge. Each guitar and guitarist is different so experiment with different positions to achieve a deep bassy 'thud'.

Tam 2 is a higher pitch percussive sound. This can be achieved with the fingertips by hitting the wood on the guitar top just by the neck joint. Again, experiment with different positions. The important issue here is the contrast in tone that these two sounds have. The slapped harmonics are played just as they were earlier.

In bar 85 the right hand reaches over to hammer the notes on the 4th fret. Again, listen to the CD track to understand the phrasing.

Eight Years

Eric Roche

CD2, Track 81

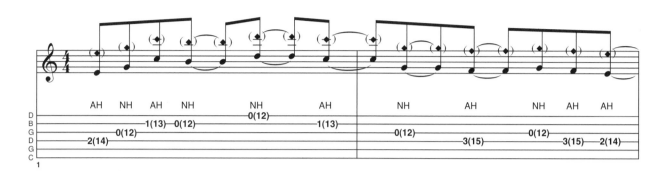

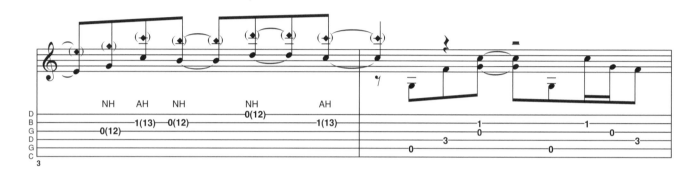

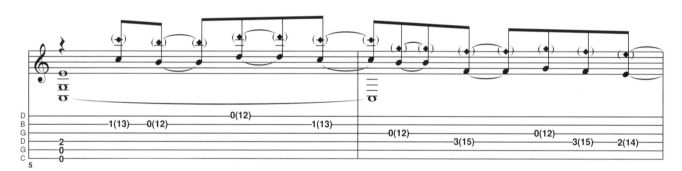

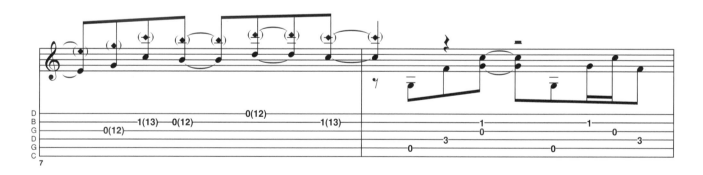

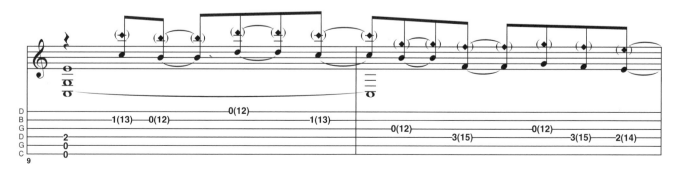

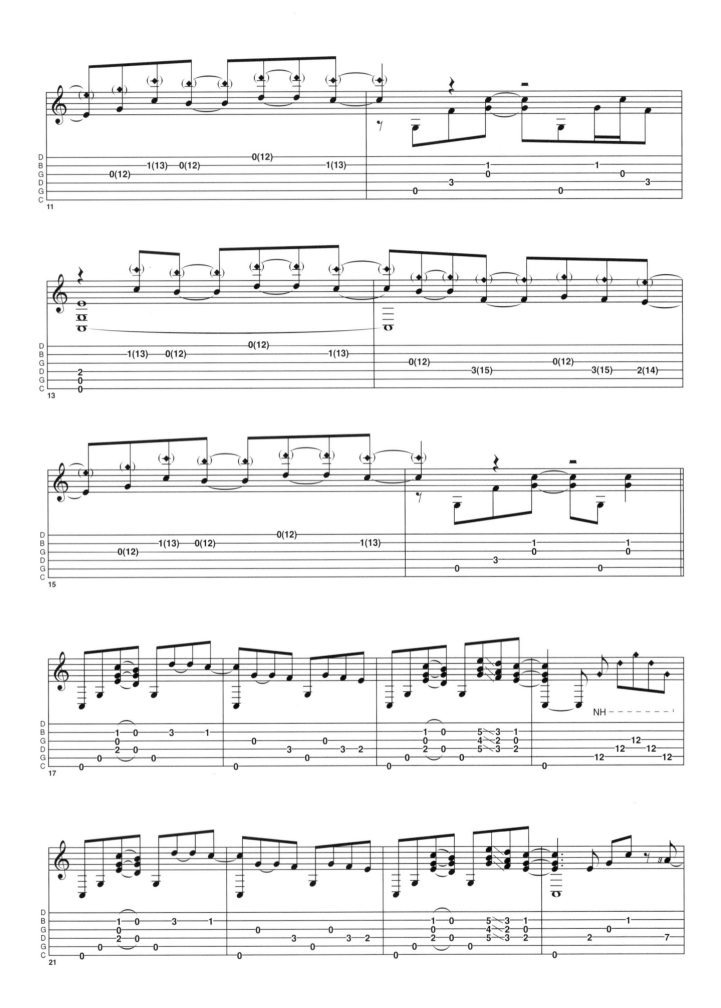

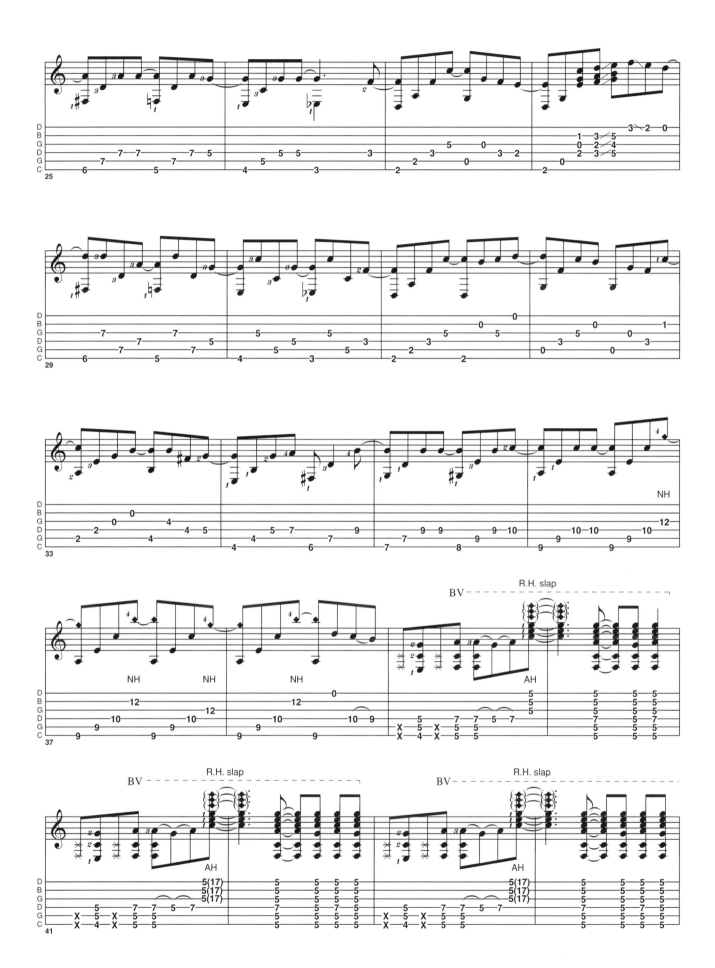

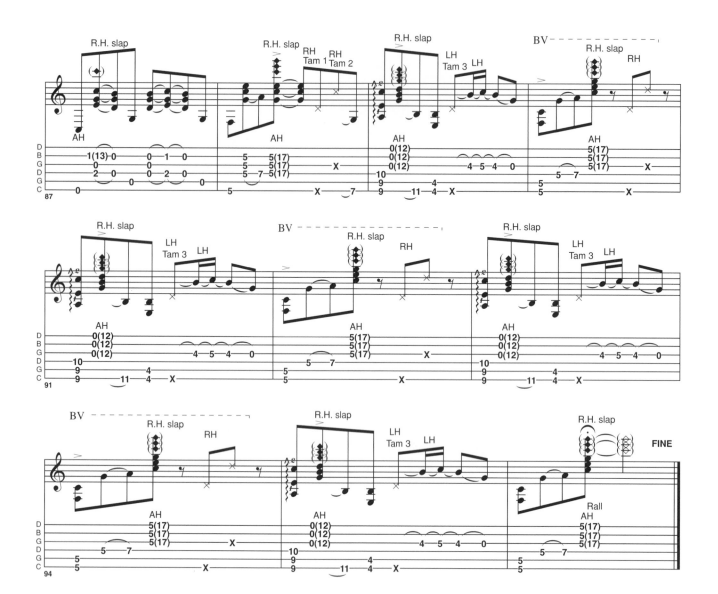

'Roundabout'

Finally the most technically challenging of these pieces. My tune 'Roundabout' was composed in an effort to try to represent in music the confusion, intensity and rhythm of rush hour on a large West London roundabout. Composed in 1998, the tune has been on the set list of every concert since.

As well being very demanding on the stability of your instrument, the tune calls for plenty of two handed and one handed tapping as well as a host of percussive sounds. I would advise the use of some sort of nail re-enforcement (but not fingerpicks!). You could try nail hardener or (as I do) false nails.

To help you with the correct intonation I would also suggest that you try a set of .013 gauge strings. A pair of goggles to protect your eyes from flying chips of wood might also be advisable!!!

The tuning for 'Roundabout' is DADGAD. 'Roundabout' is essentially in G Mixolydian mode and the opening bass line captures a lot of the rhythm and harmony that follows. The bass is harmonised in octaves and is played with both hands on the neck. I've introduced a few new symbols to help you achieve the correct technique. The first octave is hammered with the left hand, while the next octave is hammered by the right hand (marked as 'T' in the tab stave). This octave is pulled off to the open strings by the right hand (RPO – Right-hand Pull Off). The fourth sixteenth note in beat 2 is a right hand hammered grace note, which very briefly precedes the slide from fret 3 to 5. I would suggest practising bar 1 in a loop until you are comfortable with the rhythm and the groove of both hands.

At the end of Bar 2 there is a set of slapped harmonics. Slapping the open treble strings with (in my case) the right hand middle finger sounds these. With practise you can begin to accurately hit the 'node point' where the harmonics are produced. The technique also produces a distinct percussive sound as your finger hits the fretboard. This sound and technique appear again and again throughout the tune. The harmonics are followed by a deep percussive beat. This is played by the heel of the right hand striking against the soundboard in the area where the neck meets the guitar body. Obviously I recommend some restraint until you are more familiar with the strength of the guitar top. Bar 3 opens with a flamenco style technique – *rasgueado*. To achieve this, strike the bass strings with the little finger (c), and then by the ring (a), middle (m) and index fingers (i) in quick succession. The A string is muted by the pad of the fretting second finger. This technique is used again and again throughout the piece.

At bar 9 the two hands separate and play two completely different techniques simultaneously. The left hand continues to play a bass line in a legato fashion (hammer-ons and pull-offs) while the right hand plays a 'bass' and 'rim shot' style drum pattern! In the notation the right hand 'drum' pattern is marked with Xs. The bass drum (the lower of the Xs in bar 9 is played with the heel of the right hand at the furthest away part of the lower bout of the guitar. This part of the guitar should produce a deep resonant boom.) The 'rim shot' sound is achieved by banging the tips of the finger nails against the side of the guitar just underneath the lower bout. This sound is represented by the higher of the two Xs in bar 9. The bass line in the left hand is slightly simplified here to create a better synchronisation.

Bar 14 is a little more melodic (in a minimalist sort of way!) and uses many of the techniques already covered. One new technique is the sound on the last sixteenth of beat 2 bar 14. The right hand index finger taps lightly on the low D string at the 7th fret. Not quite a note or harmonic, the sound has a more of a rhythmical function. The rake at the end of the bar is similar to the earlier rasgueado. Bar 18 is very similar with the addition of some left hand tapped percussive sounds. These are played by lightly tapping the bass strings with the extended left hand middle finger. There is no need to produce a pitch, the sound is there for rhythmical effect. Bar 22 introduces some strummed rhythms. Follow the 'up' and 'down' directions carefully!

The most challenging part of the tune (if you aren't already frustrated!!) is bar 28 to 35. The two handed tapping *and* percussion will require some serious time in the wood shed. Once again I've had to use some new symbols to represent some of the sounds. The phrase actually begins on the last note of bar 27 with a percussive bass drum sound similar to that played at the end of bar 2. The first X in bar 28 is played on the upper bout of the soundboard just below the area where the neck meets the body. The Xs in brackets are produced by lightly tapping the bass strings with flat of the extended left hand middle finger (around the 7th fret). Again this sound is rhythmically important – don't try to produce a pitch. As the right hand index arches over the guitar neck to hammer the three bass strings at fret 3, the left hand leaves the neck to slap a 'snare' (X on the fourth tab line) sound on the side of the guitar just below the neck. I recommend a definite hard, sharp slap – this is a particularly strong part of the instrument. As soon as the 'snare' sounds the right hand pulls off, the left hand returns to hammer the 3rd fret again and the right hand slaps some harmonics at the 12th fret. The (still) fretted left hand slides up to the 5th fret. Be careful or you'll have your eye out!! The pattern repeats four times and is marked by a strummed jazzy altered dominant chord (bar 29). The altered dominant is always followed by a right hand rasgueado on the first beat of the following bar.

Roundabout

Eric Roche

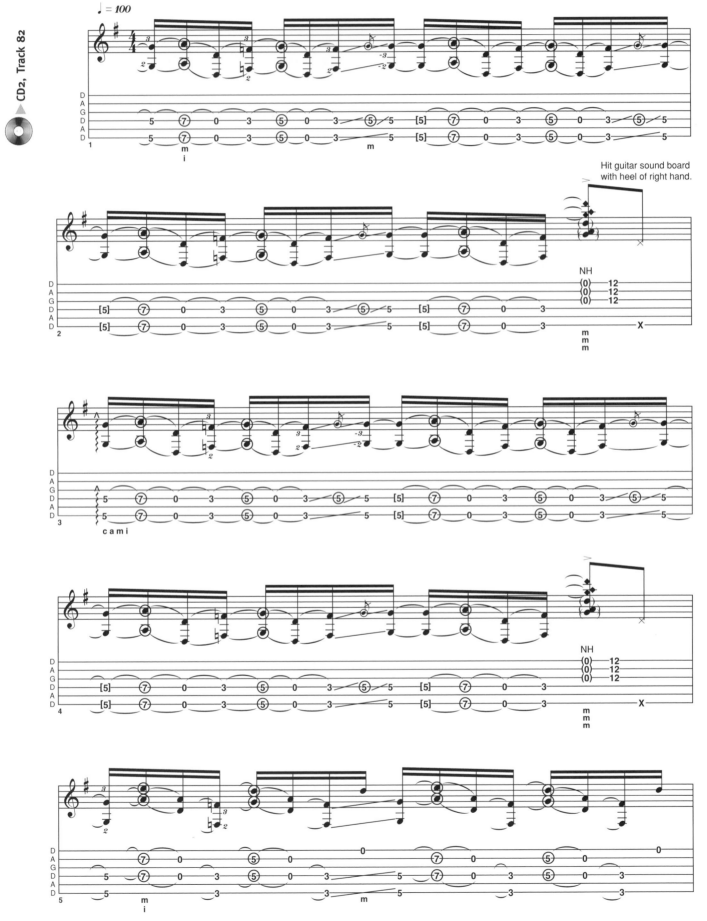

Hit guitar sound board
with heel of right hand.

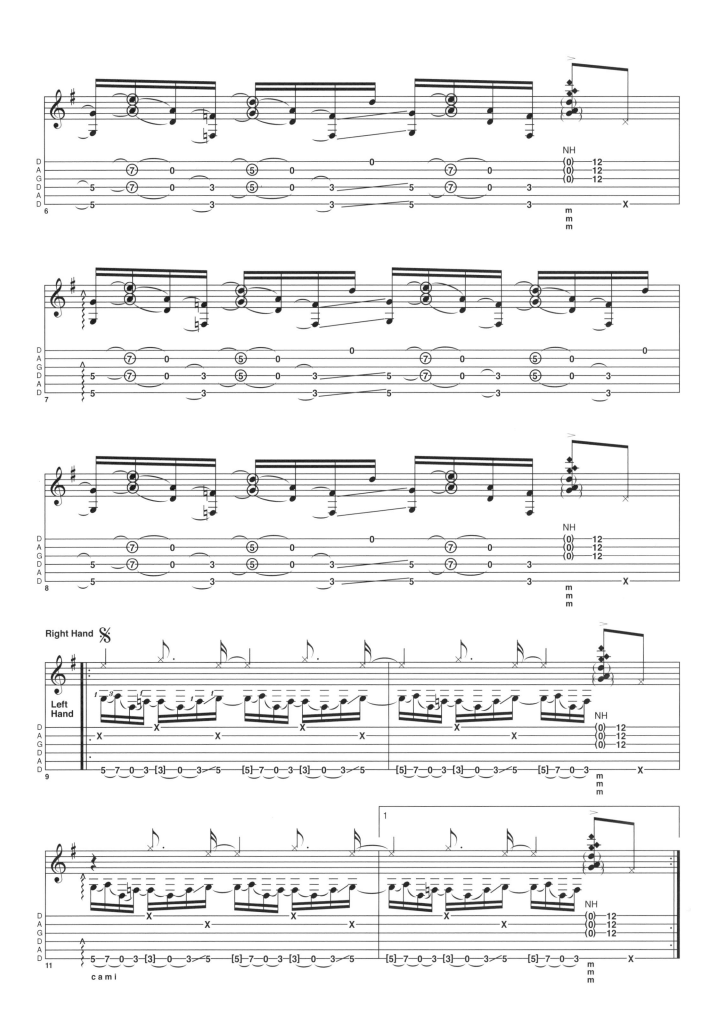

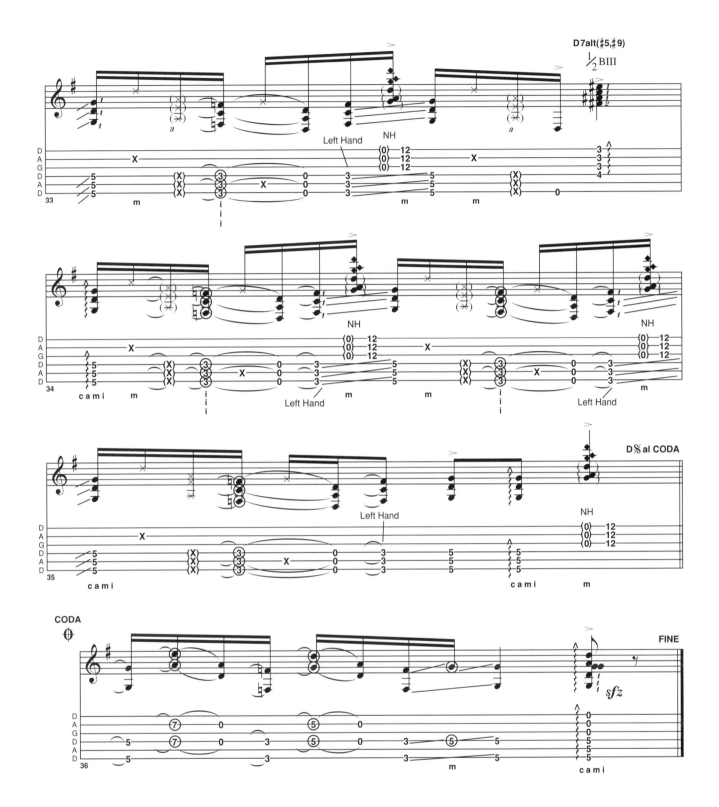

10 AND IN THE END...

Revelations, Truth And Some Commandments

'I'm not trying to play the guitar; I'm trying to play music. That's the difference.'

– Michael Hedges

Although so much emphasis has been placed on technique and theory in this book, I hope that you have also picked up on the strong theme throughout all the exercises and paragraphs – that technique, theory and exercises are tools to help you become a better musician. Use the understanding and ability that this book has given you to transform your playing and your music. It can take some time for the technique and theory to become a natural part of your approach. After all it has to fit in with your experience and goals. In my experience you have a 'Eureka!' moment where the penny drops and you can see more clearly. Remember the saying about the fruit – it ripens slowly but falls suddenly.

Learn to listen more deeply to all styles of music. The more I learn about music, the more deeply I understand that there is only music and that any labels are purely man-made. I am as happy listening to sincere thrash music as I am to honest folk music or authentic be-bop. These categories are useful when you are searching for an album in a large record store. However: Should Miles Davis really be in the *jazz* section? Or Leo Kottke in the *folk* section? Or David Gray in the *rock* section? Or Chet Atkins in the *country* section? Or Kelly Joe Phelps in the *blues* section? All of these artists, in fact *every* artist, crosses these imaginary boundaries in music. This is especially true over the years – as an artist grows their music grows and changes.

The best I can hope to do as a musician is to be available for the music and to be technically and musically developed enough to do a good job in transmitting it. How it's received by the audience is pretty much outside my control. I can practise and make sure that all my tools are up to the job, but after that the listener has the responsibility. If I am sincere and honest in my broadcasting, then the reception should be fine. Sometimes it takes a while for people to tune into your station.

I am now convinced that music comes from outside of us, although I am unsure as to from where exactly. In the great musicians I have seen, heard and been fortunate to share time with, I have understood that although many are called, few are chosen.

Regardless, guitar playing is great fun and a source of great pleasure (and occasional pain) for so many around the world. I love teaching and one of the great thrills is watching people struggle and succeed in their passion. Guitar does that to people – it gives them a passion and simple way to discover themselves through music. The more I play, the more I realise that music is a gift. The guitar is a tool – an awkward one! – that allows us to explore music. Watching and listening to the great masters is one of the key ways to teach ourselves how to explore our music through the guitar. Working with a great master or teacher is an even better way to discover yourself through music.

Good luck in your search.

The Ten Acoustic Guitar Commandments

I prefer to think of these as commitments by you rather commandments from me. After all I am still a student myself. However, I have managed to pick up a few tips and pointers from other guitar journeymen on the dusty roads. Just think of me as a fellow traveller who found these large stone tablets along the path. Let me just brush them clean here and see what they say.

1   Thou shalt create a practice schedule (and stick to it).

2   Thou shalt memorise all the note names on the guitar neck. In this practice lie the secrets of the fretboard.

3   Thou shalt only use one finger to create a barre. You have only been given four fingers on thy fretting hand. Do not waste any of them for they are precious.

4   Thou shalt make thyself familiar with the basic concepts of music theory for it will give you deep understanding of your art.

5   Thou shalt learn the major scale, in many positions all over the neck and memorise them.

6   Thou shalt invest in a metronome or similar device. To play with good timing fills me with great joy.

7   Thou shalt endeavour to keep your instrument in tune at all times. To do not so will displease me greatly.

8   Be aware of your tone at all times. Audiences will praise you forever throughout all lands.

9   There are no wrong notes, only notes from other songs.

10 Thou shalt keep your instrument in good order at all times. You know not the day nor the hour...

NOTES

NOTES

NOTES

NOTES

NOTES